A HISTORY OF BOURNEMOUTH

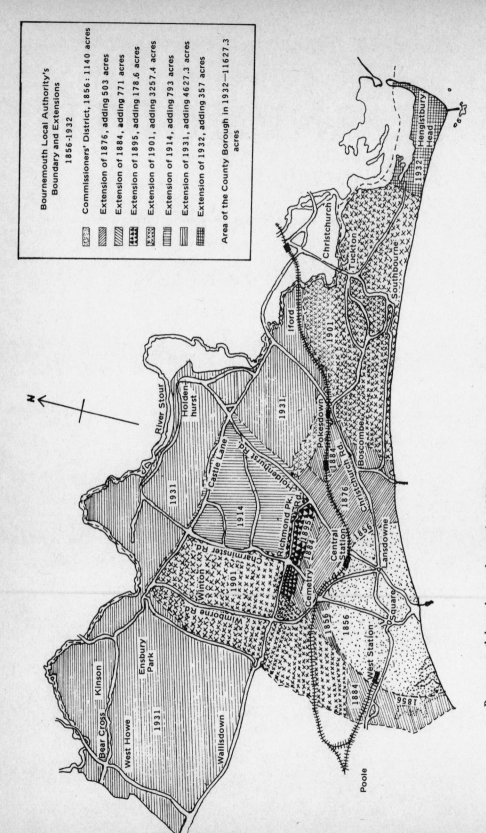

Bournemouth boundary and extensions 1856-1932 (drawn from an original in the possession of Dorset County Library).

Bournemouth Local Authority's
Boundary and Extensions
1856-1932

Commissioners' District, 1856 : 1140 acres

Extension of 1876, adding 503 acres

Extension of 1884, adding 771 acres

Extension of 1895, adding 178.6 acres

Extension of 1901, adding 3257.4 acres

Extension of 1914, adding 793 acres

Extension of 1931, adding 4627.3 acres

Extension of 1932, adding 357 acres

Area of the County Borough in 1932—11627.3
acres

A History of
BOURNEMOUTH
The Growth of a Victorian Town

Elizabeth Edwards

PHILLIMORE

1981

Published by
PHILLIMORE & CO. LTD.,
Shopwyke Hall, Chichester, Sussex

ISBN 0 85033 412 8

Phototypeset in 11/12 pt. Baskerville by
INPUT TYPESETTING LTD.,
London SW19 8DR
Printed and bound in Great Britain by
THE CAMELOT PRESS LTD.,
Southampton, Hampshire

CONTENTS

To my husband
in appreciation of his
encouragement and help

LIST OF PLATES

(between pages 84 and 85)

1. Memorial to Charles E. Smith
2. Thatched cottages, Iford, 1896
3. Kinson Church
4. 'Smugglers at Bourne Mouth'
5. Lewis Tregonwell (1758-1832)
6. The Mansion, the first house in Bournemouth
7. The *Tregonwell Arms* in 1883
8. Sir George Ivison Tapps, 1st Bart.
9. Miss Georgina Talbot
10. Lady Tapps-Gervis, wife of the 3rd Bart.
11. Sir George Eliott Meyrick Tapps-Gervis, 3rd Bart.
12. The *Belle Vue* Hotel, library and baths, 1856
13. The *Bath* Hotel in 1845
14. St. Peter's Church, from an engraving published *c.*1860
15. The *Mont Dore* Hotel, *c.*1886
16. Southbourne pier in 1894
17. Boscombe Spa, 1876
18. The *Ragged Cat* inn, Boscombe, *c.*1860
19. Rustic Bridge, 1855
20. Bournemouth pier approach in 1899
21. Bournemouth pier approach, *c.*1890
22. The Square, Bournemouth in 1909
23. The first office of Fox & Son, 1889
24. The old Winter Gardens, Bournemouth, *c.*1898
25. The original part of Stourfield House, Southbourne
26. Sir Merton and Lady Russell-Cotes in 1909
27. The Russell-Cotes Museum and Art Gallery, Bournemouth
28. The original Fancy Fair, founded by John Elmes Beale in 1881
29. An early Beales van, *c.*1924
30. John Elmes Beale and Mrs. Beale
31. Percy Bysshe Shelley
32. The original part of Shelley Park
33. Skerryvore
34. Lillie Langtry

Photographs have been reproduced by kind permission of the following: Miss P. Angus (plate 39); A. H. Barnes (plate 1); Beales of Bournemouth (plates 28, 29, 30); Dorset County Library (plates 2, 4, 5, 6, 7, 12, 13, 14, 16, 17, 18, 19, 20, 21, 22, 24, 33, 36); Fox & Sons (plate 23); Mr. H. W. Kiddle (plate 40); The Marconi Co. Ltd., Chelmsford, Essex (plate 37); Sir George Meyrick (plates 8, 10, 11); the Rolls-Royce Enthusiasts' Club (plate 38); the Russell-Cotes Museum and Art Gallery (plate 26); Miss M. Brown, Hon. Keeper of Casa Magni Shelley Museum, Boscombe (plate 31).

Plates 3, 32, 41 and 42 were photographed by H. L. Edwards, and plates 8, 9, 10, 11, 25, 27, 34 and 35 by Doreen Forshaw.

LIST OF TEXT FIGURES AND MAP

Map

Text figures

The map has been reproduced by kind permission of Dorset County Library.
The text figures were drawn by H. L. Edwards.

PREFACE

How often has it been remarked that Bournemouth, a mainly Victorian town, a former spa and watering place for the wealthy and those with delicate constitutions, has very little history worth mentioning. It certainly does not have the antiquity of its two venerable neighbours, Poole and Christchurch, whose occupied existence dates back continuously to Saxon, or even earlier, times. Whilst Bournemouth evolved and developed during the 19th century, much of importance has occurred both before and since that period.

Today this modern and fashionable town, with a population of about 154,000, is slowly and inevitably losing its Victorian and Edwardian period character, to be replaced by monolithic and characterless blocks of flats, offices and motor roads. What better time to record its history and early fame before it is completely lost to the demolition man!

ACKNOWLEDGMENTS

So many people have shown interest in my book, giving me both help and encouragement, that I wish to express my gratitude for their assistance, without which it would not have been possible to write it.

I am indebted to the two major works on Bournemouth; – *Bournemouth, 1810–1910*, by Mate and Riddle, and to David S. Young's detailed topographical book, *The Story of Bournemouth* (1957), which have been a source of reference to me. I wish to thank Robert Hale Ltd., for their permission to quote a few extracts from the latter book; and the Dorset Publishing Co. for permission to quote extracts from *Bournemouth Symphony Orchestra* by Geoffrey Miller. I would also like to thank Mr. Lawrence Popplewell, Mr. J. A. Young, Rev. E. J. G. Forse, Mrs. S. J. Lands, and Mr. T. N. Michael for permission to quote from their books (see Bibliography and Notes). Another book that was of great value to me in researching Holdenhurst and the neighbouring villages was the well-documented *Holdenhurst, Mother of Bournemouth*, by Kathleen M. Chilver.

I am especially indebted to Mr. M. A. Edgington and the staff of Lansdowne Reference Library, Dorset County Library, for their willing assistance and helpful co-operation at all times.

I also wish to express my gratitude to Mr. Graham Teasdill, Curator, Miss A. Findlay, Secretarial Assistant, and Mr. T. Rees, former Assistant, of the Russell-Cotes Art Gallery & Museums: and Mr. D. Shepherd, Public Relations Officer, Bournemouth Town Hall, for his helpful advice: Mr. Frank Beale, Mrs. P. Wentzell and Jayne Owen (Publicity Consultants for Beales' Centenary): and Mr. H. Insley-Fox, Mr. W. H. Mooring Aldridge, Mr. H. A. Mellory Pratt, Mr. I. McQueen, Mr. Lavender, former Curator of Red House Museum, Christchurch, and Mrs. Basil Druitt, who all willingly allowed me to look at privately printed books about their family backgrounds, and gave me access to documents, maps and papers collected over many years.

I also wish to acknowledge the kind assistance given by the following: Mrs. J. Ridley for the chapter on prehistoric times; Mrs. P. Bowring, Dr. J. Fisher, Miss Goddard, Mr. L. Loader, Mr. E. R. Morris, Headmaster of Hurn Court School, Miss C. Noll, Mr. and Mrs. Storey, Mr. J. Wallis, former Agent to Lord Malmesbury's Estate for the chapters on Holdenhurst and the villages; Mr. J. D. Armitage, Headmaster of Talbot Village School, Mr. and Mrs. A. H. Barnes, Mrs. M. Burrows, Mr. & Mrs. Brash, Mr. L. W. Chisman and Mr. R. Haskell, Chairman and Secretary of Kinson Historical Society. Mr. and Mrs. K. H. Gray, Mrs. S. J. Lands, Miss C. Noll, Mr. Nigel Nicolson, of Weidenfeld & Nicolson, Miss P. Mantell, Mr. and Mrs. J. Fulford,

Mr. B. J. Pickering, Mr. J. A. Young for the chapters on Bournemouth and districts; Mr. J. D. Armitage, Counc. Bessie Bicknell, Bursar, Talbot Heath School, Mr. D. Griffith Harries and Mrs. Lorraine Masefield, Principal and Secretary of Bournemouth Community Arts Centre, Mrs. S. Gibson, Old Girls' Assocn. of Wentworth Milton Mount, Mr. Jenkins, Victoria Hospital, Boscombe, Miss Laidlaw, Mr. Peter Morse, Western Orchestra Society, Mr. E. R. Morris, Mrs. P. Schollar, Mr. and Mrs. R. Warren for the chapter on education and other services; Mrs. S. M. Burney, Mrs. P. Sibley, Miss J. Woodhams, Mr. and Mrs. R. Warren for the chapter on the war years; Sister Catherine, Convent of Mercy, Sister Felicity, House of Bethany, Sister Helen, Convent of the Cross, Mr. Malcolm Fox, Lansdowne Baptist Church, Rev. J. Grattick, Punshon Memorial Church for the chapter on religion; Miss P. Angus, Mr. W. Beeching, Miss Margaret Brown, Mr. and Mrs. H. Kiddle, Mr. John Piper, Programme Controller of Two Counties Radio, Mrs. M. Walsh, and Mr. Stewart Daniels of Rolls-Royce Enthusiasts' Club for the chapters on famous people.

I wish to thank Doreen Forshaw for providing many of the high-class photographs used in the book, Lansdowne Reference Library, Dorset County Library, for their loan of original, early photographs of Bournemouth, and my husband, Harry L. Edwards, for the line drawings and for preparing the Index. I with to thank Sir George Meyrick for his kindness in allowing Mrs. D. Forshaw and myself to visit Hinton Admiral to take photographs from original paintings of his ancestors, and also the many people who have kindly loaned, or even given me, booklets and original photographs.

Chapter I

PREHISTORIC TIMES

ALTHOUGH BOURNEMOUTH is still considered a new town, beneath its soil have been discovered many valuable traces of antiquity of great interest to archaeologists. In 1934 J. B. Calkin wrote; 'Probably no other seaside resort in the whole of the British Isles can furnish so complete a record of the prehistoric age'.[1] Thousands of prehistoric flints and stone axes have been (and still are) discovered in many parts of Bournemouth and the surrounding area, usually in river and plateau gravel deposits.

One of the greatest archaeological sites in the country is Hengistbury Head and its stark, jutting headland, Warren Hill, which forms the most south-easterly part of the boundary of Bournemouth. The area is much appreciated for its flora, fauna, and magnificent sea views by countless visitors and residents, many of whom are unaware of its great antiquity and habitation by early man.

The first occupation of Hengistbury would seem to have been during the latter part of the Old Stone Age when, c. 9,000 B.C., primitive groups of hunters began to arrive periodically for short visits in order to slay reindeer and other animals. It is thought that these nomadic cave dwellers came from more southerly regions of the Continent, of which Britain was then a part. During a period of warmer weather, probably in about 8,000 B.C., this country became disconnected from the continent, forming its present island, and the milder, humid weather resulted in the growth of dense forests.

As a result, later Stone Age man preferred to live near the coast and on the banks of rivers. By about 4,000 B.C. farming skills were developed, and the existence of the people was less nomadic. Although flint finds of this period have been discovered, to date no evidence of their huts and villages has been traced in the Bournemouth district. A skull known as 'the Bournemouth man', and thought to date from the Neolithic period, was later discovered to be that of a woman. It was unearthed at Longham in 1932 and is considered to be the earliest remains of a human found in Bournemouth. (It is now in the Rothesay Museum.)

As early man's knowledge increased he discovered how to make metal tools, using an alloy by fusing together copper and tin. Thus came the Bronze Age, from about 1,900 B.C. to 600 B.C. These people were mainly of Germanic origin and buried their important personages in round barrows or tumuli: usually they were first cremated and placed in large urns inside the mound. Offerings and possessions such as ornamental cloaks, beads and amulets found inside the barrows show their belief in life after death. Barrows and burial urns have been discovered at Moordown, Iford and Longbarrow Road (Bournemouth), and complete cemeteries at Hillbrow, Pokesdown.

1

The Iron Age people came mainly from the south-west of France. They were skilled in forging iron, and traded with the Continent and elsewhere from Hengistbury, which developed into a busy and prosperous port. For defence purposes they built banks and ditches, the Double Dykes at Hengistbury being one of the famous. They lived in circular houses with a smoke fire in the middle, and had their own mint. Over three thousand coins have been discovered on the Head, which was referred to as Hengistbury Class, as have numerous fragments of pottery, some from France and Italy. Iron Age settlements have been discovered in several areas, including Strouden, Kinson and Iford. The most important settlement is considered to be that on the East Cliff, between what are now the *Carlton* Hotel and the Riviera flats, which was discovered in 1969 mainly due to the prompt action of two workmen who were building a retaining wall in that vicinity. Banks, ditches, pottery, a pedestal base, animal bones and other items were revealed.

After the Romans invaded Britain in A.D. 43 they seemed to live on friendly terms with the Iron Age settlers. Hengistbury coins continued to be minted, and were later found intermingled with Roman ones. Although they traded together, a recently discovered Roman fort at St. Catherine's Hill, Christchurch, showed that the Romans were able to watch the activities of the Hengistbury folk.

During this period frequent attacks were made by pirates from the Continent. After the Roman forces withdrew in about A.D. 400, some of the raiders settled in the area, preferring the river valleys to the lonely heathlands. Small Saxon communities were formed, but there have been few traces of their occupation. The trading settlement and port at Hengistbury declined, whilst the heaths and forests continued to flourish unopposed, until in the early 19th century Mrs. Lewis Tregonwell, charmed by the beauty of Poole Bay and the Chines, suggested that her husband should build a summer residence by the Bourne stream. This became the first house in Bournemouth.

In the 16th century an attempt by James Blount, sixth Baron Mountjoy and Lord of Canford Manor, to form the first trading venture in the area proved unsuccessful. On discovering that alum lay beneath the soil at Parkstone, he began to produce calcanthum or copperas and to boil alum. As alum, which was then used in tanning and other trades, was imported from Italy, Mountjoy was hopeful that he might be able to supply the whole of the British market. Mining work was carried out at Parkstone, Allom Chine, Baskaw and Brounsey (Brownsea) Island, and a company was formed, but with disastrous results: investors lost their money and Mountjoy was ruined. An appeal for financial assistance to Queen Elizabeth I was rejected. He died in poverty in 1581.

The only reminder of this early venture is in 'Alum Chine', the name given to a well-wooded, narrow ravine in the mining area, which leads to the sea and which is now a favourite walk with the many visitors to Bournemouth.

Chapter II

HOLDENHURST, THE MOTHER OF BOURNEMOUTH, AND ADJACENT HAMLETS

THE DEVELOPMENT OF BOURNEMOUTH as a fashionable seaside resort commenced in the 19th century. As it expanded it absorbed several old communities whose forefathers, living on the banks of the River Stour, had tilled the soil for many generations. Thomas Hardy accurately describes Bournemouth as a 'pleasure city and glittering novelty' which had sprung up on 'a tawny piece of antiquity . . . a new world in an old one'.[1]

The old world consisted of parts of the parish of Christchurch, and mainly of the ancient village and chapelry of Holdenhurst, the mother of Bournemouth. Today it is sometimes referred to as the 'forgotten village', and has hardly been mentioned by previous writers on Bournemouth. It seemed to me, therefore, that a history of Bournemouth should begin with the parish and hundred of Holdenhurst, out of which Bournemouth, then wild heathland, slowly grew. The village of Holdenhurst and adjoining farming communities still preserve their rural atmosphere on the outskirts of present-day Bournemouth. Despite considerable loss of farmland and the growth of neighbouring housing estates, its narrow, muddy lanes, extensive views of the open country and remaining scattered farms still have an air of peaceful tranquillity.

The village first appears in the Domesday Survey of 1086 in the following words:

> The King himself holds HOLEEST. Earl Tostig held it. It was then assessed at 29 hides [unit of assessment for food rents] and half a virgate [quarter of a hide] . . . There is land for 20 ploughs. In the demesne are 4¹/₂ ploughs, and there are 37 villeins and 25 bordars with 19 ploughs. There is a Chapel and 14 serfs and a mill worth 15 shillings and 3 fisheries for the use of the hall; and 181 acres of meadow . . .

The word 'Holeest' is derived from the Old English 'holegn', or 'holly', and 'hyrst', or 'copse', and at one time holly grew in profusion around the village. In succeeding centuries, the name was spelt variously Holehurst, Holhurst, Holeherst, Hollehurst, Holnehurst and Holnest.[2] By the 18th century it was known as Holdenhurst.

In the time of Edward the Confessor, Holdenhurst was held by Tostig, Earl of Northumbria, brother of King Harold II, (against whom he rebelled) who was killed at the battle of Stamford Bridge in 1066. William the Conqueror held the village for a time, then granted it to Hugh do Port, one of the greatest feudal landowners in Hampshire. By 1100, Holdenhurst had passed into the hands of Henry I who gave it to his cousin, Baron Richard de Redvers, Earl of Devon, in whose family it remained until 1293, when it became the property, including Christchurch, of the Plantagenets. Edward III granted it to William de Montague, Earl of Salisbury, whose descendants

3

owned it for many years. In 1540 Henry VIII granted Hurne, then the manor farm of Christchurch Priory, to Thomas Wriothesley, together with some 'acres of meadow in Holnehurst otherwise Holnest'. Between 1661 and 1795 much of Holdenhurst was owned by the Hooper family of Boveridge. On the death of Edward Hooper in 1795, his land, including the manor of Hurne and his estate of Hurne (Hurn) Court, passed to his kinsman, the first Earl of Malmesbury.[3]

At the time of the Domesday Book, Holdenhurst was part of the district of Egheite (which comprised Tuinam [Twynam] Holeest, Herne and other small areas), which was part of the hundred of Christchurch. By 1176 Holdenhurst had become a hundred in its own right, and in 1263 it also included the liberty of Westover, in which it was situated. By 1316 the whole area became known as the hundred of Christchurch, including the manor and honour of Christchurch. From about 1500 Westover became a separate hundred, although for some purposes it was still included in Christchurch hundred, and in 1571 it was known as the hundred of Christchurch Westover. The liberty, together with the hundred of Christchurch, has always belonged to the lord of the honour and manor of Christchurch.[4]

The liberty of Westover (the name means the west bank of the River Stour, and derives from O.E. 'ofer', or 'ofre' – a bank, shore or boundary) was divided into six tythings, which included Muscliff, Muccleshell, Throop and Holdenhurst, in the chapelry or parish of Holdenhurst, and Iford (with Pokesdown) and Tuckton (with Wick) in the parish of Christchurch.

In Saxon and Norman days life was comparatively simple, the villagers living in primitive mud and wattle cottages surrounded by a stockade or thick holly hedge. Many of the surrounding meadows were swampy, including Townsend (O.E. 'Tun', or end of enclosure), a popular area for wild ducks, geese and other water birds, where the fields were divided into strips on the open-field system. Corn was taken to the manor water-mill to be ground, whilst baskets were made from osiers and rushes, the latter being used also for strewing on floors and for thatching. Ploughing was done by oxen; swine were kept, which at pannage time (the right of free pasturage for six weeks from the end of September) were taken into the woods to fatten on acorns and beeches. Bee-keeping was popular, and sheep, cattle and hens were also maintained.

From time immemorial the villagers had wandered on the heaths and common land to collect turf and peat for their fires and also heather for bedding cattle and for thatching. In the low-lying parts of the heathland they dug clay for the walls and floors of their houses. Holdenhurst and the adjacent hamlets were situated by the banks of the River Stour, where fish were abundant.

The focus of such village life was the Saxon church, which is first referred to in the Domesday Survey. In 1137 it is mentioned in the charter of Richard de Redvers the Elder, and in 1150 in the charter of Baldwin de Redvers and his son, Richard, concerning the introduction of Canons Regular to Christchurch Priory.[5] At the Dissolution in 1539 the chapel was put in the charge of the vicar of Christchurch, who was allowed a stipend of £26 to provide priests for Christchurch and Holdenhurst.

The churchwardens' ledgers,[6] which start in 1685, give interesting information about the chapel's cost and repairs until its demolition in 1834 and its replacement by the present church. We read, for example:

1688 charge of 8s. 7d. for nails and mending the 'speare' or tower.
1707 'leding' the tower £1. 13s. 0d.
1755 leading tower £4. 3s. 1$^{1}/_{2}$d.

1702 a new Tibile bell and bellrope £7 5s. 11d.
1720 Renewing the roof £51. 17s. 3d.

The Norman font of the old church is now in the present one. During the Middle Ages the font was locked to prevent holy water being stolen for witchcraft, and to ensure that people with skin diseases could not touch the water.

The churchwardens had many duties, one of the strangest being the extermination of vermin. Sparrows heads appear annually in their accounts at '2d. a duzzen', and foxes at 1s. per head.

There was no burial ground in Holdenhurst until 1829, when Sir George Ivison Tapps, Lord of the Manor of Christchurch, gave land for that purpose. Previously part of the graveyard of Christchurch Priory had been set apart for burials of Holdenhurst people, for which the churchwarden paid a rent of 2s. annually to the Priory. Some Holdenhurst parishioners were buried in the choir aisle of the Priory. A tomb to James Welshman of 'Muscleft' (Muscliff) who died in 1714, aged 58, reads: 'Who lived to be the joyful father of seven sons and four daughters by his wife Elizabeth.

> The better part of me is gone,
> The sun is sett, my turtle flown.'

By 1829 the old Saxon church, which seated 200 parishioners (the population then being about 620) was badly in need of repair. The enlargement of the church was found to be impracticable and the building of a new church was discussed. A plot of land near the old church was given by Sir George Ivison Tapps, and a sum of £562 was raised towards its building by voluntary efforts, a further £600 being donated by the churchwardens, the Dean and Chapter of Winchester and the Church Building Society. The foundation stone for the new church was laid on 18 July 1833 by the second Earl of Malmesbury, and the church was consecrated on 9 November 1834 by the Bishop of Winchester. The new church seated 472 people and was dedicated to St. John the Evangelist (its present name).

On the site of the Saxon chapel stands a row of three old cottages, the rear walls of which are made mainly from ironstone with tooled stones in places, and adjoin the consecrated ground on one side. Elderly inhabitants state that the cottages were actually built with stones from the Saxon church.

A Christchurch guide of 1838 described the new church as being of Tudor style, with walls and roof covering of 'stone, combining convenience, solidity and beauty. The West facade with its elegant turret of Bath stone and the inside appearance of the roof, are worthy of high admiration . . .'

Originally the church lacked a chancel and a west porch. These were erected in 1872 at the expense of Rev. F. Hopkins, curate from 1846 and its first vicar from 1875 to 1903. He also built a fine brick vicarage in 1883 (now an hotel) for Rev. Biver the assistant priest of the parish. For himself and his family in about 1870 he built Holdenhurst Lodge on Haddon Hill, where there was a wooded estate of 20 acres. The estate was broken up for building after the end of World War 1, with the exception of the house. During 1936, when there was a serious outbreak of typhoid, this was used as a temporary hospital. After World War 2 a further building scheme resulted in its demolition.

We will return to the lives of the people of Holdenhurst. The yeomen were the prosperous members of the community, with business capacity, who managed the church funds and poor rate. Unfortunately, the problems of vagabondage and poverty

Fig. 1.   The Church of St. John the Evangelist, Holdenhurst.

date back many hundreds of years. The first Poor Law Act was passed in the reign of Queen Elizabeth I (Poor Relief Act, 1601), which made the parish the unit of administration. Churchwardens and substantial householders were appointed annually by Justices of Peace to be Overseers of the Poor. Their duties included training pauper children in a trade, buying materials to put those who were fit but poor to work, and providing direct relief for the old and infirm in workhouses, the costs of which were to be met from a local poor rate.

From the accounts of the overseers between 1685 and 1829, a poor rate of 1d. in the pound of the rateable value of land was levied on all property, in addition to a church rate. In some years the poor rate had to be levied several times and in 1827 there were actually 48 collections. Out of this charge the overseers also paid county rates, gaol money, and also had to maintain two pairs of stocks and repair highways and bridges. In the accounts for 1722 we read; 'mending ways at Boorne [Bourne] and Walsfoard – 16s.' (Walsford Bridge is North of Wimborne.) The bridge over the Bourne was still called Holdenhurst Bridge in 1856 (now the Square). The overseers were also responsible for punishing 'beggars, rogues and vagabonds' who, at one time, had to wear a badge with a letter 'P' for 'pauper'. In the overseers' accounts for 1697, badges cost 5s. 3d., whereas in 1707 the amount was only 1s. and in 1712 2s. In order to receive poor relief, applicants had to be villagers of Holdenhurst, otherwise they had to put their claim before the Justices of the Peace in Christchurch. The old poor house, with its thatched roof and adjoining turf house, has long since disappeared. It was said to be on land to the west of a Victorian red-brick house called 'Manor House'.

During the 18th century there were several smallpox epidemics, which resulted in increased charges on the poor rate. In 1706 £9 11s. 7½d. was allowed to Charles Troke and his family when they had smallpox, and in 1787 1s. was paid to Betty Pike 'for Brandy for Laying out Clarke's Maid'.

Facing the centuries-old village green, where fêtes are still held, are two attractive houses called the New House and the Old House. The New House is thought to have been built by William Clapcott (a Wimborne banker and a Commissioner of the Christchurch Inclosure Award) during the 18th century. Picturesque Magdalen Cottage (the Old House) with its thatched roof and beams is probably 17th-century. Formerly some of its small back windows were blocked up, which indicates that it was built prior to 1697 when a window tax was imposed on houses with more than six windows.

In the gardens of Magdalen Cottage is a low, thatched, half-timbered building, probably over five hundred years old. The use of this building, which is said to be the oldest one in Holdenhurst, has always been a mystery. Old inhabitants have referred to it as 'the Lepers' Hospital', whilst in the deeds of the Old House it is named as a 'Hospice of St. Mary Magdalen', that is, as a house of rest for the sick and destitute. Originally there was an upper room reached by a ladder. A huge fireplace stands at

Fig. 2. The Village Green, Holdenhurst, showing Magdalen Cottage and part of the Lepers' Hospital.

one side of the ground floor with skilfully-chiselled stone verticals where a cauldron chain and hook formerly hung. A large bread oven with out-built thatch is on the right of the fireplace. The door of the building, studded with large nails, is thought to be the Saxon porch door of the old church that was purchased from the churchwardens in 1764 for 2s. The most unusual features of the building are the two carvings on large stone blocks on its outside wall. One is of a grotesque, emaciated head, and the other is of a human chest, revealing its ribs. Although numerous tales are told of this building, there seems to be no definite record of its having been a leper colony; it is known, however, that there was a leper hospital in Christchurch during the 14th century at the corner of Magdalen Lane and Barrack Road.

According to Taylor Dyson,[7] an endowment was made during the reign of Edward III by 'Deed Poll, being a grant from John Feron of Poole to the Master of Lazar House and lepers and other sick there of 2 acres of arable land situate in Holdenhurst in frankalmoign . . .'. It has also been suggested that a leper colony could have been managed by canons of Christchurch Priory during the Middle Ages, and that those who had to be isolated were brought up the River Stour to this retreat. Life in the Old House is described by Kathleen Chilver in her book on Holdenhurst.[8] Harry King's father became the farm bailiff to Squire Dean in about 1880, and the family moved to the Old House. The children were all given duties. His was to whiten the front door steps every Saturday, whilst his brother had to clean all the knives. Another brother had to get the faggots of gorse to heat the brick oven in the Lepers' Hospital for his mother to do the weekly baking. The oven, filled with dry gorse, was lit and its iron door shut. When the fire had burnt itself out, the wood ash (lye) was brushed aside and the loaves put in. Then he had to seal the doors all round with moist cow dung, which set hard and kept the heat in the oven. Afterwards the wood ash was raked out and he cleaned the pewter and copperware with it.

Opposite the old vicarage was the village school (it ceased to be used as a school in about 1948), which was built by subscription in about 1846, mainly by the then Earl of Malmesbury of Hurn Court, who also provided the land, and by Mr. Clapcott-Dean of Littledown House, the two principal landowners in Holdenhurst village. In 1868 an inspector reported that the village school was managed by a totally untrained mistress, and that while the children were neat and clean, instruction was elementary and arithmetic was defective. He also commented on the fact that no log book was kept and that this was essential if they were to receive a grant. As a result of this, a log book was commenced from August 1868, and a certificated teacher was appointed. The children were expected to bring 'school pence' to pay towards their tuition. It was not until 1878, however, that the inspector was able to report that the children were intelligent, well-behaved and that the school was one of the most pleasing ones in the district.

Adjoining the grounds of the old vicarage there used to be a village smithy, but by 1930, as cars slowly replaced horses, its work diminished and eventually it closed down. The old pump, bellows and forge have gone. After being used as the village post office for many years, it was purchased and modernized, and in memory of its past history it has been named 'The Old Forge'.

Two of the oldest cottages in Holdenhurst are by the Townsend Estate. Originally there was one farmhouse cottage, to which the second was added, as was a cob and thatch shed for turf and logs. A large brick fire and chimney now separates the two thatched cottages, and the old lead pump, which is said to have the date 1707 inscribed inside it, has disappeared.

The chief landowners in Holdenhurst were the Earls of Malmesbury and the Cooper-Dean family. After inclosure in 1802, more land was acquired in the liberty of Westover, which later became Bournemouth. As the development and style of Bournemouth was mainly dependent on the progressive plans of estate owners, an indication of their backgrounds would seem appropriate to a history of Bournemouth.

Hurn Court, the seat of the Malmesbury family from 1800 to 1950, was originally the country house and manor farm of the Priors of Christchurch. After the Dissolution of the Monasteries in 1539, the property was owned by various people until the 17th century, when it came into the possession of Edward Hooper, J.P. When he died in 1795 at the age of 95 the estate was inherited by his relative, James Harris of Salisbury, who in 1800 became Viscount Fitzharris and the first Earl of Malmesbury. The first Earl was a famous diplomat, serving his country admirably in Russia, Prussia, Spain, Holland and France. He became known as the White Lion, or *Lion Blanc*. Under the Inclosure Act he purchased more land in the liberty of Westover, and was awarded other land in respect of loss of common rights or tithes. Most of his life was spent at his main seat in Henley, or in London where he died in 1820.

James Edward, the second Earl, was a naturalist and huntsman who spent most of his life at Hurn Court enjoying the country life and improving his estate. As a farmer, the weather was of great concern to him as well as to the tenant farmers. In his book *Half a Century of Sport*, he wrote: 'March 29th 1818 – Prayers for dry weather in Holdenhurst Church; 1828 – very wet summer, prayers said three or four Sundays for dry weather. July 13th 1828, July 19th 1829 – Stour too high to allow of us going to Church'. To go to church the family had to cross the River Stour at the ferry, which often proved most dangerous during the period of winter floods. In January 1825 they almost lost their lives when the ferry boat overturned and sank.

His wife was said to be one of the most beautiful women in Europe; when she died in 1815 at the age of 32 he was disconsolate and became a recluse. After his death in 1841 his remains were interred with those of his wife in the family vault below the chancel of the Priory Church at Christchurch, and near the high altar stands a large marble monument to her memory.

The second Earl was responsible for changing the name of Hurn Court (in Old English, 'hurn', 'hurne' or 'herne' mean 'a bend in the river') to Heron Court, but the original name was restored by the fifth Earl in 1935.

James Howard (1807–89), the third Earl of Malmesbury, was a famous statesman and was Foreign Secretary during Lord Derby's administration. He was a colleague and friend of Disraeli, who often visited Hurn Court. In his book *Memoirs of an Ex Minister*, the Earl writes of the lonely area of gorse and heath in the liberty of Westover, adding that 'in this wild country black game were abundant and in 1826 I shot an old blackcock on the very spot where St. Peter's Church now stands'.

On one occasion his horses and carriage were practically washed away as he was crossing the ford which traversed their grounds to attend church. After this experience he built a wooden bridge over the river, which in 1926 was replaced by the present concrete bridge.

On his death the estate passed to his nephew, Edward James, whose father, Admiral E. A. J. Harris, had been M.P. for Christchurch. His eldest son, James Edward,

9

became the fifth Earl, who died in 1950. Hurn Court was then sold and became a boarding school for boys in 1952; the heron was still adopted as the school badge.

Names commemorating the Malmesburys include the district of Malmesbury Park (the land was acquired by the first Earl under the Inclosure Act of 1802 in lieu of tithes); Orcheston Road (named after Orcheston St. George, Wiltshire, the home of their ancestor, Wm. Harris), which is a continuation of Avon Road, Winton, the latter refers to Salisbury, where the first Earl was born); and Fitzharris Avenue (the name given to the eldest son and heir to the Earldom), which is off Heron Court Road, Winton.

Littledown House, a fine, massive Georgian house standing in rough heathland on Great Dean Common near Holdenhurst, was built in the latter part of the 18th Century by John Dean (1715–1794). The family, together with the Meyricks and the Malmesburys, were the three greatest landowners in the liberty of Westover. Extensive areas of land were acquired, especially after inclosure by William Dean, 1737–1812, (see chapter V), particularly on the West Cliff, in Holdenhurst Road, the King's Park area and around the Wimborne and Charminster Roads.

His descendants included William Clapcott Dean (d. 1833), of Dean, Clapcott and Castleman, Bankers, of Wimborne, who married William Dean's daughter, Mary, and later succeeded to the Bournemouth estate. He became one of the three Commissioners responsible for executing the Inclosure Act.

Mr. Clapcott Dean was fortunate in having the services of his surveyor and agent, Mr. C. Crabbe Creeke, who was deeply interested in the well-planned development of Bournemouth, and in improving it by careful tree-planting. As a supporter of the advantages of the West Overcliff Drive, Mr. Clapcott Dean granted the Corporation a 999-year lease of the West Cliff and Chine area, also leasing to them at a rental of £50 per annum two acres of land for a recreation ground, now known as the Argyle Pleasure Gardens and Bowling Greens. Mr. Clapcott Dean also insisted on the preservation of Horseshoe Common as a park and pleasure ground when it became Corporation property. Besides showing interest in the civic life of the town, he gave financial assistance and provided land for several hospitals and churches in the town, and provided the site for the original vicarage at Holdenhurst.

The succession eventually came to James Edward Cooper (1840–1921), who married Elizabeth Dean, the daughter of Richard Dean of Holdenhurst. He took the name of Cooper-Dean. Like other members of the family, he took a keen interest in the development of the town. After his death at Littledown House in 1921, the property passed to his son, Joseph Cooper Dean (d. 1950) and afterwards to the two daughters of the latter, one of whom died in 1977.

The Dean Estate is commemorated in several districts and roads, including Dean Park, Dean Park Road, Littledown Road and Avenue, and Littledown Estate. Names commemorating the villages of their Bishops Waltham origin also occur in Durley Chine and Road, Deanmead, Droxford, Exton, Durrington, Meon, Swanmore, Waltham, Warnford and many other roads, whilst Bethia Road was named in memory of Edith Bethia Cooper-Dean (d. 1922), the wife of Joseph Cooper-Dean.

Throop
About a mile along the narrow, winding lane from Holdenhurst is the hamlet of Throop. Between the 14th and the 16th centuries it has been spelt variously as La Throp, La Thorpe, Throupe and Troppe.[9] From Saxon times, the hamlet grew around

10

the Holdenhurst watermill (later called Throop Mill) and until 1974 milling was carried on there. Until 1939, flour was ground by water power. A diesel engine was then installed, and in 1960 new owners changed to electricity.

Throop House, built in 1807, stands on raised ground to the east of the mill. This was the house of Sylvia, Dowager Countess of Malmesbury from 1929–39, and has a fine view over the River Stour. Through the branches of its large cedars Pigshoot ford can be seen. The name 'Pigshoot' is mentioned in the Christchurch Award of 1805, but could have been used since Saxon days. According to Kathleen Chilver, 'shute' (usually written as 'chute') is said to denote a piece of land detached from the main settlement. The muddy stretch of land by the ford was only considered suitable for pigs to root up.[10]

Sir Walter Tyrell fled across the Pigshoot after killing King William Rufus, having previously crossed the River Avon at a spot now known as Avon Tyrell.

The Pigshoot and Leaden Stour fords were crossing places often used by smugglers (see chapter IV), who were aware of dangerous and deep holes in the river. Here they used to sink contraband goods until they were able to dispose of them with safety. Most of the villagers aided the smugglers in some way, regarding it as a satisfactory method of supplementing their meagre wages of seven or eight shillings per week.

From about 1896, holiday-makers from Boscombe would enjoy drives in 'four-in-hand' brakes to picturesque Holdenhurst. Attractive wayside rills flowed through the village, many cottages having their own tiny bridges to the front garden gate. As the horses splashed through the Pigshoot ford, the attendant used to hoot merrily on his three-foot horn. The complete journey, via Hurn, over the old Iford Bridge and back to Boscombe cost 1s. 6d!

Amusing stories have been told of dog carts and horse charabancs being stuck in Pigshoot ford, and also of horses that refused to go any further into the water. There is one tale of a Bournemouth dairyman who accused a Hurn farmer of watering his milk. The reply given was: 'When I drove over the Pigshoot yesterday the river was so rough and the cart rocked so much that the lids of the churns jolted off and the water must have splashed in!'[11]

Muccleshell
Lying between Throop and Muscliff is the hamlet of Muccleshell. It was known as Mukeleshulle in the 13th century, Mukelshull in the 14th century, Mulkeshull in the 15th century and Mokylshyll and Muggeshyll in the 16th century.[12] The word probably derives from the Old English 'muckel', meaning much or big, and refers to the 'big hill', i.e. Bury Hill. At the beginning of the muddy path known as Berry Lane stands Muccleshell Farm, formerly known as Muccleshell Hall. Originally this was a thatched building; the date 1729 carved on a brick is said to indicate when the roof was slated. The black and white timber work and two bricked-up windows show that it dates from the 17th century, or even earlier. One legend says that Charles II hid there for one night, whilst elderly residents claim there was once a secret room in the old Hall. When gas was laid on in the 1950s, workmen had difficulty in piercing a $2^1/_2$-foot wall, and it was also discovered that one bedroom had two floors, the boards running in opposite directions, with a space between them.

Nearby is an attractive thatched cottage, over three hundred years old, with pictur-esque 17th-century-type windows, called 'The Shack'.

Walking towards Throop we came to Vine Cottage, which was probably built in the early 19th century. This delightful cottage, with its tiled roof, was once owned by Rev. F. Hopkins, the first vicar of Holdenhurst, the rent for it then being 1s. 6d. per week.

Almost opposite Vine Cottage is Stour View, a fine 18th-century house with a Georgian porch upheld by slender columns. At one time this was the home of a maltster and ships' biscuit maker. The malt was processed in a long, low-lying building adjacent to the house that is now used as a small bore rifle range. Below, on the ground floor can be seen a large iron-cased oven.

The manufacture of biscuits was conducted mainly for vessels engaged in the Poole-Newfoundland trade. It is also said that these ships' biscuits were supplied to the *Victory* in the days of Nelson and the Battle of Trafalgar. The bricked oven at the back of the house has been walled up, but judging from the double floors and double joists in one of the bedrooms, it is thought that the biscuits, which were taken up by ladder or pulley, were stored here, whilst in the stone-floored kitchen and adjoining room were two big iron ranges, where the biscuits were probably made. The large, spacious rooms indicate that Stour View belongs to an era of well-built and elegant buildings.

All these buildings are listed under preservation orders.

In 1828 a chapel was built in the hamlet, and was known first as the Independent Chapel, then as Throop Congregational Church, and today as Throop United Reformed Church. In 1978 it celebrated its 150th anniversary. In its early days, according to Kathleen Chilver,[13] a white flag which could be seen all over the Stour valley was hoisted when a minister was coming to take a service. The service was also announced by speaking-trumpet in Muccleshell, Throop and Muscliff.

Many old, formerly thatched, cottages, have disappeared; Hopkins farm, owned by Rev. Hopkins, was demolished in 1979, despite protests from the villagers, whilst the nearby ancient enclosures of Willow Mead and Dumple Close are now part of the Willow Mead housing estate.

Muscliff

At the western end of Holdenhurst parish is the hamlet of Muscliff, whose name originated from Old English 'mus-clif', or 'mouse cliff'. Early versions of the name include Museclyve, which was used in the 13th and 14th centuries; Moseclyve, in the 14th and 15th centuries, and Moseclyre, in the 15th century. The manor of Muscliff, which was later absorbed into the manor of Christchurch, was held until 1414 for one-eighth of a knight's fee of the lords of Christchurch.[14]

There used to be several attractive thatched cottages in the hamlet, but through delapidation and neglect they have all now disappeared. One of the last to be demolished was a large thatched farmhouse, over the front door of which was carved the date 1729. From 1800 to 1804 this was the home of Farmer West and his family, who was often referred to as 'the wise farmer of Muscliff' (see chapter V). When a cob-wall cottage which adjoined the wall of the farmhouse was pulled down, an old prayer book dating from the reign of Charles I was discovered.

Farmer West was soon concerned about the appalling conditions of the nearby roads, particularly Muscliff Lane, which became a quagmire in the winter and a multitude of deep hard ruts in the summer. With the help of neighbouring farmers and some of his own men, the track was improved by ploughing a border on each side, thus throwing the soil to the centre of the lane and forming a convex surface, which allowed the water to drain off at the sides. Gravel from a nearby quarry was then thrown on to the centre part of the lane, making it wide enough for two carts or two carriages to pass. According to Farmer West's son, this was the method which, 12 years later, was used by Macadam and brought him fame as a road maker.[15]

The hot, dry summers of 1800 and 1801 resulted in arid, sandy soil and poor crops, which became exceptionally dear in price. Farmer West's son wrote of the fearful summer of 1801. 'The sun looked out of the steel, blue sky as if he had no pity.' Many labouring people lived on barley, bran or oatmeal. The Government issued a proclamation recommending that bran be mixed with flour, when ground, that no person should consume more than one pound of bread per day, and that those who ate vegetables with their meals should not eat bread as well. It was owing to these conditions that much of the common land was inclosed (see chapter V).

Prior to the inclosure of Poole Heath, there were numerous common snakes, vipers and adders in the area, the latter two types being dangerous and venomous. Because of this, many farmers made holes in their gate posts where they kept a small bottle of 'adder oil' which would neutralize the poison of snake bites.

In 1804 Farmer West was elected as an overseer of the poor when, because of the extreme poverty of the peasants, 17 poor rates were demanded. This was also the time when people were scared by the threat of a possible invasion by Napoleon along the coast of Bourne. 1804 was also a year of drought, causing the only three ponds in the hamlet to evaporate to complete dryness. Cattle had to go a quarter of a mile to the river for water; turnips were the size of small oranges and barley was fit only for cattle food.[16] The relatives who had lent money to Farmer West to finance his big farm died and the executors called in the loan; the farm was broken up and the worthy farmer, depressed and unhappy, left the district, to the regret of all.

Sydenham's *Guide to Bournemouth* (1890) describes Muscliff as:

> A charming spot, and which should form a principal object in the inland drive to the Stour valley. Leaving the carriage at one of the little wayside inns, at the adjoining hamlet of Throop, a gully or slope to an old fording-place opens to the footpath and the winding course of the Stour is seen opening at the foot of a lofty bank or cliff . . . The visitor should follow this footway to the village which stands clustering its rustic cottages upon the banks further on . . .

Today, the fields and farm lands of the hamlets of Throop, Muccleshell and Muscliff, are slowly but inevitably disappearing, as more and more land is taken over for building sites and estates, while cars and buses have, long since, replaced the carts and carriages of yesteryear.

Chapter III

OTHER ANCIENT VILLAGES

Iford

TODAY IFORD is a busy conurbation and suburb on the eastern boundary of Bournemouth. Shops and business premises extend along the length of Pokesdown Hill (at one time known as 'Pub Hill,' since the *New Inn* [now *Iford Bridge* Hotel], was the only public house in the area). Housing estates have proliferated around Pokesdown Hill, Castle Lane East and Iford Lane, while an almost perpetual stream of traffic passes the enormous Iford roundabout. All traces of this ancient community of Saxon origin have disappeared. Apart from low-lying fields which extend to the banks of the River Stour, where a few cows still graze peacefully, it is difficult to imagine that up to the 20th century this was once an attractive hamlet consisting of pretty thatched cottages.

On the desolate wasteland, which was to become part of Bournemouth, were a few scattered cottages and farms, whose inhabitants were chiefly concerned with agriculture and fishing in the Stour. Their thatched cottages with mud walls were mainly in Iford Lane, along Old Bridge Road and a narrow, stony track, Water Lane, both of which lead to the Old Iford Bridge. From the moorland and surrounding marshes bedding was obtained for their animals, rushes for thatches and basket-making, and turf for fuel.

Iford (originally a ford) and Tuckton (including Wick) were tythings in the parish and hundred of Christchurch. Later they became the tythings of Pokesdown and Iford, and Tuckton and Week.

In a charter of Baldwin and Richard de Redvers c. 1150, the name was written as Huver, while Norman-French versions appear during the 12th to 14th centuries, including Huvre and Luvre. During the 15th and 16th centuries it was referred to as Ever, Yver and Iver. From that period it was mostly known as Iforde or Iford. In the Hampshire map of John Norden, published in about 1600, and in the Christchurch poor rate assessment book of 1756, it is written as Iforde,[1] although in the minutes of Justices of Peace at Hampshire County Quarter Sessions it appears as Ifford and Efford.[2]

The ancient Iford Bridge dates back to the 12th century, and possibly even before that time. Before the bridge was constructed, Iford or Iver was known as a fording place over the Stour, and was the only means of getting to and from Christchurch for the farming communities situated along the banks of the river. The earliest written records concerning the Bridge appear in the charters of Baldwin de Redvers in about

14

1140 and 1160, which refer to 'pontem de Huver'.[3] In the 16th century Leland referred to the 'Iver Bridge of stone', of which nothing now remains; this could have been the original bridge.[4]

Until the Statute of Bridges in 1530, the building and maintenance of bridges was regarded as a charity or as the duty of the local people using them. The Act made the county or borough liable for the repair of bridges and empowered Justices of the Peace to levy a rate at Quarter Sessions for that purpose, although legacies and alms were still needed. In 1560 John Howkie of Holnehurst left XXd to Iver Bridge, and in 1590 John Corbyn of Holnehurst, also left XXd for the 'reparation of Iver Bridge'.[4]

The part known today as 'Old Iford Bridge', which is preserved as an ancient historic monument for use by pedestrians, consisted of several sections, with causeways, over the Stour and intervening islets of marshy land. The first section, known as 'the Great Bridge', consisted of two segmental arches built in 1784. Between the two arches can be seen the inscription

BUILT BY THE COUNTY,
G. HOOKEY, MASON 1784.

The next section, sometimes referred to as 'The Causeway Bridge', consisted of two smaller arches, and also dates from the 18th century. Carrying on from this section was a causeway of about 40 yards leading to another bridge of four spans, which was also built in the 17th century. The final section (near Christchurch Road) consisted of six arches and was known as the 'Flood Bridge'.

In J. A. Young's carefully detailed booklet of the history of Iford Bridge a full account is given of the problems of its repair and maintenance. In 1792, in a report of the Justices at Quarter Sessions, one reads; 'I find the same [Iford Bridge] in very bad repair and dangerous for persons passing either on foot or Horseback and particularly Carriages without going round part of a field thereto adjoining, and in great floods it is entirely impassable for Man, Horse or Carriage . . .'.[5]

As the roadway was only 12 ft. wide in parts, heated arguments frequently occurred. At one time, farmers were preceded by a man on horseback who blew on his horn to announce the arrival of a team of horses or oxen that expected to have the right of way.

To relieve congestion, lay-bys or passing bays were constructed, and a patrol post manned by an R.A.C. guide, or a policemen, was established. With the increase of motor traffic, a new bridge became essential, and in 1933 the present 'new' Iford Bridge was constructed in a different position by Hampshire County Council, which fortunately decided to preserve the old bridge. After the opening of the new bridge on Christchurch Road, the Causeway Bridge was demolished and rebuilt with arches the same size as those in the Great Bridge, to which they were then joined, making it the first of the present four-span bridges in Old Bridge Road. In 1972/3 the 'Flood Bridge' was badly in need of repair, and was no longer required against flooding; to preserve the arches, it was decided to fill them in.

By 1872 the population of Iford was about 130, and as there was no church in the village, Rev. Elijah Pickford (see Pokesdown in chapter VII) arranged for cottage services to be commenced in that year. Mrs. Brake, the wife of the postman, offered a room and even sent her children to invite neighbours on the nights when the service was to be held. This continued for several years.

Up to the 20th century, despite the continuing growth of Bournemouth, Iford remained a rustic community, with thatched cottages, the blacksmith's and wheelwright's workshops, a few farms, the *New Inn* and Iford House.

Iford House was an outstanding building, which stood alone in three acres of ground adjoining Castle Lane East and Christchurch Road. A long drive led to the house, where several maids, a coachman and a gardener were employed. The house was built in 1795 by Dr. William Dale Farr, who had purchased part of Westover hundred in Iford and Springbourne. The house became known as Iford Manor and Dr. Farr as the 'squire of Iford'. From 1795 to 1813 it was tenanted by John Sloman, who later lived in his own property at Wick House. Iford House eventually became the property of Dr. Farr's grandson, William Windham Farr, after whom Windham Road, Springbourne, was named. After Mr. John King, a magistrate and the last owner, died in 1930, the property remained empty and neglected. In 1936 it was demolished for building development, when the date '1823' was discovered cut in the roof timber, and '1825' and the name of William Barnes of Southampton impressed in the plastering.

Almost opposite Iford House was Iford Farm, managed by the Ellison family, whose land extended into Iford Lane, where there were numerous pigsties, a stable for several farm horses and usually 60 or 70 cows (all milked by hand), several barns and extensive grazing land. When the last farmer, William Alfred Ellison, died in 1919, mourned and greatly respected, he was carried to his funeral on one of his own farm waggons drawn by two horses suitably draped. Shortly afterwards the farm changed to dairy farming. In 1923 the business was purchased by Malmesbury & Parsons, when all the farming implements were sold by auction. By 1931, the last occupants of the farmhouse (the Hunt family) had moved out and the building was demolished.

Adjacent to Iford House was Clingan's Charity Farm, established under the will of John Clingan of Christchurch, who died about 1716, as part of the Trust for the benefit of poor children of the parish of Christchurch, i.e. to apprentice children with particular regard to sea service. From 1948 the scope of the Trust, which is still active today, was considerably enlarged.

The farm stood 'four square like a sentinel on the hill leading to Old Iford Bridge'.[6] In 1877 there was no kitchen at the farm and all baking was done in a big brick oven using furze and brushwood to heat it. Later a coal-burning kitchen stove was fixed up by the Clingan Trustees. When the farm was to be demolished (probably in the 1930s) the Trustees allowed Miss Harvey, the last occupant (who had managed the farm alone since her father's death in 1907), to take 'anything within reason'[6] from the farm to her new home. The Trustees were more than surprised when she decided to take the front and back doorsteps so that she would continue to cross the same thresholds, together with the flagstones of the hall and dairy floor for her garden paths, and the cobblestones of the stable floor for a new rockery.

Further down the hill from Clingan's Farm was a narrow stretch of land below road level and by the edge of the Stour. Here stood a mysterious little cottage. Only one window could be seen from the road, and this was always covered with a curtain. Elderly inhabitants used to say that it was the home of a witch because the occupant wore strange clothes and spoke in a peculiar way. On moonlight nights she could be seen sailing down the Stour, standing in a covell or wooden two-handed tub which she propelled with a long-handled heather besom. On one stormy night she set out and was never seen again. According to F. W. Barnes,[7] from the early 1900s a Miss Beech lived there with her dozen Persian cats and several ducks. When the ducks stayed on

16

the river too long she would fetch them home and sail downstream in her 'tub', using her besom for propulsion – hence the witch story.

In 1958 it was decided to alter the course of the Stour to prevent recurring erosion of the cliffs over which Castle Lane East extended and to avoid further flooding. The loss of several beauty spots in the area resulted, including an attractive valley where there was a small concrete jetty known as Sheepwash. Here sheep were brought from Holdenhurst and other hamlets near the Stour to be washed prior to shearing, and sometimes 500 sheep were washed in a day. The shearers travelled from all over the country and charged 4d. a sheep for shearing.

It is greatly regretted that the attractive little village of thatched cottages with pretty gardens had completely disappeared by about 1929, due to development of the area and the need for a new bridge to accommodate increasing traffic. Their destruction was strongly criticized at the time by local residents and historians. Taylor Dyson wrote 'it was vandalism to sweep away the old cottages even though progress demanded the new bridge'.[8]

Wick

Wick and Tuckton were even smaller hamlets than Iford. The first Ordnance Survey map of 1811 shows the isolated hamlets of Wick, Tuckford (Tuckton), Iford and Stourfield, whilst an older map of 1791 shows the area of Christchurch hundred, comprising Holdenhurst, numerous Dorset villages near the River Stour, and wild heathland known as Poole Heath; Bournemouth was then unknown.

The original name, Wic (Old English for a village or dairy farm) was first mentioned in the charters of Baldwin de Redver in about 1100, and Richard de Redver in about 1161. The word Week appears in John Speed's Map of England of 1611; Wyke, Weeke and were used Week during the 17th and 18th centuries, and Week again in the Christchurch Inclosure Award of 1805.

In his descriptive booklet about Wick,[9] Mr. L. Popplewell refers to it as 'the last village on the Dorset Stour'.[10] Whilst not far from the ceaseless traffic on Stour Road, it has still retained a village atmosphere of peace and tranquillity. Protected by the river and its banks, with its overhanging, lush, green trees, and the narrow, twisting Wick Lane (originally Tuckton Lane), referred to by Popplewell as 'a rural gem of a country lane', it has missed the fate of Iford and Tuckton and remained a secluded oasis. The many attractive modern bungalows in the area, mainly built during the last 30 years on farmland and meadows, help to maintain a mixture of 'old and new' in the picturesque village.

Its main focal point is the tiny triangular-shaped green, around which are well-preserved Victorian and Edwardian buildings. The green itself hides the site of an old village well which used to be covered by a trap door. A long pole, with a bucket attached, was used to obtain the water, which was only about 6 ft. underground. Nearby a stretch of swampy land indicates the site of an old pond.

The oldest houses are to the right and front of the green, all are listed to be historically preserved. Wick House, the local manor-house, is a distinctive, well-constructed house of the Queen Ann period, built c. 1691. An extension known as 'Wick Cottage' was added later. The first written mention of it is in the Christchurch poor rate book of July 1813, when it was occupied by John Sloman and his family. Three generations of Slomans lived there until 1939, when it was sold to Mrs. M. McConnell and was turned into four terraced maisonettes. It is said that Nelson dined there, and also that he stayed at Wickmeads. Lord Lascelles is also reputed to have stayed at Wick house, hence Lascelles Road. A subterranean passage used to lead under the back of Wick House, under the River Stour, to the crypt of the Priory – another of the smugglers' secret underground routes.

Next to Wick House is Wick Farm, a long two-storey building with a slate roof, which was originally the property of the lord of the manor. From 1729 it was owned by Lady Mews and then by her heirs, Benjamin Clarke, Joseph Jarvis Clarke and George Ivison Tapps. Prior to 1777, it was shown in the Christchurch poor rate assessment book as 'Knaptons' and 'Holloways', the rates being 8s. 6d. for the former and 10d. for part of the latter. Later it was known as 'Kemptons' and 'Holloways', while from March 1777 the name 'Wick Farm' was used.

Behind the green are the quaint, semi-detached houses known as 'Quality' and 'Tranquillity', the latter having served as the village shop for a short period. Today there is neither church, shop nor inn in the village. Nearby are some old cottages, and it is thought that all these buildings date from about 1820. A more recent house is the stylishly-built Well House of 1908, at the back of which is an old barn where church services were held for a time during the 19th century.

To the left of the green is another well-constructed house known as 'The Sanctuary', behind which is an older cottage, together with remnants of old farm buildings and a barn with the date 1846 engraved in its brick work.

Laurel Cottage is perhaps the tiniest and the most attractive of the 'listed' buildings, and was built in 1851. Until the early 20th century an old, thatched 'one-up one-down' cottage (now demolished) was joined to it. It was known as 'Uncle Tom's Cabin', and was inhabited by Rosie and John O'Brien (and their parents before them), who worked on the Wick ferry service. It is said that he was so big that his sister had to have special boots made for him. He was also the first pier-master of the ill-fated Southbourne pier (see chapter VII). His pier-master's hut, somewhat dilapidated, remains in the grounds of Laurel Cottage.

The only thatched cottage remaining in Wick today is 'Riverside', a picturesque 17th-century building, brick-faced and half-timbered at the back.

Gordon Selfridge (of Selfridge's, London), once owned parts of Wick and neighbouring Hengistbury Head, and even planned to build an enormous castle on the headland. For financial reasons, the area was sold to Bournemouth Corporated on 6 May 1930 for £25,250, on the condition that the buildings and scenic beauty were preserved.

Before the advent of bungalows and 'laid-out' lanes and drives, Wick consisted of low-lying fields, swamps, gravel and several farms, each with their pigsties and cowsheds, and also orchards and profuse wild flowers. There were woodlands of tall, straggling pine trees, frightening in their density; an ill-defined track through them led to the desolate headland of Hengistbury Head. This was the area which became Branders Lane, and where a spring-fed pond which caused frequent flooding had to be drained before the site was suitable for building.

Prior to the last World War, the river by the ferry was dredged to avoid recurrent flooding from the tidal waters of the Stour. On an old ordnance map of 1871 is the warning 'river liable to flooding', and it was also said that the river took at least one life a year. Although reclamation of salt and reed marshes have resulted in the pleasant Tuckton Riverside Walk, the dangers of flooding have not been entirely overcome.

Even in 1979, the heavy rainfall caused the banks of the Stour to burst, flooding meadows on either side of the river in Christchurch, Wick and other areas.

A ferry has existed in Wick for centuries, and water transport has always played an important part in the lives of the villagers. Before Tuckton Bridge was constructed in 1882, the only other route to neighbouring Christchurch (for supplies, business or to attend the Priory) was via Wick Lane (originally Tuckton Lane), Iford Lane, crossing over Old Iford Bridge and on to Christchurch Road,

Before the dredging of the river there used to be a ford which would be crossed on horseback or on foot at low tide. Local residents mainly crossed the river by means of their own boats. The first ferry service commenced from the Christchurch side from about 1800 and was established by Eli Miller, in whose family it remained until 1903. The ferry from Wick was introduced in 1814 by Mr. Marshall, a worker on the farm tenanted by John Sloman of Wick House. When Marshall broke his leg and was unable to carry on with farm work, Mr. Sloman provided him with a boat and gave him land at the river side which has been used as a landing stage since that time. The original charge was a $1/2$d. each way, villagers travelling free on the return trip!

Off Wick Lane, not far from the bungalows in Riversdale and Magnolia Roads, is a Bronze Age burial site. I wonder how many people are aware of the round barrow, which lies practically hidden among the pines?

Hengistbury Head

Hengistbury Head, with its magnificent, panoramic views of the Purbecks and Isle of Wight, attracts thousands of visitors each year. To the authorities it is an area that causes grave concern due to the continual erosion, which takes place at a rate of about three ft. per year. It has even been stated that the whole hill could disappear within thirty years, or that part of it could virtually become an island. Frequent cliff falls cause more and more deterioration, whilst Mr. Teasdill, Curator of the Russell-Cotes Museum, and others are becoming deeply concerned that prehistoric finds and evidence are disappearing. It is to be hoped that some way will be found of preserving and protecting this ancient and famous piece of Dorset's heritage, which is of both national and international importance, for future generations.

Tuckton

The tiny hamlet of Tuckton (Old English Tocketon and Touketon – the Ordnance Survey of 1811 has the name as Tuckford) consisted, until recently, of scattered farms and a few cottages.

Until 1872 there were about sixty inhabitants in Tuckton, and as there was no bridge or direct route to neighbouring Christchurch until the building of Tuckton Bridge in 1882, it remained completely rural until after that time. The only access was by way of the Wick Ferry or by taking a long walk (or ride on horseback) to Old Iford Bridge.

As the nearest churches were Christchurch Priory or St. James's Church, Pokesdown, Rev. Elijah Pickford (see Pokesdown) managed to obtain a room in one of the farm-houses. Well-attended services were held during the winter months for several years from about 1872, and later, through the kindness of Mr. Moser, a mission hall was built.

Besides Tuckton Farm, Elford's Farm and the inevitable smithy, there were several large houses in the area. There was Carbery House (owned by Mr. F. Moser), a large estate between Pokesdown and Tuckton. A winding drive, with thick bushes and firs

19

on either side and magnificent rhododendrons in the Spring, hid the house from the road. (The house is now demolished.) Beyond and around was farmland. There was also Heatherlea, Tuckton, owned by the Hon. Ed. Wm. Douglas, J.P. (4th son of 19th Earl of Morton), now demolished, and Stourcliffe House and Farm, owned by George Kellaway, another large estate comprising gardens, barns, stables and several fields, which has also been demolished.

For a time in the late 19th century, Tuckton achieved fame as the area where Count Tchertkoff and other Russian exiles stayed and printed the works of Tolstoy. (See chapter XXI.)

Kinson

Traces of Palaeolithic man have been found in the ancient village of Kinson. Early records reveal its original names: Cynestanstun ('tun', or farm, of 'Cynestan', a Saxon chief) is the earliest form, and Chinestantone appears in the Domesday Survey of 1086, when Edward of Sarisberie (Salisbury) held the land, together with Canford, in fief for the Normans. Other names include Kynestanton, Kinstanton and Kynston; in the 19th century Kingston was used, and then Kinson. Kinson used to be a tithing belonging to the large manor of Canford (Cheneford), which also included Hamworthy, Parkstone, Longfleet and Poole, in the county of Dorset.[11] As Bournemouth later absorbed the ancient villages around it, so Poole incorporated these villages, including the original manor of Canford.

Kinson lies on the northernmost boundary of Bournemouth, and was one of the last villages to be added to the growing town, when it was taken from Poole. Today Kinson, straddling either side of Wimborne Road, consists of a busy shopping area, a shopping precinct and a modern library, which in 1940 replaced an old, corrugated one.

On leaving the main road, however, one is soon among lanes where the countryside remains, in spite of housing estates and urban sprawl. In Kinson Road, Brook Road, East Howe Lane, Poole Lane, and others, one is almost surprised to see the untidy, straggling hedgerows, high banks and ancient oaks. In this area, too, one comes across some of Kinson's architecturally listed buildings, of which the residents are justly proud. The *Thatched House* in East Howe Lane, a pretty cottage ornée c. 1820, now a public house, was formerly a villa called 'The Shrubberies'. Nearby are Primrose Cottages, a pair of symmetrical, picturesque, thatched cottages c. 1800. In Poole and Manor Farm Lanes are several attractive Canford Estate cottages, c. 1850, in Tudor style with buff bricks and stucco dressings, originally built by Lord Wimborne for estate workers.

Unfortunately many of Kinson's fine buildings were demolished in the days when building development was considered more important than historical preservation. Among them was Howe Lodge, an elegant 18th-century house built by the smuggler, Gulliver. Despite many protests it was demolished in 1958 for road widening and the erection of flats, when a concealed room, trap door and bricked tunnel were discovered. Next door was 'Woodlands', its original parts dating to the 1700s, with thick cob walls and period windows, which was also demolished. Kinson House, Horsham Avenue, was at one time the home of the great uncle and aunt of Dame Sybil Thorndyke and her brother, Russell. The oldest parts were again said to be linked with the smugglers, and as a result of happy holidays spent riding about the wild heathland, Russell later wrote a book about a clergyman smuggler, Dr. Syn. Some large oak trees mark its grounds by the flats which have replaced the house. Until about 1840 nearly everyone in the village was connected with smugglers, and any present residents who can trace their ancestors to that time are probably descended from them.

Kinsonians are determined that the village's original community spirit shall be kept alive. Research by the members of its active Historical Society continues to provide interesting evidence of the bygone days in this once rural district. In the heart of the shopping centre is the Village Green, another mixture of the old and the new. The Green was established in 1968 on the site where two attractive thatched cottages once stood near the old horse pound. A swinging sign stands in the centre of the green, which reads; 'Any person causing damage to any part of the village green may be liable to chastisement by being placed in the village stocks'. Next to the post are the stocks!

Another unspoilt area noted for its natural vegetation and many wild flowers is Kinson Common, where prehistoric implement have been discovered (they are now in the Rothesay and Dorchester museums), and also Bronze Age barrows.

For many generations village life has centred around the church, St. Andrew's, sometimes known as 'the smugglers' church' (chapter IV), and the oldest church in Bournemouth. It is of Saxon origin, although only the tower foundation remains. Its Norman tower was constructed of ironstone rubble, surmounted by a crenellated parapet. The 13th-century font is of Purbeck marble. At one time the cover had to be locked to prevent its use for black magic, and also during a period of interdiction during the reign of King John. The nave, aisles and three gables were rebuilt in 1893 at a cost of about £1,500! Interesting graves include one with a face, moth and skull, and another dated 1667 which is in memory of Johne Weare of Little Canford, 'a glover, a man industrious, peaceable and charitable', who left 10s. to be paid annually to the poor of Kinson. The smugglers' altar tomb with its moveable lid bore the false names, Jane and William Oakley, 1718 and 1724.

A monument in the churchyard, as well as pictorial windows in the church, commemorate members of the Fryer family, some of whom lived at Pelhams (see below). Gulliver's respectability was further enhanced when his daughter, Elizabeth, married William Fryer of Wimborne and Lytchett Minster, a banker and esteemed member of a Dorset family.

Village life has also centred around a well-proportioned, elegant Georgian house, in white stucco, with two Tuscan columns, called 'Pelhams', which was built in 1793. The house, together with the land and farm known as Kinson (later Kinson Manor), Farm, was previously owned by Gulliver. By 1840, when the estate was divided among Gulliver's descendants, the farm was separated from the house. From the late 19th century the house was owned by Rev. A. M. Sharp and was known as Kinson Vicarage, until 1930, when he sold the house and park to the Council at a moderate price on the condition that it was used for the benefit of Kinson people. During the last war it was used as a civil defence and fire centre, after which it had become delapidated. Both renovation and demolition were considered. Happily, it was decided to repair the building, and it was transformed into the present, gleaming white mansion. During restoration, reed and plaster panelling was discovered, as was a George III halfpenny dated 1806, which was embedded in the brickwork. Today the fine Kinson Community Centre, in its spacious grounds among magnificent trees, offers a variety of activities, including a playing area for children, and fulfils a need in the district.

Kinson Manor Farm, c. 1700, consisted of 140 acres in 1840 and extended to what is now New Road. The long, two-storeyed building of mellow bricks was originally thought to have been a hunting station for the Earls of Shaftesbury. Demolished farms commemorated in road names include Cudnell Farm, Cudnell Avenue, which was farmed from 1816 to 1956 by the Elliott family; Durdell's Farm, Durdell Avenue, farmed by Abbott family, and Pitts Farm (between Durdell Av. and Kinson Farm), which was once owned by Gulliver.

The demand for more houses in Bournemouth and Poole and the surrounding districts resulted in the growth of brick and building industries, which were fostered by the discovery of several different types of clay. Flue bricks were even exported to Canada, where some were recently discovered bearing the words' Kinson, Poole' (these are now in the archives of the Elliott Industrial Estate, West Howe, which developed on the site of one of the Pottery Companies).

There are several historic public houses in Kinson. The *Dolphin* inn, Wimborne Road, is thought to be a 17th-century coaching inn, and the *Royal Oak* inn, known as the *Travellers' Rest* until 1840, was a halting place for travellers. For 23 years after this it was known as the *Five Alls*, and had a sign which read:

> I rule for all
> I pray for all
> I work for all
> I fight for all
> I plead for all

(The motto refers to five different professions.) The low, L-shaped building was originally lit by oil lamps, and care had to be taken that the smell of oil did not flavour the beer. In 1863 it became known as the *Royal Oak*, which was demolished some years ago to be replaced by the present modern building.

The *Bear Cross* Hotel, built in 1931, replaced a picturesque thatched cottage known as the *Old Inn*. Supplies were brought in from Poole, and when extra beer was required a donkey cart was dispatched. In the days before the huge roundabout, a simple signpost indicated the direction. (The name 'Bear Cross' is thought to be a corruption of the Dorset place-name 'Bere', as in Bere Regis.)

Another listed building is the Longham Bridge, built in 1728, and rebuilt and widened in 1792. A plaque threatens transportation to anyone damaging the bridge. The Longham Pumping Station was built in 1885 and is thought to be the site of an old mill recorded in the Domesday Survey. The cottage on one side of the bridge was an old smithy, worked for many years by the Cherrett family. (It is now part of the Longham Mower Service.)

Ensbury (formerly Eynesburgh, Emsbury and Emsberry) was another ancient village adjoining Kinson.[12] It is greatly to be deplored that the fine Ensbury Manor, belonging to Kinson Farm, the foundations and deeds of which were 700 years old, should have been demolished and replaced by another housing estate. When one reads of the Jacobean fireplace, the panelling, a maze of passages and brick-lined cavities and tunnels used by the smugglers, it seems reprehensible that this and other buildings have not been preserved to add to the heritage of Bournemouth. Fortunately the Dower House remains, which was built about two hundred years ago for the Dowagers of Ensbury Manor, and is now occupied by Joy Lands, the author of the well-researched book *Old Kinson*.

East of the Manor was Ensbury Vicarage, built in 1785. The mellow, red-brick house was once surrounded by tall trees and was the vicarage for St. Andrew's Church until 1895, when Rev. Arnold Sharp moved to Pelhams. After the Second World War the vicarage became a restaurant and guest-house known as *The Old Vicarage*. During alterations subsidence in the grounds revealed tunnelling leading from a chamber under the kitchen, which was thought to be one of the many used by smugglers. For a short time the licensed restaurant was renamed the *Cayman Arms* by the brewers, but due to strong protest it has now reverted to its former name of *The Old Vicarage*.

In 1895 Kinson became a parish council under Dorset County Council and Poole Rural District Council. In about 1929 Bournemouth decided to make its final, major boundary extension, which was to include Kinson, East and West Howe, Ensbury, Wallisdown Road and Talbot Village, all of which were part of the Rural District Council of Poole. For a time there was strenuous opposition, particularly to the 'poaching' of land from another county, when five local authorities – Dorset County Council, Poole R.D.C., Poole Town Council, Kinson Parish and Bournemouth County Borough – were engaged in the bitter fight. Finally, by a plebiscite, the people of Kinson decided that there were more advantages in incorporation into Bournemouth, to which it was becoming more and more closely allied, than into Poole Borough, which also tried to claim the area. Some Bournemouth residents expressed doubts concerning the expenses involved in bringing Kinson to the standard of the County Borough. It certainly seemed a mixed blessing, as Bournemouth took over 36 miles of roads, in one of which pools were so deep that ducks swam, and in another a child was almost drowned; and in September 1931, after extension, 150 lamps were lit for the first time. Kinson agreed, however, to pay a differential rate of 3s. 4d. in the pound over Bournemouth rates, which was to be eliminated over a 10-year period, in order to pay for the benefits received.

The boundary extension of 1931 was a unique example of a town increasing its acreage of 6,643 acres by two-thirds of its size to 11,270.3 acres. In taking Kinson from Dorset into Hampshire, the Borough encountered many sentimental objections as well as prosaic ones. The extension also took in Holdenhurst, the 'mother' of Bournemouth; the fashionable young adult thus swallowed its ancient, countrified mother.

Chapter IV

SMUGGLING AND THE DISCOVERY OF BOURNEMOUTH

Five and twenty ponies
Trotting through the dark –
Brandy for the Parson,
'Baccy for the Clerk,
Laces for a lady, letters for a spy,
And watch the wall, my darling, while the Gentlemen go by!
– *R. Kipling*

IT SEEMS STRANGE that modern Bournemouth owes its discovery mainly to the efforts of the Government during the 18th and early 19th centuries to eliminate the practice of smuggling, which was then rife along the south coast.

This was a period of high taxation of many commodities, including tea, coffee, silks, wines, brandy and other goods. It was also a period of economic depression with high unemployment and low wages, thought mainly to be caused by the numerous wars in the 18th century, and especially the long struggles against France. There were blockades on foreign goods, or the tax exacted by excise officers made the price prohibitive to most people, the result being that more and more goods were smuggled into the country, particularly during the reign of George III. In fact it was said that almost as many goods were smuggled into the country as came in legitimately!

In the 18th century there was no such place as Bournemouth, although the words, 'la Bournemowthe' are shown in the Christchurch cartulary of 1407, but this is a geographical reference only and refers to the area of the mouth of a stream, or 'burna'.

In a Calendar of Domestic State Papers of 1574, Lord Thomas Poulet, Earl of Southampton, and others issued a certificate of dangerous places where an enemy could land on the coasts of Hampshire, from Bourne mouthe in Westover Hundred to the East Haven of Hayling Island. The report stated: 'we finde at Bourne mouthe within the west baye at Christchurche a place very easy for the enemye to lande there conteyning by estimacion oon quarter of a myle in length, being voyde of all inhabiting'. (Public Record Office.)

The area which became Bournemouth was then merely a wild, barren stretch of heathland with precipitous cliffs interspersed by narrow, rocky chines leading to the sea, and lying between the historical and ancient towns of Poole and Christchurch. Here the only roads were rough cart tracks, and a traveller could pass the entire day without meeting a single person. Occasionally children from nearby farming communities in the hamlets of Holdenhurst, Throop, Tuckton and others came to play and picnic among the heather and gorse or to scramble down the steep cliffs and run on the golden sands. This desolate area, with its deserted beaches, rugged cliffs and thickly-wooded chines, proved an ideal place for smugglers to land their illicit cargoes.

To defeat the smugglers in their widespread tax avoidance, the Government appointed excise officers who were stationed at Christchurch. Also stationed in the nearby barracks, built in 1795, were the Dorset Rangers or Dragoons under the command of Captain Lewis Tregonwell and his lieutenant son, St. Barbe Tregonwell. Their duties were to guard the coastline, an area of seven miles known as Poole Bay, and to warn the authorities of any intended invasion by Napoleon and his troops; when requested they were to assist the customs and excise officers in the prevention of smuggling on the coast. Lewis Tregonwell was later to become the founder of Bournemouth.

Although the word 'smugglers' was commonplace in that period, it has to be remembered that practically every member of the scattered rural communities around Dorset, Hampshire and Wiltshire – fishermen, owners of small boats, farmworkers, carpenters and poachers – either actively supported or were in sympathy with the smugglers. Even parsons, squires and other members of the gentry were rarely averse to receiving gifts of laces or contraband brandy. As illiteracy was widespread, it was necessary to have a 'writer' or 'quill' man in their midst, often a well-respected clerk who might be employed in the offices of a wine merchant, whilst seamen were sometimes financed by wealthy tradesmen known as 'venturers'.

Goods purchased on the Continent were brought to this country by small, fast-sailing craft which steered surreptitiously into the rocky and dangerous coves. Usually they were met by men with pack-horses, known as 'landers', who hid the goods in one of their many secret hiding places until they could be disposed of with safety. The men took great risks; an Act of 1736 imposed the death penalty for wounding an excise officer, and five years' transportation for resistance to arrest. But the rewards were great; even the land-men could expect to receive ten shillings for a night's work, which compared favourably with the pay of farm labourers, which ranged from about seven to ten shillings per week.

Although large sums of money, sometimes over £500, were offered for information leading to the arrest of notorious smugglers, the rewards were rarely claimed. Informers who were caught were roughly handled by the smugglers and even murdered. The attitude of the gentry and local people to smugglers is summed up by the following words, which appear on a smuggler's grave at Kinson (then Kingston). Robert Trotman was killed in a clash between revenue officers and smugglers.

> To the memory of Robert Trotman, late of Rond [Roud, Rowde] in the county of Wilts who was barbarously murdered on the shore, near, Poole, the 24th day of March, 1765.

> A little tea, one leaf I did not steal
> For guiltless bloodshed I to God appeal
> Put tea in one scale, human blood at t'other
> And think what tis to slay a harmless brother.

Many are the stories told of the smugglers' daring and cunning. The belfry of the parish church (known as 'The Smugglers' Church') in the ancient hamlet of Kingston was used for storing casks and bales of smuggled goods, whilst the grooves in its stone parapet were said to be produced by the constant friction of ropes hauling kegs of brandy and other merchandise to the tower. Near the church porch is a large tomb, with a moveable lid, in which contraband goods were audaciously hidden.

25

In 1870 Lord Shaftesbury was dining at Heron Court, Hurn, with the owner, Mr. Hooper, when they were disturbed by the clatter of horses and waggons. Lord Shaftesbury rushed to the window to see what was happening, but his host, the Squire, refused to turn round and carried on with his meal. When soldiers arrived, breathless, the Squire was able to say that he had seen nothing at all. The smugglers had evidently dashed through two deep fords in the river Stour. The soldiers, not being certain of the depth of the river, had hesitated and so lost their prey.

Another tale is told of an elderly lady wearing a long, flowing cloak, who was seen by coastguards standing on the summit of Mount Misery (see chapter VII). On being asked if she had seen any men with loads on their backs, she replied 'Yes, in that direction'. The men dashed off while the old lady carried on her way home, with a keg of brandy hidden under her ample cloak.

One smuggler, Isaac Gulliver (1745–1822), even earned fame through his illegal activities for his daring and organising ability in controlling a gang of fifty or more tough men as well as a fleet of ships. His followers, loyal to the last degree and ready to take part in any daring escapade, wore a special livery (an improvement on their own poor clothes). They grew their hair long and wore powdered wigs; the white powder, which was then taxable, was provided by Gulliver and gave them an aristocratic appearance. They were referred to locally as the 'White Wigs'.

Even a smuggler had a code of conduct, and Gulliver was regarded by his gang as a strict disciplinarian who forbade violence. Sometimes he boasted that his men had never killed an officer in any of their fights with authority. For his fair-mindedness he became known as the 'gentle smuggler', whilst others referred to him as the 'King of Smugglers'. With pack-horses, boats and men, he smuggled on a wide scale along the south coast and inland, where there were many secret hiding places, including the cellars and vaults of farmers, where merchandise could be hidden. It is said that at times Gulliver was bringing in over £20,000 worth of contraband goods per year. Through his ill-gotten gains he became a wealthy man and bought properties in various areas; for example High House at East End, Corfe Mullen, was built so that he would have a clear view of approaching excise men through the windows. He owned several houses around Wimborne, often bearing the name 'Gulliver', some of which stand today. He built Eggardon Farm, or Manor, near Dorchester, where he planted a clump of trees as a sign and landmark for certain ships.

In 1782 a free pardon was bestowed on any smuggler who would serve in the Navy, or provide a substitute. Although Gulliver availed himself of this generous offer by providing a substitute, his pardon was a special one, as it is said he disclosed a French plot against the life of George III. The King was reputed to have said 'Let Gulliver smuggle as much as he likes', and there were some occasions when Gulliver led his army of men along the deserted beaches in the Bourne area and it seemed that the authorities had turned a blind eye.

Many are the tales told of Gulliver's exploits. There was one time when he only just managed to disappear into his house after being closely chased by Excise men. When the officers returned later with a warrant for his arrest, they were met by a distressed woman who informed them tearfully that Gulliver had just died and was lying in his coffin. Incredulous at the sudden death, they demanded to see the coffin, but when they saw a white-faced Gulliver stretched out stiffly, they were not only shocked but also frightened at the sight of the dead man. With due solemnity the heavy coffin was buried. Afterwards friends were able to congratulate a robust Gulliver, who had removed the white powder from his face and was soon enjoying a hearty meal.

Gulliver retired to 'Gulliver's House' at Wimborne, where he entered into partnership with a banker and even became a churchwarden. He died on 13 September 1822 and was buried in the centre aisle, under the clock tower, in Wimborne Minster.

By 1860 reduced taxation and the introduction of free trade, together with improved coastguard and customs services, had lessened the need for smuggling.

To return to Lewis Tregonwell, the founder of Bournemouth: the name 'Tregonwell' derives from an ancient seat in Cornwall, prior to the Norman period. In a footnote in Hutchins' *History and Antiquities of the County of Dorset*, Pollen states, 'Tregonwell of Bellarmine builded many places and had many lands and manors ante conquestorem'.

One of his Cornish ancestors was Dr. (later Sir) John Tregonwell, who, because of the support he gave to Henry VIII in connection with the divorce of Catharine of Aragon received a pension of £40 a year. In 1538 he was appointed a Commissioner, and in 1539 Henry granted him Milton Abbey Estate in Dorset, on payment of £1,000 and relinquishment of the pension. Dr. John Tregonwell (knighted by Queen Mary I) was Sheriff of Dorset and Somerset for many years. He was buried in Abbey Church, Milton, in 1565. His grandson became the owner of Milton Manor and also purchased other estates, including Anderson Manor in Dorset. From the 17th century two branches of the family developed, namely the Tregonwells of Milton Abbey and the Tregonwells of Anderson. It was to the latter branch that Lewis Tregonwell belonged.

Lewis Dymoke Grosvenor Tregonwell (1758–1832), J.P., Squire of Cranborne Lodge, Deputy Lieutenant for Dorset was the son of Thomas Tregonwell of Anderson, Dorset. His first wife was Katherine, daughter and sole heiress of St. Barbe Sydenham Esq., of Priory, Devon and Coombe, Somerset; she died on 14 February 1794. His second wife, also very wealthy, was the daughter of H. W. Portman Esq., of Orchard Portman and Bryanston, Blandford, Dorset.

After retiring from the Army in 1810, Mr. and Mrs. Tregonwell spent some time in Muddiford (Mudeford), which was then a select sea-bathing area that had achieved much fame from visits by George III and other fashionable people. Mrs. Tregonwell was suffering in health and still grieving after the death of her baby son, Grosvenor, in 1807, on the day he should have been christened. In the afternoon of 14 July 1810 they drove to the Bourne area to revisit the lonely countryside formerly patrolled by her husband. Whilst Bourne still consisted of swampy valleys, wild heathland and a haunt for birds and game, Mr. Tregonwell remembered also the beauty of the coastline and attractive glens near the mouth of the Bourne. Nearby was the decoy pond, i.e. Coy Pond (then at the beginning of the Upper Gardens, and later resited at its far end), which was used to lure ducks and fowl for game shooting. Adjoining was a hut called the 'decoy house' where sportsmen could wait for game to arrive; but it was also frequently used by the smugglers.

Mrs. Tregonwell was charmed with the place, the beauty of the bay, with its calm, blue sea and golden sands, and suggested it would be ideal for a holiday residence near to the beach. Mr. Tregonwell readily agreed. His first step was to purchase 8½ acres of land between the decoy House and the sea from Sir George Ivison Tapps, Lord of the Manor of Christchurch, for £179.11s. The piece of land purchased is described in the Inclosure Award Map, 1805, part of Lot 31 as 'all that piece or parcel of common land or heath land situate, lying, being at or near Bourne, in the Parish of Holdenhurst, containing by estimation 8 acres and 2 roods and 8 perches . . .'. It was

27

here that the first house in Bournemouth was built: it was originally known as The Mansion. In 1814 Tregonwell made further purchases from Sir George at £40 per acre, and in 1822 he bought land (above the present Cranborne Road) at £60 per acre. As his estate, referred to as Bourne Tregonwell, by then extended from the sea to Yelverton Road (off Old Christchurch Road), he also acquired the *Tapps Arms*, built in 1809 (in Post Office Road, formerly Beckford Road), the only place after the *New Inn*, Iford, where travellers from Christchurch could rest and take refreshment: it was also a favourite meeting place for smugglers. The inn was practically rebuilt and renamed the *Tregonwell Arms*.

The Mansion was first occupied by the Tregonwells on 24 April 1812 and became their summer residence. From that time they divided their time between their Cranborne estate and the Bourne. A four-room thatched cottage was erected at about the same time for their butler, Symes, and it was known originally as Symes Cottage. Later, as extensions were added, the picturesque thatched cottage became known as Portman Lodge (after Mrs. Tregonwell's maiden name), and she lived there after the death of her husband. On 3 June 1922 Portman Lodge was damaged by fire. It was restored, but in 1930 it was demolished, the site then becoming part of the Hants and Dorset Bus Co., until it was again mostly destroyed by fire. When Portman Lodge was demolished, an underground chamber, three feet below ground level and entered by a trap door was discovered. It has been suggested that Symes might have been in league with the smugglers.

On the Cranborne Road site, an old cottage, known as Terrace Cottage, became the home of the Tregonwells' gardener; today the site is occupied by the *Hotel Merville*. Lying between Commercial Road and Upper Terrace Road is Orchard Street. Its designation as 'street' has caused considerable speculation since it is the only one in Bournemouth, and David Young suggests that it seemed a suitable name for an area where working-class houses were being built for those who would serve the leisured classes living in more fashionable parts of the town. The name 'Orchard' has a family connection, for Mr. Tregonwell's first wife's family owned the Manor of Orchard Wyndham, Somerset, and his second wife's father was Henry William Portman of Orchard Portman, Dorset. A further connection is said to be that the gardener was responsible for looking after their orchards.

To share the delights of sea-bathing and a leisured existence, friends of the Tregonwells were invited to stay at Bourne. Soon Mr. Tregonwell built extra cottages for summer letting, and the beginning of a popular and fashionable seaside resort had commenced.

In 1820 an advertisement in an old newspaper stated that The Mansion was to let, furnished. It was described as:

A modern, detached convenient house at Bourne Mouth, midway between Poole and Christchurch, consisting of three parlours, . . . six or seven bedrooms, kitchen, scullery, housekeeper's room, servants' hall . . . coach-house, stable for two horses, a garden full cropped, a well of good water, and a bathing machine. . . . A butcher and baker will bring provisions. Cows are kept on the spot. . . .

As a result of the advertisement, the Marchioness of Exeter became the first tenant, and the names 'Exeter House' and 'Exeter Road' were given to commemorate her stay. Exeter House was to become The *Royal Exeter* Hotel (also *Newlyn's Family* Hotel) after it was purchased in about 1876 by Mr. Henry Newlyn, who extended the hotel in that year and again in 1886, and who was responsible for its success as one of the main hotels in Bournemouth. A plaque on the wall of the hotel reads:

> To the memory of Lewis D. Tregonwell, who erected the first house in Bournemouth on this site in 1810. He died on January 18th 1832, aged 73, and was buried in St. Peters' Churchyard, Bournemouth. He was descended from Sir John Tregonwell, a member of an ancient Cornish family.

Lewis Tregonwell spent much time developing his estate, planting trees and particularly improving the glen, which he called Cranborne Gardens (now the Winter Gardens). On his death in 1832 his wife erected a cenotaph, consisting of a huge pedestal, surmounted by an urn, which was encircled by iron railings. The inscription read:

THIS URN
marks the favourite spot of
L. D. G. TREGONWELL,
Late of Cranborne Lodge, Dorset, Esq.,
The first proprietor resident
at Bournemouth,
And to his beloved memory
is Dedicated
by his Widow Henrietta,
Daughter of Henry William Portman Esq.,
1832.

Unfortunately the monument has disappeared and no one seems to know where it has gone. Tregonwell was originally buried at Winterbourne Anderson, near Cranborne, but after the consecration of St. Peter's Church (the first parish church in Bournemouth), his remains were transferred there on 26 February 1846 at the request of his widow.

After her husband's death, Mrs. Tregonwell sold part of their land and received £800 per acre! She died soon afterwards, on 5 April 1846, at Portman Lodge, where she was then residing.

Chapter V

THE MARINE VILLAGE, INCLOSURE MOVEMENT AND THE FIRST CHURCH

WHILST LEWIS TREGONWELL was the founder of Bournemouth, much of its growth and development is due to the foresight and enterprise of the Tapps-Gervis-Meyrick family.

Sir George Ivison Tapps (ancestor of the present Sir George Meyrick) became Lord of the manor of Christchurch and liberty of Westover, in which Bournemouth is situated, on the death of his cousin, Joseph Jervis Clerke in April 1778. The honour of Christchurch had been purchased by Sir Peter Mews, M.P. for Christchurch (who married Lydia Jarvis or Gervis) from the Earl of Clarendon and his trustees in 1708. Hinton Admiral, the family seat, was built by Sir Peter Mews.

The early 19th century was a period of poverty and even famine (see chapter IV). As a result, concern began to be felt that such a large proportion of Britain remained uncultivated waste land. Corn was in short supply, wheat costing 21s. per bushell and a 4 lb. loaf being sold for 25s. in 1801. The need, evidently, was for more food and better crops to provide for the increasing population. The open-field or strip system of farming was unsatisfactory and uneconomical, whilst the common land, on which sheep and cattle mingled, resulted in thin, unhealthy animals. The era of Inclosure Acts was inevitable, and by the 19th century at least one thousand seven hundred private Acts had been passed which dealt solely with particular local areas. In 1801 a General Inclosure Act, outlining a number of provisions which could be included in private Acts, received the approval of Parliament. As a result, a further 300,000 acres of waste land were enclosed that year.

In 1802, two Acts were passed affecting the vast, desolate heathland which stretched between Christchurch and Poole. The Canford Inclosure Act dealt with land in the county of Dorset, whilst the Christchurch Inclosure Act was entitled 'An Act for dividing, allotting and inclosing certain Commonable lands and Waste Grounds within the Parish or Chapelry of Holdenhurst in the County of Southampton.'

Although common land belonged to the lord of the manor, his tenants held grazing rights for their cattle and sheep and also rights to wander over the land, especially to collect unlimited supplies of turf for their fires. When news of the proposed inclosure reached the poor tenant farmers and labourers, they were greatly concerned at the thought of losing their common rights of 'turbary', for centuries their animals had grazed on the heaths, whilst the turf which could be 'cut from one to four inches thick'[1] was almost the only fuel. The men felt aggrieved that this ancient right should suddenly be threatened by groups of lawyers and commissioners.

Farmer West of Muscliffe (see chapter II) had earned the reputation of being a wise man who was sympathetic to the labouring classes. After groups of labourers had met together to discuss their problems, they decided to go 'en masse' to Farmer West's place to ask for his advice. At that time there were only ten houses in the hamlet of Muscliffe, and when the farmer saw the large crowd congregating outside his farm he became alarmed. Repressive Combination Acts of 1799 and 1800 forbade meetings of groups of workers for strike purposes or to improve their conditions. Farmer West drew their attention to the fact that they were acting illegally and could be prosecuted. On hearing, however, of their concern over loss of grazing and 'firing' rights, which they had possessed from time immemorial, and of their sincere wish for his advice, the farmer consented to draw up a petition which they were to present to the commissioners at their next meeting in Ringwood.

The request was accepted by the commissioners, resulting in 425 acres being placed in trust with the Lord of the Manor, Sir George Ivison Tapps, for the benefit of those in the area of Poole and Bourne Heath for the purposes of grazing and cutting turf. The preserved common land of yesterday is responsible for some of Bournemouth's fine, open spaces and parks of today, as Meyrick Park, Queen's Park and King's Park testify.

The three commissioners who were appointed to carry out the requirements of the Act (the Award was completed in 1805) were Richard Richardson of Lincoln Inn Fields, John Wickens of Mapperton, Dorset, and William Clapcott of Holdenhurst, together with the lord of the manor. One of the first tasks was to construct roads where, before, there had only been rough tracts across the heath, the main ones running between Christchurch and Poole (originally known as Poole Road), Holdenhurst, Charminster Road and Bourne and Iford to Wimborne. These formed the basis of our present-day roads.

The cost of presenting private Acts to Parliament was high, and was the responsibility of the presenters of the Act. To meet these costs, some of the enclosed land was sold to wealthy landowners.

Sir George Tapps paid £1,050 2s. 10d. for 205 acres on South and East Cliffs; land above 'the Bridge' (now 'the Square'), including Redhill and Meyrick Park areas was sold to Mr. William Driver for £887 2s. 10d; 500 acres on the West Cliff and Queen's Park area were sold to Mr. William Dean for £639 1s. 2d; Mr. Philip Norris paid £653 1s. 7d. for 500 acres in Boscombe and Strouden areas, whilst the Earl of Malmesbury paid £359 15s. 6d. for land near Iford Bridge and also at Moordown. Further plots were awarded to landowners in compensation for loss of common land, especially to the lord of the manor, as owner of the soil, who acquired extra land on the East Cliff and Southbourne area. The new owners were to be responsible for the maintenance of the roads in their areas.

As a result of these Acts, the principal pine planting was commenced on the barren wasteland, resulting in dense pine forests. The aroma from the pine resin and the balmy atmosphere helped to gain wide renown for Bournemouth as a health resort and a fine watering place.

Sir George Ivison Tapps died in March 1835 and was suceeded by his son, Sir George William Tapps-Gervis. In 1825 the latter had married Clara, eldest daughter of Augustus Eliott Fuller, resulting in the estates of the Meyricks of Anglesey coming into the Gervis family. The new Baronet continued the work commenced by his father to a more advanced level. He not only envisaged a marine village, a watering place for the genteel elderly, but also felt that a fashionable and select seaside resort could be developed, which could become as famous as Brighton or Weymouth whilst still retaining its exclusiveness, and in which it was essential that a church should be included. The growth of Bournemouth increased greatly during this period owing to the Baronet's interest and active participation in the planning and construction of the new town.

With these plans in mind, in 1836 he commissioned a young architect, Benjamin Ferrey of Christchurch, a pupil of Augustus Pugin, to design the marine watering place. This was Ferrey's first major engagement, although he was already well known as an architectural draughtsman, especially because of his drawings of Christchurch Priory. Ferrey's suggestions resulted in the construction of the Westover Villas in 1837, the first villas to be erected in the Bourne, facing one of the splendid pine woods. Sir George stipulated that every residence must be detached, standing in its own grounds and surrounded by trees and flowers. Ferrey was also responsible for the planning and laying-out of the Westover Gardens, which still continue to give pleasure and enjoyment to the many thousands of visitors to Bournemouth annually. The same year an elegant and commodious hotel designed by Ferrey known as the *Bath* Hotel (now the *Royal Bath* Hotel) was constructed. It was opened, with ceremony, on the Coronation Day of Queen Victoria on 28 June 1838, by Sir George Gervis, having only been completed a few weeks before.

Ferrey had envisaged a large, centrally-placed, pagoda-like building, which would dominate the gardens and the marine village. The resultant centrally-placed *Belle Vue* Boarding House (later Hotel) was, however, somewhat more modest. In the *Visitors' Guide* of 1840, it was described thus: 'For the appropriate accommodation of those numerous visitors who may prefer the retired and quiet mode of life available in such establishments, the Belle Vue Boarding House situated close to the beach, has been fitted up with every regard to elegance and comfort, to which the attentions of Mrs. Slidel, the conductress, are very conducive . . .'. Casual visitors were welcomed; picnics were catered for and there was even a billiard table. It was not until 1929 that the hotel was replaced by the fine Pavilion and Assembly Rooms of today, thus, belatedly, carrying out one of Ferrey's main ideas. His plans also included a number of villas to be erected on the cliff front in different architectural styles, including Elizabethan, Italian and Gothic. In *Tess of the D'Urbervilles* Thomas Hardy writes admiringly of 'the lofty roofs, chimneys, gazebos, and towers of the numerous fanciful residences of which the place was composed', and describes the place as 'a city of detached mansions; a Mediterranean lounging-place on the English Channel'.[2]

The *Hampshire Advertiser* of 16 June 1838 reported that 'the new romantic watering place called Bourne is progressing at a railway pace . . . in a few short years it is conjectured that it will compete with the renown of Southampton'. Some weeks later, there was a sale, by auction, of 'marine villas' at the *Bath* Hotel, whilst in the same year an advertisement in the *Salisbury and Winchester Journal* appealed to 'gentlemen, builders and others desirous of investing capital advantageously'.

Ferrey's design for a church for the Bourne village was based on an eight-sided building with lancet windows in groups of three and an ornamental porch, turret and spire, which he intended should occupy a position much further up the hill than the present St. Peter's Church. Despite its artistic merit, his scheme for the church was not accepted. (The church design later accepted was criticised as 'ugly and small'.) Bournemouth residents continued, therefore, to make the journey to Poole, Holdenhurst

Fig. 3. Typical Gazebo of Victorian Bournemouth.

or Christchurch for Sunday worship. Dr. A. Granville, whose book *Spas of England* (1841) was mainly responsible for the acceptance of the area as a spa, remarked scathingly of Ferrey's design that both the building and the proposed site were un-suitable, and that invalids would be completely blown away before they were able to reach the house of God.

But there had to be a church of some kind, so in order to provide a central place of worship a small, temporary building was erected in 1838, consisting of two semi-detached cottages (near what is now Debenhams at the foot of Commercial Road) which were knocked into one building, and which were used as a church on Sundays and as a schoolroom during the week. Services were held at 11 a.m. and 3 p.m. each Sunday, Rev. Hugh Wyndham of Salisbury usually being the officiating minister. The building, however, with its pointed turret containing a single bell, was pitifully small and accommodated less than two-thirds of the people. Whilst some of its windows had been rounded in a mock-Gothic style, others were left in their original state, flat and square. The upper floor of one of the cottages was left as a minstrel's gallery. By 1850 the building was no longer required as a church and became the first national day

33

school and a Sunday school. (Later it was sold to Miss Georgina Talbot, owner of Talbot Village Estate, and demolished, some of the stones being used in the Talbot Village Schools.)

As more seaside villas were built and more people were attracted to the new watering place, the need for a permanent site became increasingly imperative. A new architect, John Tulloch of Poole and Wimborne, who had designed other churches in the vicinity, was engaged by Sir George, and the commencement of a permanent church on the site of the present St. Peter's slowly became a reality. On 28 September 1841 the foundation stone was laid, an inscription on the corner-stone reading; 'This church was built at the sole expense of Sir George William Tapps-Gervis, Bart, of Hinton Admiral in the county of Hants. and proprietor of this estate.' Sir George had hoped that the new church would be completed and consecrated in 1842. Unfortunately he did not live to enjoy the full fruits of his enterprises, as he died on 26 August 1842, aged 47, before the work was finished.

Tribute to his pioneering work is expressed by David Young: 'An important factor in the rapid progress made in the development of the marine village was the interest and enthusiasm of Sir George Gervis himself. He was personally concerned in much of the detail connected with the building and road work and never lost the conviction that his venture would be a success.'[3] As his estates were left in trust for his eldest son, then a minor of 15 years (the 3rd Baronet, Sir George Elliot Meyrick Tapps-Gervis), private Acts had to be passed to endow the church, which was completed the following year, and to allow the trustees of the Gervis Estate to continue the work of the town's development.

Decimus Burton was appointed as supervising architect in succession to Benjamin Ferrey. Burton had gained a name as the designer of the Triumphal Arch at Hyde Park Corner in 1828, and he carried on the work of beautifying and arranging the Pleasure Gardens, especially towards the sea front, thus following the advice of Dr. Granville.[4]

He was also responsible for the construction of a brick bridge in 1849 over the Bourne Stream. Before then, in order to get from one side of the stream to the other, people had to go over a small, wooden, rustic bridge, which was criticized by Dr. Granville, who said that 'the present insignificant wooden bridge ought to be replaced by a handsome stone one'.[5] Costs were borne mainly by the Gervis Estate, assisted by contributions from residents, including John Tregonwell. The area became known as 'the Bridge', or Holdenhurst Bridge, until after the development of open spaces and the building of more villas and shops, when it was called 'the Square', its present name. As the area has never resembled a Square, it is not surprising to learn that in the past frequent complaints were made by people who had wasted time in looking for the 'elusive square'.[6] Today, the Square, with its attractive, well-kept garden centre-piece, is still a mystery to visitors to Bournemouth.

But we shall return to St. Peter's, where there were further problems. For two years the completed building, although licensed for divine worship, remained empty, as no clergyman could be persuaded to accept the unattractive living. There was no parsonage (its first vicar had to build one at his own expense, which, then cost about £1,500); there was no church school; the small endowment was £50 per annum and the income from pew rents was under £200.

In 1845, to the relief of many residents, Rev. Alexander Morden Bennett was inducted as the first vicar of St. Peter's, and on 7 August 1845 the new church was consecrated by the Bishop of Winchester. One reason given for the vicar's acceptance of St. Peter's was that his second wife was the daughter of Captain Henry Hopkins of Christchurch and sister of Rev. F. Hopkins, curate, then vicar, of Holdenhurst Parish Church. Until the vicarage was constructed in 1846 the new vicar lived at Mudeford, riding over the desolate wastes between Christchurch and the Bourne almost every day.

Rev. Morden Bennett later remarked that when he first came to Bournemouth the church was a very poor structure. Indeed the structure of the church was both disappointing and ugly, whilst its mock-Gothic style came under considerable criticism from the clergy of the period. There were no decorations, and the interior was plain and austere. By 1848, it did, however, possess a clock – the first public clock in Bournemouth! The church, which was described as being 'all height and no length', seated 150 people, plus an additional 90 in its gallery.

Shortly after the consecration of the church in 1845, it was the strong wish of those connected with it, and particularly of Mrs. Tregonwell herself, who was then old and infirm, that the bodies of Captain Lewis Tregonwell, the founder of Bournemouth, who was buried in 1832 in Winterbourne Anderson, Dorset, together with that of their child Grosvenor, who died when he was 10 weeks old, should be transferred from Anderson and re-interred in a new family vault at St. Peter's church. On 26 February 1846 the bodies were reburied, with great ceremony, in a place selected by Mrs. Tregonwell near the top of the 39 steps, which had been erected by Rev. Morden Bennett to recall the 39 Articles. Part of the inscription reads; 'Their remains were removed from Anderson to this spot on February 26th 1846, Bournemouth, where Mr. Tregonwell was the first to bring into notice as a watering place by erecting a mansion for his own occupation, having been his favourite retreat for many years before his death'. When Mrs. Tregonwell died two months later, she, too, was buried in the same family vault.

The continuing development of Bournemouth soon meant that the new church was too small. Census reports for 1851 show that Bournemouth District had a population of 695, which increased to 1,707 by 1861. Morden Bennett was a man of ideas and action. He realised that it was essential to have a fine church, the size and architecture of which would match the promise of the growing town. Although some alterations and improvements had been made to the church, the structure and general ugliness of the building made it impossible to extend indefinitely.

Another architect was appointed to design a new church, George E. Street, diocesan architect of Oxford (later to become famous as the designer of the Royal Courts of Justice in the Strand); but owing to the expenses and difficulties involved, it was decided that the work should be carried out in three stages.

By 1856 a new north aisle had been completed with 12 lancet windows, showing representations of the 12 apostles in coloured glass. An octagonal font, supported by eight pillars, was designed by Street and given to the church 'In memory of James Meyrick – presented by his mother – 15th October, 1854' (i.e. the date of his death, aged 37 years). By 1858 the Bishop of Salisbury had officiated at the opening of an enlarged church, and now the first stage had been completed.

However, Morden Bennett was still far from satisfied, and in 1869 he wrote; 'All that is needed to render the church one of the grandest structures in the south of England is a tower, which will be erected at the west end and surmounted by a spire'.[7] In the following year the tower was completed, some distance away from the remainder of the church (thus leaving a space for a transept or vestibule). A temporary wooden covered way was built to link the church with the tower. It was intended that a peal of bells be placed in the tower, but at about this time Morden Bennett became seriously ill, mainly due to overwork and worry about the new building. A special appeal was made, with the intention of providing the bells to honour him on his return home from convalescence abroad.

The dedication took place in 1871. A brass plate under the tower reads; 'To the Glory of God and as a mark of respect and esteem for the Rev. Alexander Morden Bennett, M.A. Vicar of St. Peter's District, Six Bells were hung in this Tower by the Inhabitants of Bournemouth – Whitsuntide 1871.'

By 1879 the spire, with its cross, was standing 202 feet above the ground, thus marking the completion of the building.

For 26 years Morden Bennett and his architect worked happily on the building of the new St. Peter's. Although their achievements were great, they were sadly only able to appreciate them for a short time. On 19 January 1880, only one month after the church was finally completed, Morden Bennett died. There was immense sorrow throughout Bournemouth at the loss of this great man. Over three thousand people attended his funeral at St. Peter's to show their love and respect for their first vicar, who was buried on the right of the steps he had built. Two large windows were installed in the church in memory of their beloved vicar, and later a new church, St. Stephens, was erected nearby as a memorial and thanksgiving for his many works to Bournemouth and its people.

Not only was Morden Bennett responsible for St. Peter's School, but also for eight other churches and schools in the area, including the erection of a school-chapel at Moordown in 1854, on land provided by Sir Tapps-Gervis, for the benefit of the poor artisans and workpeople who lived in the area.

George E. Street, the architect, who had worked so well and tirelessly with the vicar, died the following year.

Many renowned people have been connected with St. Peter's Church; foremost among them was John Keble, vicar of Hursley in the New Forest for 30 years, Professor of Poetry at Oxford University, author of the well-known book *The Christian Year* and a pioneer of the Oxford Movement, who came to Bournemouth on 11 August 1865 with his wife, in the hope that the mild climate and healing qualities of the watering place would benefit her poor health.

They stayed at a boarding house called *Brookside*, in Exeter Lane, near the Pleasure Gardens (now the *White Hermitage* Hotel; the original white Italian-style tower still remains). Each morning the Rev. John Keble attended St. Peter's for the daily service, usually sitting in the recently built south transept. Unfortunately, he died at *Brookside* on 29 March 1866, and both he and his wife, who died six weeks later, were buried at Hursley.

In memory of this devout and renowned preacher two stained-glass windows were erected, one near his favourite place, in the south wall of the transept, illustrating the *Te Deum*, with a portrait of him robed in cassock, surplice and hood, in the lower right-hand corner; and the other, depicting the Resurrection, at the east end of the transept. In 1906 the south transept was made into a side chapel, named in his memory. Today, worshippers come to the chapel for private prayers and peace.

In 1898 the former Liberal Prime Minister, William Ewart Gladstone, took his last communion at St. Peter's shortly before his death. At that time Phyllis Bottome, a well-known authoress, was living in Bournemouth with her father, Rev. W. M. Bottome, at the Quadrant, opposite the church. As she was attending church when Gladstone made his last communion, she was requested by Mrs. Gladstone to kneel besides the elderly statesman and help him to rise. Because of his feebleness, he occupied the end choir stall, near the altar rail, where a brass plate now commemorates the event; 'From this stall Gladstone made his last communion on Thursday, March 3rd A.D. 1898.' He died shortly afterwards at Hawarden, at the age of 89.

Chapter VI

A NEW SPA

COASTAL SPAS AND SEA-BATHING became fashionable during the late 18th and the 19th centuries. A treatise called *Dissertation on the use of sea water*, published in 1752 by Richard Russell, a Brighton physician, was responsible for the beginning of 'seaside mania'. Dr. Russell advocated sea-bathing and even sea-drinking as a panacea for most ills. The bathing machine had recently been invented by Ralph Allen of Bath. Doctors urged their wealthy patients to visit coastal areas for the benefit of their health or to relieve their nerves or boredom after the excitement of the London season. Besides the beneficial effects of sea water, people were attracted by the reputed value of mineral springs. Brighton's popularity developed mainly during the Regency period, whilst that of Weymouth was assured after a visit from George III in 1789.

Bournemouth was then unknown, its tranquil blue sea and long stretches of fine, sandy beaches still only frequented by smugglers, fishermen and families from nearby hamlets who brought their children to play on the cliff tops or sands. Not far away was Mudeford, which, at one time, showed promise of becoming a major health resort. By 1803 it already had three bathing machines and a dipping lady, the formidable Jane West, who charged one shilling per person for 'dipping' her clients into the sea. Distinguished families came here for a restful or health-giving holiday, but as Bournemouth became more widely known, the popularity of Mudeford as a watering place waned.

Bournemouth's possibilities as a seaside resort began to be realised after Lewis Tregonwell, its founder, began to let a few of his villas to select acquaintances or visitors. The idea was further developed by Sir George Ivison Tapps (first Baronet) and then by his son, Sir George William Tapps-Gervis, who realised the opportunities for building up and planning a holiday area for wealthy and delicate persons. Bournemouth was created solely with this in mind, its fine villas, gardens and plantations of pines all being designed to create an atmosphere of luxury, ease, and health-giving qualities.

By 1838 'furnished and papered' villas were advertised at four guineas per week, if taken for a month. A mansion, thought to be that of Mrs. Tregonwell, was described as 'the property of a lady and suitable for a family of distinction'. There was a kitchen garden, two cows, three bathing machines with guide, all of which were included in the rent of eight guineas weekly.

It was a great disappointment to the chief landowners and developers of that period when, on reading the book *Spas of England*, written in 1840 by Dr. A. B. Granville, a

38

fashionable and well known London physician, which recommended watering places on the south coast, they found that there was no mention whatever of Bournemouth. Fortunately, in February 1841, Doctor Granville was again in the vicinity of Bournemouth when a pressing invitation was sent to him requesting him to visit the almost unknown terrain and to give his professional opinion on the area.

At that time, Bourne, as it was then referred to, comprised The Mansion, Westover Villas, the *Bath* Hotel, the *Belle Vue* boarding house, a simple church consisting of two cottages joined together and the Sydenham Library, where, for a subscription of 3s. 6d. per person, the latest books and journals could be borrowed. Mr. Sydenham, who also sold soft drinks, tea, coffee, sheet music, perfume, bathing caps, etc. – surely a very early beach stall – was inspired to write the first guide-book in 1840, in which, besides acknowledging the active part played by Sir George William Tapps-Gervis, he wrote poetically:

> Thus on spots where, before, the foot of man rarely pressed, but the lowly heath flower blossomed and faded in unnoticed solitude, where no sound was heard but the rustling of the rank grass and the wild shrub as they waved in the light sea-breeze – there a number of detached villas, each marked by distinct and peculiar architectural features, have sprung into existence. . . . To all these are attached ample gardens, whilst in front are shrubberies tastefully laid out and walks arranged with due regard to convenience and effect.

For the small number of élite visitors who came to Bourne, perhaps the pleasure of sea-bathing, driving in the carriage, and visiting the Library and the reading room sufficed, but this was not so for one domestic servant employed by a London family on holiday in one of the Westover villas. She wrote in August 1840; '. . . there is nothing to be seen here but woods and fir trees we shall not be able to go Donkey riding for there is no Donkeys to be had . . . its a very Prettey place to look at but not to stay at there is a sermon every other sunday morning . . .'.[1]

Dr. Granville was lodged in one of the Westover villas. Soon he had written a second volume in which he extolled the virtues of this undiscovered haven. In his book he explained how he was wined and dined at the Great Hotel (i.e. the *Bath* Hotel) 'in a style of excellence seldom surpassed even in the metropolis', and that the only reason Bourne was not included in his previous volume was that he was entirely unaware of its existence. The Doctor's examination of Bourne was thorough and was conducted under varying conditions, during periods of delightful sunshine and those which were wet and windy. The outcome was an ecstatic report: 'I look upon Bourne and its yet unformed colony as a perfect discovery among the sea nooks one longs to have for a real invalid and as the realization of a *desideratum* we vainly thought to have found elsewhere on the south coast of England'.

He continued that in his opinion there was no place along the south coast that possessed so much potential, including excellent sea bathing, for being the first invalid sea-watering place in England, and particularly as a winter residence 'for the most delicate constitutions requiring a warm and sheltered locality at this season of the year.' 'This might seem at first view,' he added, 'an exaggerated and sweeping opinion had it been uttered by one less accustomed to judge localities, climates and topical peculiarities than the author of these pages can be after having visited *all the resorts* of invalids, abroad and in England'. With enthusiasm he described 'the cliffs clothed in verdure running from the sea inland with a smiling vale watered by a rapid brook or bourne . . . ideal for a convalescent free from positive disease but also for patients in the most delicate state of health as to lungs and for the wealthy afflicted with disease'.

Although the stress is on the consumptive invalid, the doctor admitted that 'there were other classes of people in easy circumstances who would benefit by its mild and temperate air'. These people should be welcomed in the summer, but the winter was for a select community of invalids and visitors.

Doctor Granville considered thoroughly all aspects of the area and warned the developers 'not to commit blunders perpetrated on other coasts by admitting strangers and brick and mortar contractors to build up whole streets of lodging houses and interminable terraces in straight lines facing the sea'. He emphasised that there was a need for more insulated villas of different sizes to attract the wealthy and also a community of craftsmen and artisans to cater for their needs. The doctor noticed that provisions could readily be obtained from Christchurch and Poole markets, five miles away from Bourne, that tradesmen would call daily for orders and that soon a regular series of shops could be established.

Dr. Aitken of Poole, described as 'a scientific and painstaking physician', was requested to examine the waters of the Bourne chemically, and also the soil through which it flows, as its waters would be essential for the new community as it grew. Dr. Granville was pleased to learn that the source of the water was from gravel and sandy beds below peat earth on adjoining heathland and was quite free from any infiltration of dung, which was found in many rivers.

To conclude, he stressed the fact that a church was essential to the new spa, and that it should be constructed in a secluded and rural spot accessible 'to the villagers in health, occupied with household tasks to the last minute and the feeble who cannot walk far. . . . An opportunity is now offered of establishing a real Montpellier on the south coast of England and better than a Montpellier in point of beauty for the upper and wealthier classes of society who ought to be enticed to remain at home and spend their income in husbanding their wealth in England.'

As a result of the publicity derived from Dr. Granville's excellent report, the little village of Bourne began to gain a reputation as a favourite and exclusive invalid retreat. By 1851 the resident population of Bourne was still only 695, many of whom were concerned with providing services for the benefit of the invalids. Fashionably-dressed ladies with parasols could be seen strolling by the beach or taking gentle trips around the coast in rowing boats. There were donkeys on the beach and 12 bathing machines. For the purchase of such important necessities as silks, linens, bonnets, haberdashery or home-brewed beer, a carriage drive to Poole made a pleasant outing. But soon more shops were opened in Bournemouth and it became less necessary to go to Poole. Shops providing silks, millinery, mantles, besides those specializing in servants' liveries, were thriving. There was an undertaker (essential for an invalid and elderly population), and mourning clothes could be provided at short notice; the first grocer and tea merchant opened, who also offered foreign cigars and snuff for his gentlemen clients. A class of polite, subservient tradesmen was slowly growing who were willing and anxious to attend to the needs of their select customers.

On the death of Sir George William Tapps-Gervis in 1842, trustees were appointed to continue the development of the area, as his son and heir was only 15 years old. A private Act was passed empowering this action.

Although Bournemouth was slowly expanding, it lacked one important amenity essential to all coastal watering towns, and that was a pier, a feature already possessed by Brighton, Weymouth and other coastal resorts. The urgency of this matter was stressed by some of the chief residents, who pointed out that when the waves were high it was impracticable to approach the shore without being swamped. So anxious were developers and residents to have a pier that it was actually described in Brannon's Guide Book of 1855, together with an engraving by him, although it was incomplete then. As money was not forthcoming for a 'real' pier, a landing-stage was built on piles with a retractable platform, the first pile being driven in during July 1855, but the work was not finished until 1856. Unfortunately this structure was damaged by a storm on 20 August 1856 and had to be repaired.

In 1861 it was replaced by a wooden pier, 800 feet long and 16 feet wide, which was opened with great ceremony and rejoicing by Sir George Gervis on 17 September. There were gun salutes, pleasure steamers, fireworks, a free tea in Cranborne Gardens, and for the more important residents there was a dinner at the *Belle Vue* Hotel. People were delighted, and fashionably-clad gentlefolk could be seen strolling along the pier whilst their carriages often awaited them at the pier entrance. Soon there was more trouble as, by 1866, the wooden piles had been attacked by the teredo or ship worm, becoming so weakened that they had to be replaced by cast-iron ones. In January 1867 its T-shaped head was destroyed in a severe gale, shortening the pier by 300 feet. A further gale the same year destroyed another 100 feet of its structure. It was evident that the pier was doomed, but it was not until 1880 that a stronger, iron pier was constructed. In 1980, the centenary of the pier, it was decided to replace the badly corroded ironwork on the foreshore with reinforced concrete as part of a new, more modern pier. Despite the unfortunate loss of many seaside piers today, Bournemouth has decided that such an amenity should be retained.

Although the railway age was developing rapidly, bringing progress and an increased population to many seaside resorts, the landowners of Bournemouth opposed the idea of a railway station for over twenty years on the grounds that it was noisy, dirty, would attract a lower class of people to the detriment of the wealthy invalids and would vulgarize the town. A line had existed between Poole and Southampton since 1847, but it completely bypassed Bournemouth; and it was not until 1870 that Bournemouth had its own railway station, when a branch line was extended from Christchurch to Bournemouth. Because of intense opposition, it had to be constructed on the very edge of the commissioners' district in an area of brick works. It was known as Bournemouth East Station. A frequently heard verse in those opposition days, dating from about 1863, was:

> 'Tis well from far to hear the railway scheme;
> And watch the curling, lingering clouds of steam,
> But let not Bournemouth's heath's approved abode,
> Court the new presence of the iron road.

When extensions to the line were proposed in 1882, the verse was further heard. In 1861 the population was still only 1,707, but by the year 1881 it had increased to 16,859, mainly due to better transport.

In 1885 a new East Station was constructed on the west side of Holdenhurst Road. As L. Popplewell writes in his well-researched book, *Bournemouth Railway History*, 'What other town would have forced the London & South Western Railway Co. at the height of its power to design its new Bournemouth station to resemble of all things – a Winter Gardens?'

Whilst Bournemouth could never lay claim to being one of the great spas of England,

41

it certainly gained renown in the 1880s, and much of its fame was due to the favourable views expressed by another physician, Dr. Horace Dobell.

Dr. Dobell was a London physician who came to live in Bournemouth from 1882, although he had previously stayed there, finding relaxation from his London practice. Previously he had also visited the Auvergne in France, where he had been most impressed by the Mont Dore cure given at the famous spa of that name. In his book *Medical Aspects of Bournemouth and its surroundings*, he remarked; 'I consider the heathland character of the site of Bournemouth of utmost importance in its medical aspects and much gratitude is due to early planners for not building houses under the cliffs but on them'.

To some of the chief medical men in Bournemouth he wrote; 'I propose to establish at Bournemouth a system of treatment to that known in the Auvergne as the Mont Dore Cure and consider that the treatment might be more successfully carried out in Bournemouth than at Mont Dore'. Dr. Dobell considered that the balmy and resinous perfume from the numerous Scotch pines in the district would be most beneficial to those with consumptive and bronchial complaints, whilst the trees' other health-giving properties, including tar, the infusion of which was important for pulmonary affections, were of vital benefit to invalids. The Mont Dore cure, when introduced, would relieve many types of disorders, including rheumatism, gout, scrofulous, syphilis, tuberculosis, asthma and affections of the throat and chest.

A great hotel and hydropathic institution was proposed, the name of which was to be the *Mont Dore* Hotel. In May 1881, its foundation stone was laid by King Oscar II of Sweden and Norway, who had been staying at the *Crag Head*, Manor Road (today a high-rise block of flats) with Queen Sophia Wilhelmina, who had been ill for many years, but for whom the mildness of Bournemouth's climate had effected a cure. The King was only too happy to extol the many curative virtues of the area.

The *Mont Dore* Hotel was opened in 1885 with every conceivable luxury. It was the first residential hotel to be built so far back from the sea front. It was constructed in an Italian style of architecture on four acres of land previously known as 'The Glen', and was described as the most magnificent in the south of England. There were superbly decorated sitting rooms, drawing rooms, billiard and smoking rooms, a covered tennis court, outdoor skating and a ballroom. The hotel possessed one of the first local telephones, its number being 3!

Above everything else, the hotel offered the Mont Dore cure. The water, vital to the health of the many patients who flocked to this palatial establishment, was imported from the springs of the Auvergne. This water contained essential constituents which could not be found anywhere else in England, including free carbonic acid gas, nitrogen, helium, mineral contents of iron and even arsenic. The Mont Dore treatment was unique. Besides drinking the healing water, it had to be gargled and its vapours inhaled. There was nasal and throat irrigation and many different types of hot and cold baths. Sea and pure water from the Bourne were pumped into the basement of the hotel to allow the additional luxury of soaking and perspiring in Turkish and salt baths. Besides being open to patients and visitors, the hotel was open to non-residents.

To ensure that the correct treatments were carried out, Dr. Dobell arranged for Dr. Edmond, chief physician to Mont Dore Spa, Auvergne, to reside in the *Mont Dore* Hotel, Bournemouth, during the winter months, when the French establishment was closed due to the bitterly cold weather. He would supervise the treatment and instruct local physicians in all its techniques. Bournemouth's reputation was firmly established as a select watering place for the wealthy, the infirm and the delicate, its image as a bath-chair town still continuing.

With the advent of the First World War in 1914, the hotel was commandeered by the army as a hospital. Hundreds of sick and wounded soldiers wandered through its fine, spacious corridors. First there were Indian soldiers, then British soldiers and sailors, and finally it became a convalescent home for officers until May 1919. Its days as a hotel were finished, for in 1919 it was put up for sale and was soon purchased by Bournemouth Corporation, becoming its fourth and present-day Town Hall.

Chapter VII

POKESDOWN AND SOUTHBOURNE

Pokesdown

POKESDOWN IS ANOTHER busy conurbation on the eastern side of Bournemouth. It adjoins Iford to the north-east and Southbourne to the south-west, whilst also being a continuation of Boscombe. Originally, Pokesdown was part of the tything of Iford in the hundred of Christchurch, and was one of the several Saxon agricultural communities which extended along the fertile plains and valleys of the river Stour.

Apart from a few cottages and an isolated farm (in the area of Herberton and Castlemain Roads), it was surrounded by wild, uninhabited heaths and dense woods. There were no roads across the heath, but there were four main tracks, one leading from Christchurch to Poole. These and other rougher tracks were of much use to smugglers in the 17th and 18th centuries. On watching the almost ceaseless stream of traffic and the multitude of shoppers in Pokesdown, it is difficult to imagine that Old Pokesdown Hill used to be a narrow, stony lane with oak trees on either side, ditches, springs of water and a profusion of wild flowers growing on the banks.

There is some doubt about the origin of the name 'Pokesdown'. It is said it could be a corruption of Pooksdown, a dialect word for a 'haycock', or of Pucksdown, connecting it with pixies among the gold and purple of the heather and gorse, whilst 'pokes' was the smugglers' word for elves. The accounts of the Christchurch churchwardens for 1663–4 refer to the receipt of '1s. from Henry Mantle of Poxdowne', and in the Christchurch Poor Rate Book for 1734 the word 'Pokesdown' is mentioned.

The first mansion to be built between Christchurch and Poole was Stourfield House (now Douglas House and a long-stay hospital). It was constructed in 1766 in Georgian style on a hillock amidst heather and moorland by Edmund Bott, Barrister and J.P. The house possessed a much-admired ornate staircase, a greenhouse, dovecote, and an underground ice-house. The estate, including farm buildings, was extensive, and was bounded by Southbourne, Beaufort, Cranleigh and Watcombe Roads.

Mr. Bott was a man of great intellect who wrote a commentary on the Poor Laws of England, whilst his house became a popular centre for literary discussion. His affection for his moorland home was so great that after his death in 1788 local folk claimed that they had seen him driving his coach and four along the narrow tracks nearby.[1]

Owing to a fight at Tuckton Cross between two swains for the hand of Mrs. Bott's maid, a popular song sung by local children of that period was:

44

A battle was fought at Tuckton Cross,
Where Wick won and Tuckton lost.[2]

The winner was Charles Pain who lived at Wick, his 'hard fought for' wife living until she was 95.

After the death of Edmund Bott the estate was purchased by Sir George Tapps, who leased it to a number of tenants, the first being the Countess of Strathmore, one of the richest heiresses in England. She came to Stourfield to seek peace and quietness and was greatly respected and loved for her kindness to the poor of the district. Before she died in 1800 she requested that she be buried in her court dress and that a silver trumpet be placed at her side so that she would be able to answer the Heavenly Trumpeter on Judgment Day. Her coffin was taken to London and buried in Westminster Abbey.[3]

The seclusion of the house was also appreciated by Sir Henry Harper, who became its next tenant in 1801. To obtain a direct route to the beach, he ordered the construction of a road from his gates. The work took two years to complete. Unfortunately their first ride proved to be their last one. Squally, wintery weather swept away the cliff end of the road, making driving to the sea impossible. Not to be deterred, Sir Henry had a footpath made down the cliffs, which was probably much appreciated by the smugglers!

Adjoining the house were two ponds; one, known as the Black Pond, was encircled by dark cedars, and the other, larger and deeper, was near the farm buildings and is now the site of All Saints' Church, Southbourne.

Many people have lived in Stourfield House, the large estate providing considerable employment for Pokesdown's increasing population. In 1844 it was purchased by Admiral William Popham, whose family lived there until the estate was broken up in 1893.

We shall return to the small agricultural community living in Pokesdown in 1820. In that year, a weekly prayer meeting was commenced under the auspices of the Christchurch Congregational Church, led by Rev. Daniel Gunn. The first services were held in a thatched cottage, owned by a Mr. Burt, near to Pokesdown Farm and Stourfield House; then they were held in a thatched cottage owned by Mr. John Troke. By 1834 it was felt that more permanent premises were needed, and when Mr. Troke offered part of his garden for a site, this was gladly accepted.

A mud and thatch chapel was constructed entirely by the local people in their spare time, and when it was opened in 1835 by Rev. Daniel Gunn it could hold fifty to sixty people. The strong religious feelings of the little community were clearly shown in their communal achievement, which was then the only place of worship of any kind between Christchurch and Poole. At the same time the first day school in the hamlet was held in the chapel, which shortly afterwards was also used as a Sunday school.

In 1850 Mr. Elias Lane, a deacon of Christchurch Congregational Church, became the lay pastor of Pokesdown, where he worked enthusiastically for the next 20 years, taking an active part in the life of the village.

Due to the success of the chapel and a growing population, a larger site of 27 acres (by Southbourne and Stourvale Roads – then Hampden and Victoria) was purchased in 1855, at a cost of £1,000. An open field had to be cleared of fir trees before the foundation stone was laid in 1857 by Rev. Joseph Fletcher. Part of the 27 acres not

45

used for the chapel was laid out as roads, the names of which reflected the outlook of these early developers, e.g. Cromwell Road, Hampden Lane and Livingstone Road.

The need for an Anglican church had also been felt, and shortly after 1850 a group of local people and landowners headed by Sir George Gervis, the Earl of Malmesbury and Admiral Popham requested the Ecclesiastical Commissioners for their permission to provide one. After some delay the request was granted. A site for an Anglican church was given by Sir George Gervis, and the foundation stone was laid by Lady Gervis on 1 March 1858. Rev. A. Morden Bennett, vicar of St. Peter's Church, Bournemouth, raised the sum of £1,750 with the assistance of his wealthy parishioners, whilst the new church, dedicated to St. James the Greater, was designed by his friend, George Street, the architect of St. Peter's. The church was built of ferruginous sandstone quarried at Lychett, with Purbeck and Bath stone dressings, and was large enough to hold a congregation of 160. By 1860 Pokesdown had become a parish in its own right; in 1888, the church was described as 'one of the most beautiful village churches in the county'.[4]

Admiral Popham of Stourfield House died on 22 August 1864 and was buried in the churchyard of St. James; a window in his memory was placed in the church.

A school was opened in 1857, and this was used for services pending the opening of the church. Records of the school exist from 1862, in which year a log-book had to be kept in all schools which received a grant. A charge of 1d. per week was made for each child, with a maximum of 4d. per family. There were then 49 children on the roll.

From about 1860 the Wesleyans, who had previously attended the Congregational Church, began to hold their own services, first in a cottage in Cromwell Road, and then, after obtaining a site in Darracott Road for £340, in their own church, which could hold 140 people and which was opened on 24 April 1872.

The first post office was eventually established in 1865 in the village shop kept by Mr. W. Bolton, who was appointed Postmaster. He, together with his family, remained in charge of the post office for over a hundred years. Three years later a Mechanics' Institute was formed, which held meetings in the school until the Cromwell Hall in Cromwell Road was obtained in 1872. The Hall comprised Reading, Lecture and Club Rooms, and in the latter room various games could be played.

On the retirement of Mr. Elias Lane in 1870 from the Congregational Church, Rev. Elijah Pickford was appointed as Pastor, He remained there for the rest of his life, and became a much respected and influential person, taking an active part in the development of the village.

Rev. Elijah Pickford had suffered greatly from frequent attacks of bronchitis and had been advised by his doctor to leave his home in the north of England for a milder climate, either on the Mediterranean or on the south coast. Later, in the Parish Magazine of October 1896, he wrote that the hand of God was shown when he received a pressing invitation to supply pulpit for two Sundays in Pokesdown. On looking at his map, he could neither find Pokesdown nor Bournemouth, but as a clear route had been indicated he set forth on his long journey. Everywhere he was given a kindly welcome, which was soon followed by a permanent invitation. Of his first day he wrote; 'I found myself in a NEW world. Flowers were blooming in the open air and the atmosphere was warm and genial, the trees were clothed in brilliant green, and not far off I could hear the murmur of the waves as they beat upon the shore.' When he left his home in Lancashire there was more than two feet of snow all around.

He continued:

When I first came to Pokesdown 25 years ago, I was struck by the sparseness of the population for I had lived most of my life in densely crowded localities. According to the Census taken in 1871, there were only 511 inhabitants [in Boscombe at the same period there were 200]. A few of these were to be found working on neighbouring farms, but most of them were artisans, employed upon the building trade, at that time very prosperous. . . . Another thing that struck me was, that there was only ONE SHOP for the whole of the village where you could get almost everything; bread, grocery, drapery, millinery, boots and shoes, drugs, crockery etc . . . for some things you had to go to Bournemouth or Christchurch. Suppose you had some legal business to transact and wanted a lawyer . . . a doctor . . . or the signature of a magistrate; in all these cases you had to walk to Bournemouth. I have said 'walk' for there were neither brakes, nor omnibuses nor cabs available in those days.

Rev. Pickford was also struck by the difficulty of moving from one place to another, as there was then no station. To go to London or Birmingham it was necessary to walk to Christchurch station, and to go to Bath or Bristol you had to find your way to Wimborne station 'as best you could'. To conclude, he wrote:

When I first came there was no Southbourne, no Freemantle, and in Boscombe, only 'the Ragged Cat' [inn] and two thatched cottages . . . a few houses in Palmerston Road and Gladstone Road. I have often walked from Pokesdown to the Crescent at Lansdowne in those early days on a footpath, under the shade of pines, a high hedge between me and the highway and I have not met half a dozen people all the way.

By 1881 the population had increased to 838, and in the 1891 census 1,871 people were recorded. This latter figure was due mainly to the growth of Bournemouth, the advent of the railway, and the need for accommodation for the artisans and workpeople employed in the new town, with the result that an active period of building development and road construction of new roads commenced in and around the village (including the areas of Boscombe and Springbourne). Soon, due to overcrowding, there was need for a new school, and on 18 July 1887 an infants section was added to St. James School. In the previous year the attendance charge was raised to 3d. a week, with a maximum of 8d. for a family. Any child who could not pay the requisite amount on Monday morning could be sent home.

Several unsuccessful attempts had been made to obtain a railway station at Pokesdown, but it was not until 1883 that the London and South Western Railway Co. authorized improvements to the existing line from Christchurch to Bournemouth, including a small station at Pokesdown, which was opened on 1 July 1886. For some unknown reason, the new station was known as Boscombe Station until that district had its own station, which was opened in 1897 in Ashley Road, Boscombe. From about 1889, a local horse omnibus service was provided by the Bournemouth, Boscombe and Westbourne Omnibus Co. Ltd, whose stables were at Pokesdown, adjoining the *New Bell* inn.

As there were several blacksmiths' workshops in Pokesdown, people often heard the sharp clanging on metal and witnessed sparks flying in all directions. One was close to the *Three Horseshoes* inn (now the *White Horse*); another was situated opposite the *New Bell* inn, and when a new railway station was erected in 1929–30, it was demolished.

As many children left school at 12, it was felt that more education, particularly in science and technical subjects, was required for the children of the increasing number of artisans in the district. The foundation stone for an Art and Technical School was laid by Abel Henry Smith, M.P., on 14 September 1898. The cost of the building was about £2,300, and the money was provided by a group of local people. The Technical School was at the corner of Hannington Road (now a children's clinic) and helped to fulfil the need for further education until the construction of the Municipal College at the Lansdowne in 1913.

An area unknown to most people is that of Freemantle, lying between Wolverton Road, Boscombe and Pokesdown Station. It is thought that the name derives from the Manor of Freemantle, between Kingsclere and Basingstoke; the names Hannington and Wolverton were also villages in the same region. A Freemantle Mission Hall still exists in Somerset Road, and from 1890 to 1917 a sub post office was known by that name, before it changed to Boscombe East.

Towards the end of the 19th century, much dissatisfaction was felt by Pokesdown's residents concerning the poor condition of the many unmade roads, the lack of main drainage and inadequate street lighting. At that time Pokesdown was in the newly-formed Hampshire County Council (L.G. Act, 1888) and was also part of Christchurch Rural Sanitary Authority.

In 1890 a Pokesdown association of local residents was formed to urge improved services, and the following year

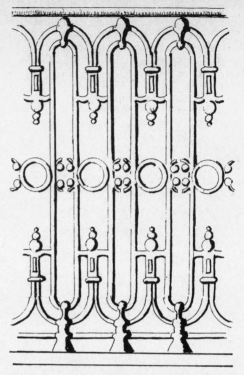

Fig. 4. Typical cast-iron balcony, c.1890, as seen in Pokesdown and Boscombe.

a request was made for incorporation into the Borough of Bournemouth. It was then the largest community within the liberty of Westover to remain outside the Borough. Although the Council tentatively agreed, no action was taken. As a result of the L.G. Act, 1894, which created urban districts, rural districts and parishes, the Pokesdown Residents' Association applied to the Hampshire County Council on 6 July 1894 for urban district status; this application was rejected. Determined that some action should be taken, the Association made a further application for incorporation into Bournemouth. To assist their case, they included a memorial signed by 370 ratepayers, but this request was also rejected. However, in September 1894, the County Council established a parish council, and as a result of further application, urban district status was conferred in October 1895. The first meetings of the newly-formed council were held in the Cromwell Hall until the council obtained a site of its own. A clerk to the council, a medical officer, a rate collector and a surveyor were appointed (Mr. Burt, Dr. Nunn, Mr. Morley and Mr. Ingamells respectively). Prompt action was taken by the little council to improve and pave roads, to convert oil lamps to gas lighting where there were gas mains, and a main drainage scheme was also undertaken. By 1900 the population had risen to 5,550, a figure about 10 times greater than that which obtained when Elijah Pickford had come to Pokesdown 30 years previously.

Bournemouth continued to grow rapidly and was seeking complete independence from Hampshire by applying for county borough status. In July 1900 it was suggested that Pokesdown should be incorporated into the newly proposed Borough, and by November 1901 Pokesdown had become part of Bournemouth. Although most rate-payers were in favour of amalgamation, there was some dissent. One member remarked prophetically; 'If it is incorporated with Bournemouth, it would simply be blotted out and in future no one would know that Pokesdown ever existed'.[5] How regretful it is that his comment should have proved to be true, and that people today are completely unaware that Pokesdown had its own council and that the residents acted with enthusiasm and vigour to improve their own district.

Southbourne

Although Southbourne was incorporated into Bournemouth together with Pokesdown in 1901, it has always retained its own characteristics. Today it is considered a pleasant, residential area, most of the houses being stylish and commodious; a variety of good-quality shops are provided in Southbourne Grove.

Originally the area consisted of a desolate tract of land in the much older parish of Pokesdown, and the name Southbourne was unknown. Nearby were the small agricultural communities of Iford, Wick and Tuckton. The terrain was often referred to as 'The Guns', as gunnery was practised there by coastguards. The only buildings were Stourwood, which belonged to Captain George Lamb; Stourcliffe, which was owned by Mr. H. J. Smith; Cellar's Farm; the coastguard's station, and three small stone cottages.

Roads whose names are familiar now were then unknown, being little more than rough, unnamed tracks often frequented by smugglers. Seafield Road was a country lane in which grew magnificent convolvus; woods and cornfields surrounded Carbery Avenue (leading from Southbourne to Tuckton); Broadway was a mass of gorse, brambles, sand dunes and dark pine woods, and a rough road known as Half Way Lane, now Cranleigh Road, led to Christchurch.

Whilst Bournemouth's commencement was partly due to the possibilities seen in it by two physicians – Dr. Granville, who recommended it as a watering place for the delicate, and Dr. Dobell, who introduced the Mont Dore spa treatment – it was a third physician, Dr. Thomas A. Compton, whose Bournemouth practice commenced in 1866, who realised that the expanse of trees, wasteland and sandhills, combined with pure and bracing sea breezes due to its high position near the cliff tops, would be most suitable as a health resort. In 1870, therefore, he purchased 230 acres of land, including just over one mile of sea frontage, for £3,000, and named the district 'Southbourne-on-Sea'. The area was bounded on the west by a sandy track, formerly used by smugglers, and now part of Clifton Road. Further to the north were the properties of Heatherlea (now demolished) and Stourfield House (see Pokesdown). Hengistbury lay to the east and the sea to the south. Adjoining were dense oak woods called 'Foxholes', and to the south was a small fir plantation. Rabbits abounded and duck shooting was also very popular.

A single path led down to the sea (through Clifton Road), known locally as Mount Misery,[6] perhaps because of the difficulty it presented in clambering down the rocky and tortuous cliffs, but generally thought to be so named as a result of the suicide of a young girl, who, after signalling from the cliff tops to her smuggler lover to bring his vessel inshore, witnessed, to her horror, the wrecking of the boat and the drowning of her future husband and his mates. Distraught and heartbroken, she threw herself over the cliffs.[7]

Nearby is Fisherman's Walk (leading from Southbourne Overcliff to the Grove), the name given by fishermen from neighbouring hamlets to the narrow path along which they walked to their favourite fishing place. There, below the cliffs, shoals of mackerel could be caught. At low tide the fishermen trudged wearily back along the path to the *New Bell* inn, the only pub for several miles.

One of Dr. Compton's earliest tasks was the construction of a roadway to make the lonely, overgrown area more accessible: Belle Vue Road was therefore commenced from the junction with Tuckton Road to the present Tuckton Bridge. As the new road ran along a duck path, the many ducks continued to waddle across it with their families! Belle Vue Road, when completed, avoided a long detour across Old Iford Bridge for vehicles and road users wishing to travel to Christchurch; the only other alternative had been the small ferry at Wick.

Foxholes was the first house to be built in the new area of Southbourne. In 1872 Henry Reeves, Registrar of the Privy Council, leader-writer of the *Times* and Editor of the *Edinburgh Review*, bought a site at Foxholes for his home in later life. The land was described as being situated on the summit of a hill in the middle of 'an untouched sweep of gorseland'. It was not, however, until March 1876 that he was able to take up residence in his new home.

Soon he was writing to his publisher, 'I enjoy my life here beyond all things. Four months have skipped by in this Olympian calm, between the sea and the sky . . . but it is time to be up and doing and next week I return to London with a large stock of health and good spirits.' In his diary he wrote, 'I have left my hill which overlooks the great seaway between the Needles and Hengistbury Head and come to London for my next three months, but I had much rather stay in my hermitage. London is as dis-agreeable as an east wind can make it.'[8] Whilst in Southbourne, he maintained his political and literary interests, and wrote long letters from Foxholes to friends in London and abroad on 'political developments in France, the Irish Land Act, Mrs. Carlyle's letters and Shelley'. In his diary he wrote of the General Election of 1880; 'It is raining heavily today – rather damp for the electors, but a capital thing for the country and for my shrubs'.

A few years after Mr. Reeves' death in 1895, Foxholes became a well known girls' school, St. Cuthbert's. As the school grew in size a new wing was added, the difference in style and architecture being easily discernible. In 1937 the school was purchased by the Galleon World Travel Association as a hotel. Visitors often comment on the style of the building, which on the southern side is reminiscent of Italy or the south of France, and also on its curious bas-reliefs in the lounge, which are replicas of the Elgin Marbles in the British Museum.

By 1874 Southbourne had its own Winter Gardens, which were 400 feet long by 40 feet wide and were constructed almost entirely of glass (several years before the erection of the first Winter Gardens in Bournemouth) on the south side of Belle Vue Road, near the present Cross Roads, and opposite the then recently completed *South Cliff* Hotel. The Winter Gardens were well heated, and filled with flowers, ornamental plants and large palms. People from Bournemouth flocked to visit them and willingly paid the 6d. entrance fee. At first water was supplied from a well 120 feet deep, pumped by a horse-driven machine.

The story behind Southbourne Winter Gardens is unusual, as the whole structure was transferred from Tedworth Park, near Andover. Tedworth Park was the home of a well-known sportsman, Assheton Smith, who was disturbed when informed by his physician that he should take his wife to Madeira for the winter, for about six months, to cure her chest complaint.

As he was a keen huntsman with his own racing stud, he had no wish to leave England for such a long period. He decided that instead of taking his wife to Madeira, he would bring Madeira to her. He ordered the erection of a huge glass conservatory in the Park, which he filled with roses and other bright flowers, maintaining the temperature at a minimum of 60°F. There, his wife, who was also a keen horsewoman, was able to have her daily rides in the atmosphere of the warm Mediterranean. When Assheton Smith died, Tedworth Park was let to another hunting man who was not, however, interested in the enormous glass structure. This was eventually sold to the Southbourne Winter Garden Co., founded by Dr. Compton.[9]

The nearest church was either the Priory at Christchurch or St. James's, Pokesdown. It was not until 1876 that a small brick building, which served as a school during the week and a church on Sundays, was erected. It was surrounded by high, straggling gorse bushes, whilst a multitude of rabbits scampered everywhere. The first verger, Mr. John Barnes, who used to plough the land on which the building stood and who lived in one of the three original cottages in Southbourne, was paid 10s. per quarter to ring the bell and to see to the paraffin lamps. His wife cleaned the church every Saturday in readiness for the Sunday service, and was also paid 10s. per quarter. Up to 1974, for almost one hundred years, members of the Barnes family have retained the tradition of serving devotedly as vergers; a fine achievement in service and loyalty!

As Southbourne developed, a larger church became necessary. In June 1882 the foundation stone of the present St. Katharine's Church, at one time called 'The Church in the Woods', was laid by Canon W. Lucas, the rural dean of Christchurch. The land (about an acre) was donated to the parish by Dr. Compton, who had previously paid £70 for it. He, together with the vicar of St. Peter's, Bournemouth, Rev. Morden Bennett, chose its name owing to the nearness of St. Catherine's Hill and also of St. Catherine's Point on the Isle of Wight. The completed church, constructed in the Early English style, was consecrated by the Bishop of Winchester in 1886 on St. Katharine's Day.

In 1881 the Tuckton Bridge Co. was initiated by Dr. Compton, who ordered the construction of the original wooden Tuckton Bridge at a cost of £4,000. It was opened in May 1883, and until 1943 it was a toll bridge, the charges initially being 6d. for four-wheeled vehicles, 4d. for two-wheeled, $1/_2$d. for bicycles and prams and 1d. for pedestrians. In 1904 the bridge was purchased by the Borough of Bournemouth, and in the following year it was replaced by a stronger structure which enabled trams to cross it en route for Christchurch.

At about this stage Dr. Compton began to find the increasing work too strenuous, especially in conjunction with his practice in Bournemouth, and sold some of the land to the Southbourne Land Co., another company which he had founded. Owing to insufficient capital the Company eventually had to wind up, but first it was able to construct a one-third of a mile length of the Undercliff Parade, and a sea wall, in 1883 (several years before the Undercliff Drive in Bournemouth), which was opened by Dr. Compton and the local M.P., Sir Horace Davey, in September 1885. A toll was charged of 1d. for adults and $1/_2$d. for children. Towards the west end of the Parade, a chalybeate spring was discovered containing 66 grains of feric sulphate and 56 grains of sodium per gallon, which it was thought would have curative value for anaemic sufferers. Unfortunately the Southbourne Land Co. lacked funds to adequately maintain the sea

51

wall, which was broken by severe gales in 1902, and the Undercliff Parade gradually disintegrated after being broken up by the sea.

It was a great occasion when Southbourne had its own pier, built in 1881 of iron with a concrete entrance, 300 feet long and 30 feet wide. It was confidently believed that the structure would withstand the furies of the sea, but on 28 December 1900 it was severely damaged by gales, and it was further demolished by another gale six days later. In 1907 the pier was dismantled by Bournemouth Corporation as being dangerous and by then completely derelict. Six fine three-storey houses built on the undercliff in 1888, in one of which Dr. Compton lived, also had to be destroyed owing to severe flooding in their basements.

The enterprise and progress made by Southbourne is praised in Bright's *Guide to Bournemouth*:

> The rapid progress of Southbourne may be judged from the fact that whereas some 15 years ago it had neither a name nor a road, much less a house, it now possesses a handsome Church, a large Hotel, numerous private residences and lodging-houses, shops, Post and Telegraph Offices, a valuable Chalybeate Spring, and last, but not least, a magnificent Undercliff Esplanade and Sea Wall, to which a well designed iron Pier of about 300 feet in length is now attached.

It seems a pity that all the splendid efforts made by the forward-looking new district were to be destroyed.

St. Katharine's Children's Home was established in 1892 under the auspices of the Church of England Waifs and Strays Society at Sandymount, Crescent Road (now part of the Overcliff Drive and near Avoncliffe Road), on a lease of £70 a year from Dr. Compton. A matron was appointed at £12 p.a., and the original 20 girls made their own uniforms, attended St. Katharine's school at a charge of 2d. per week, and assisted in the Home, as well as cleaning the church on Saturday mornings. When they were older they were placed in approved services as domestics at about £6 p.a., as opportunities for children at that time were very limited.

By 1911 concern was felt in the Home due to continual cliff erosion, and the following year it was discovered that it was only 113 feet from the cliff edge. When the First World War commenced, there was the further worry of bombardment and danger to the children, and the matron was ordered to lay in a stock of food, including 2 cwts. of rice and 2 cwts. of oatmeal. Despite the ever-increasing problem of erosion, part of their southern boundary having completely broken away by 1917, the Home remained on the cliff edge until the present Home on the corner of Church and Wildown Roads was completed in 1920. Today St. Katharine's Home accommodates about twenty boys and girls. It is a delightful place, light and airy, where an atmosphere of love and understanding is more than apparent and where educational opportunities are fully developed.

The following extracts are from early Minute Books in the Home:

1898 Butcher charging more than 8d. lb. for meat, contract price.
1912 30 bath towels purchased at $8^3/_4$d. each.
1927 33 top coats purchased for £25.
1934 500 eggs purchased at 9d. per dozen.

The first boys' school in the area, Pembroke Lodge House School, was opened on 8 May 1880 by Mr. Theodore Cornish, M.A., commencing with two pupils! Later there were to be about thirty boys. The fine Victorian building with extensive grounds occupied the area from Seafield Road, near the Crossroads, to the Southbourne Water

Tower. Older residents of Southbourne remember the boys playing cricket in their magnificent grounds or clambering over the cliffs and enjoying the delights of sea-bathing, whilst a former sewing maid remembers being severely reprimanded for walking along the school drive without wearing a hat!

The first girls' school, Grassendale, started over a shop by Miss Tucker (succeeded by Misses Amy and Mary Lumby). In 1886 Miss Tucker took over a newly-built house, 37 Belle Vue Road (originally called Locksley, then The Bealings, and today a block of flats, known as Channel Court), with a few day children and five boarders, who were soon joined by four or five others. In 1888, needing more accommodation, the school moved to larger premises in St. Catherine's Road (now St. Peter's School), which had to be extended after one year. An atmosphere of trust, confidence and loyalty was developed amongst the pupils, whilst a healthy mind and body were considered to be of major importance.

Although St. Cuthbert's School and Grassendale were so close together, due to their extensive grounds and the dense forest of pines and oaks separating them, many people were practically unaware of their existence, especially around 1891 when the population of Southbourne was only 607.

In 1936 Pembroke Lodge moved to Fordingbridge, its headmaster feeling that the area was losing much of its original charm and was in the process of becoming too built-up. Grassendale moved on to Belle Vue Road, Southbourne, and changed its name to St. Mary's Gate School, by which it is known today, whilst the original school was purchased in 1936 by the Jesuits as a boys' school, and in 1947 by the Da La Salle brothers. The school has been greatly extended since the Grassendale days. (Today it is the only comprehensive school in Bournemouth.) Over the doorway of one of the original buildings was engraved the message:

> Come in with Love, stay long,
> Then bid farewell in peace.

In an account of the early history of Grassendale, its Founder wrote; 'The Grassendale spirit is here and is to be found by now in all corners of the earth'. Today, Southbourne still prides itself on its high standard of education, both private and public.

Chapter VIII

BOSCOMBE AND SPRINGBOURNE

AS THE NUMBER of stylish, detached villas in Bournemouth continued to increase, so did the demand for artisans, including carpenters, plasterers, builders, shopkeepers and painters, who were required to work in the new watering place but who were expected to live outside the area. No working-class quarters had been provided in Bournemouth, resulting in the growth of districts outside its boundaries where suitable houses for artisans were built.

The name 'Boscombe' seems to be of doubtful origin, and has appeared in several forms over time. In proceedings in the Court of Chancery during the reign of Elizabeth I, reference is made to 'certain mines of alum and copperas called Baskaw'.[1] In the state papers of June 1574 in the Public Record Office it is spelt 'Bastome';[2] Nordens map of Hampshire c. 1600 indicates 'Boscombe Copperas House', and during the 18th century it was written as 'Boscomb'. In the journal of a Riding Officer, 1803, a reference is made to 'surveying the heath of Little Down and Boskum'.[3] It is said that 'Bos' could be Cornish for 'a house',[4] and 'Cumb' is Old English for a narrow valley, 'coombe, coomb, comb, combe' also denoting a short valley running up from the coast.[5]

Boscombe was originally separated from Bournemouth by dense pine woods and moorland. This desolate area contrasted greatly with the development then taking place in Bournemouth, where residential villas had extended beyond what is now Derby Road and on the East Cliff to the end of Manor Road.

By 1850, on the lonely Boscombe heathland stood a picturesque wayside inn bearing the strange name of the *Ragged Cat*, which was later changed to its present name of the *Palmerston Arms*,[6] and a few scattered mud and thatch cottages. The first estate, Boscombe Cottage, comprised 17 acres, and is shown on the Award Map of 1805: it was built in 1801 for Philip Norris, near the site of the old Copperas House. As a result of the Inclosure Awards it was considerably enlarged, but the building owes its fame to the fact that it was occupied by Sir Percy Florence Shelley (son of the poet Percy Bysshe Shelley) from 1849 for 40 years. (See chapter XIX.)

In order to provide workmen's homes, Dr. William Dale Farr, the owner of land in the area of Iford, Pokesdown and the greater part of Springbourne, made land available on building leases in about 1864, forming a suburb along Cleveland Road (then Princess Road) and Windham Road (named after Wm. Windham Farr). After Dr. Farr's death Peter Tuck of Bournemouth and James Druitt Snr. leased from the Farr estate land for building, and began constructing roads and developing the area. At about the same time, John Sloman of Wick, who owned adjoining land on the south side, commenced the development of his property. By *c.* 1880 about fifty houses had been built in the Springbourne area, including a mission chapel (later replaced by St. Clement's Church), a Wesleyan chapel and two inns, the *Dolphin* in Holdenhurst Road and the *Cricketers Arms* in Windham Road, whilst a dozen or so houses had been erected along the newly-constructed roads in the adjoining Boscombe area. All these roads were given the names of statesmen, for example Walpole, Gladstone, Churchill, Salisbury, Palmerston and Ashley.

The growing popularity of Boscombe was mainly due to the foresight of Sir Henry Drummond Wolff, a diplomat and politician, who hoped to make the district a rival watering place to Bournemouth. After retiring from a governership abroad with the Foreign Office, he purchased land, mainly consisting of pine woods, from Lord Malmesbury; this land lay between Boscombe Chine and Shore Lane, (now Sea Road) and adjoined the Shelley Estate. For his own occupation he built a stately villa in 1868 called Boscombe Towers (now part of the *Burlington* Hotel). In his house was born the Primrose League (given in memory of Disraeli, who loved primroses).

The name 'Boscombe Spa' was given to his estate owing to the properties of a ferruginous stream near the Chine. The impregnate waters of this small spring were

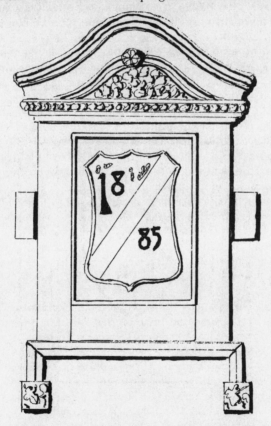

Fig. 5.   Dated crest, *Clock House* Hotel, Boscombe Spa Road, Boscombe.

55

said to be completely pure and mildly chalybeate. Physicians recommended their patients to drink the waters for their mineral contents, which were said to contain properties similar to those of Harrogate waters. Sir Henry erected a small thatched building [7] around the spring which attracted visitors from neighbouring Bournemouth to partake of its waters. Many of these enthusiasts walked all the way through the lonely country, finally to climb up steep Boscombe Hill and along the narrow Boscombe Spa Road (its present name). The water was also sold, bottled, as aerated table water, and its taste was said to be similar to Seltzer's water, an effervescent mineral water that was considered a fashionable drink.

Other villas were built on the estate and roads were constructed, some of which he named after personal and literary friends. Sir Algernon Borthwick (later Lord Glenesk), a neighbour and friend of Sir Henry, also played an active part in fostering the progress of Boscombe. When Sir Algernon founded a satirical social-political magazine called *The Owl* in 1864, Sir Henry became one of its first subscribers, and this is why the unusually-named Owls Road was so called. The names Borthwick and Drummond Road were also bestowed by Sir Henry.

In addition, he was responsible for laying out Boscombe Chine as gardens and building a rustic bridge across it. (Boscombe Chine, first known as Boscombe Bunny or Boscombe Mouth, was a deep, narrow ravine, cut by a stream and leading to the sea.) Tennis courts were provided, and an old brick kiln in the chines was demolished to be replaced by a rustic building for the accommodation of tennis players.

To cater for visitors who came to the area, the *Boscombe Spa* Hotel was erected in

Fig. 6.   Dated crest, Montague House, Owls Road, Boscombe.
The original Montague crest was defaced by property developers who, for a joke, made up this crest with their initials, G. W.

1874. (It has now been considerably enlarged and is known as the *Boscombe Chine Hotel*.)

St. Clement's was the first parish church to be built in Springbourne, in an area which was then mainly surrounded by woods and moorland. As Bournemouth and parts of Boscombe developed residentially (mainly on the south side), the church drew a large proportion of its congregation from wealthy and titled people who lived in stately and detached villas. Today, over a century later, it is surrounded by working-class houses, overcrowded flatlets and a number of badly maintained buildings, whilst the church itself suffers from the ravages of time and is, badly, in need of repair.

The church, with its tall, majestic tower, owes its inception to the genius, foresight and generosity of three men. Rev. Morden Bennett, the first vicar of St. Peter's, was always aware of the spiritual needs of Bournemouth and the surrounding area, and was responsible for the selection of eight sites for eight new churches, one of which was St. Clement's. By subscription, in 1867 he was able to obtain sufficient money to buy four acres of land from Mr. Sloman, who owned land to the south of Springbourne. On this land was built the church, a vicarage and a school for boys and girls. Originally the parish of St. Clement's was part of the parish of St. Peter's (the latter having been formed in 1845 from the ancient parishes of Christchurch and Holdenhurst).

To meet the requirements of the district before the new church was built, Morden Bennett hired some cottages in Holdenhurst Road as a temporary church (nos. 290, 292 and 294), from which a mission church was created which seated 200 people. The first service was held in the little church on 10 November 1867. Through the generosity of Edmund Christy, who came to Bournemouth from Aberdeen, a gift of £30,000 was received for the building of the church, vicarage and schools. He made one condition: that a separate district should be formed for the church. This was agreed, and by Order in Council of 19 August 1871 the new parish of St. Clement's was formed.

Mr. Christy was a wealthy bachelor, a lover of beautiful *objets d'art* who had a vocation to devote some of his great wealth to the service of God. After deliberating for several years as to whether to found a religious community home or to endow a church in a new parish, he decided on the latter. Part of the site of the church was in the same road as his fine Tudor-style home, The Knole, which was built as a manor-house in 1873 by his friend J. D. Sedding, a great and talented Bristol architect. (The Knole later became the home of Sir Henry Page Croft, M.P. for Christchurch and the first M.P. for the Borough of Bournemouth. Today it is a Freemasons' Hall.) The Gothic design of St. Clement's Church, the decorative style and the exquisite lace-work of the screens were due to the genius of John Sedding, whose name 'is as great in the history of English Architecture as Rosetti in English painting'.[8]

The foundation of the church was laid by Morden Bennett on St. Clement's Day, 23 November 1871, and the church was consecrated by Bishop Wilberforce of Winchester on 15 April 1873. The service was based on the Oxford Movement, i.e. Anglo-Catholic or Tractarian. In its early days there was opposition to this type of service, which involved a mass and vestments. At the consecration Bishop Wilberforce was quite perturbed, and asked for two candles by the Holy Table to be extinguished and for the wafers to be replaced by bread. Early vicars and members were stoned and heckled by irate crowds outside, and even Rev. Morden Bennett was abused and an effigy of him burnt in the streets.

Closely associated with St. Clement's Church is the Convent of the Sisters of Bethany, an Anglican religious community founded in 1866 by Etheldreda Anna Bennett, originally under the title of the Sisters of the Order of Retreat, whose premises were then in Lloyd Street, London.

Rev. E. F. Russell of St. Alban's Church, Holborn, London, and also chaplain to the Sisters of Bethany (their title from 1871) at the Mother House in London, visited Bournemouth in 1872 to meet the Rev. Mother Foundress, and to inspect with her a proposed site for a convent and an orphanage. Rev. Russell described the site as part 'of the untamed, unbroken moorland of the New Forest which descends in low hills and shallow valleys, heather-clad. The surface was in all its native wildness and I remember how we gathered here and there the characteristic moorland plants, the stag-moss, the bog asphodel and, in moist places, the wonderful little sundew. Looking southward, the heath continued unbroken by a single building to the sea cliff.'[9]

A site adjoining St. Clement's Church was purchased, and in the following year, 1873, Rev. Tinling, the first vicar of St. Clement's, invited the Sisters to undertake work in the parish and placed under their care St. Clement's Home, a small orphanage which had been started by Miss Emma Mordaunt and Rev. Morden Bennett. The large, well-proportioned, three-storeyed Victorian building of mellow red-brick tiles could accommodate about a hundred children. The orphanage was completed in 1875, and after it was blessed by Rev. Russell the Sisters began their work in the larger orphanage.

An attractive sloping roof, tall stately chimneys and a wide Gothic-style porch are features of this 'listed' building, designed by Norman Shaw, who was also the architect for St. Michael's and St. Swithun's Churches; a convent wing was added in 1880 and further additions at later periods. The substantial House of Bethany was well-hidden from the road, in about six acres of ground, among chestnut, sycamore and oak trees. Its site on open moorland was considered ideal for a children's home, whilst its secluded position bore out the precepts of the Mother Foundress; 'In quietness and confidence shall be your strength and "Be hidden, efface yourself".' The children ranged from two to ten years, and some of them had parents who, for various reasons, were unable to look after them. Their training and education, including commercial and domestic work, and also nursing, were undertaken by the Sisters, and it must have been a considerable task for this small group (originally there were three Sisters), who were also concerned with retreat and mission work in London and Bournemouth.

Credit is given to the work of the Sisters in a pamphlet of 1899 by Horace Dobell, M.D., Consultant Physician to the Royal Hospital for Diseases of the Chest. After writing of the wonderful effects of Bournemouth air on children, especially those with delicate chests, he continues:

> But I do not know of any evidence so good as that of the Bournemouth Orphanage, to which the Sisters of Bethany in London send destitute children for care and education. The beneficient effect upon their health is wonderful. There is no prettier sight in this neighbourhood than these nicely clad children, who are to be met in troops of 20 to 50 in charge of one or two Sisters, rambling unrestrictedly through the heath and pinewoods or along the beach, laden with country treasures, their ruddy faces beaming with health and pleasure . . . I never saw a host of poor children who looked so full of joyous life as these.

By 1892 there were 105 children in the orphanage, 26 of whom were entirely free; 33 were partially paid for and the remainder paid 5s. weekly. As the total amount received did not cover the expenses of the Home and the education of the children, outside laundry work was undertaken in addition to that for the Home, whilst subscriptions from the public were welcomed. The control of the work was in the hands of a

Sister-in-Charge under the guidance of Etheldreda Anna Bennett, the Mother Foundress, a distinguished, courteous, high-born lady who had forsaken her wealth and possessions for Christ and the poor. She died in her ninetieth year, in 1913, and was buried in St. Clement's churchyard.

By the mid 1930s it became clear that the days of large orphanages were over; their equipment was out of date, there were fewer children, and the cost of maintaining them had increased. The state, too, was becoming more responsible for the welfare of orphans. The orphanage was eventually closed when more accommodation could be provided for retreatants, a work undertaken by the community since 1866. Fortunately, by the outbreak of the last World War all the children had been placed elsewhere, as in September 1940 a passing German bomber demolished the orphanage wing, which was then out of use until 1950. A separate house, known as St. Gabriels, was used as a convalescent home during the war years for sick children from London. In 1955 this building was altered and re-established as a home for elderly ladies. In 1962 the Mother House moved from London to Bournemouth, and the House of Bethany was further enlarged to give additional accommodation for conferences, visitors and retreatants.

Adjoining Boscombe Manor and extending from Wentworth Road to Fisherman's Walk, Southbourne, was the summer residence and estate of Lord Portman of Bryanston, Blandford. Wentworth House was built c. 1873 and remained in the family until 1922. The large, ornamental gates to the original drive of the house can be seen today leading into Woodlands Walk; the former lodge still exists in Christchurch Road and is now owned by Deric Scott Ltd., Funeral Directors.

The well built, impressive Victorian house, with its stables, cobbled stable yard and walled kitchen gardens, was considerably extended over a period of years after being purchased in 1922 by the Collegiate School for Girls. The school commenced in 1899, when Dr. J. D. Jones, Minister at Richmond Hill Congregational (now United Reformed) Church from 1898 to 1937, and other Free Church members opened a girls' school to provide a sound Christian education without sectarian bias in a house called 'Towerfield' in Poole Road. When the house became too small for the growing school, they were able to acquire Wentworth House, when much of the surrounding estate was sold to finance extensions.

In 1962 Wentworth School was amalgamated with Milton Mount, a Surrey school, whose building had been purchased for development, and became known as Wentworth Milton Mount, its present name. Lord Portman is commemorated in several roads: Portman Road, Portman Crescent, Wentworth Avenue and Bryanstone Road.

By 1875 Bournemouth was seeking to expand the limited area granted under the Improvement Act of 1856 (see chapter X). As Boscombe and Springbourne adjoined its boundary, it seemed natural that the first petition for extension should seek to incorporate them, and in 1875 the commissioners made a request to the L.G. Board for the inclusion of the two districts under their jurisdiction. Their appeal was strongly opposed by Boscombe, which counter-petitioned to be formed into an urban sanitary district together with Springbourne. An inquiry was held in 1876, and the L.G. Board assented to the wishes of the commissioners. This extension was to be the first of many; the seafront area was increased and Bournemouth gained another 503 acres.

Although houses were continuing to be built, up to 1885 Boscombe remained an outlying district with no railway station and no pier, and piers were, of course, a great attraction in the Victorian era. A resolution was put to the commissioners for the provision of a pier, but without success. In 1888 a Boscombe Pier Co. was formed, with Sir H. Drummond Wolff and other important people as its directors; the independent attitude of the district and its determination to rival Bournemouth was again in evidence. On 17 October of that year there was jubilation as Lady Shelley fixed the first pile. The pier was 600 ft. long and 32 ft. wide, with landing stages on either side, and was built of iron. The opening ceremony was performed on 29 July 1889 by the Duke of Argyll, accompanied by the Marquis of Lorne. In his speech the Duke explained his acquaintance with Bournemouth before the time of the commissioners. In 1846, when he had been feeling ill, he was advised by a medical friend who was also the author of *Notes of a Wanderer in search of Health* to go to Bournemouth, the only place where his health would be improved. His friend then described it as a place he had seen on his travels and that he had never seen any place on the English coast that eclipsed Bournemouth. The Duke took the train to Winchester (the nearest station to Bournemouth), posted through the New Forest and eventually arrived at Bournemouth. There, all he saw was the *Bath* Hotel, a few houses and practically nothing else. A large fir wood extended from the hotel to Boscombe, where he and his friend took long walks without meeting a single human being, only numerous squirrels. After 10 days his health was restored.

Although the pier was an attraction and a social amenity, providing roller-skating facilities and music, it was not a financial success. In 1903, in response to several requests, it was purchased by Bournemouth Corporation, but it still remained unprofitable.

Following the erection of the pier other developments took place, mainly due to the progressive ideas and activity of Mr. Archibald Beckett, the Boscombe representative for the ward, who was also a strong advocate of the Boscombe pier and promenade. He was responsible for the erection of the *Salisbury* Hotel in 1890, the Arcade in 1892 and the theatre in 1895, all of which were part of the same structure. The feeling of rivalry with neighbouring Bournemouth remained; since Bournemouth had an arcade (1866–72) and a Theatre Royal (1882), Boscombe must also have them.

The magnificent L-shaped Victorian glass edifice was named 'The Royal Boscombe Arcade'. It had two entrances, one in Christchurch Road and another in Palmerston Road, and cost over £40,000 to build. The Arcade was opened on 19 December 1892 by the Duke of Connaught. The 1,000-guinea organ was played daily at 11.30 a.m., whilst orchestral concerts were given at 3.30 p.m. As the building was designed with a double front the organ could be played either in the theatre or from the balcony in the arcade. Until about 1930 people could shop whilst listening to pleasant music in an arcade that was often adorned with palms and cacti growing in tubs. (At this time there were no shops beyond Palmerston Road or Sea Road on either side of the main Christchurch Road, the area still being mainly residential and rural.)

The Grand Pavilion Theatre, also known as the Boscombe Theatre, was built by Mr. Beckett at a cost of £16,000, and was opened on 27 May 1895. The superb building was luxuriously furnished; it had a floor space of 13,000 sq. ft. and could accommodate 3,000 people. There was an 'open' or 'lantern' roof and clerestory lights. The seating arrangements consisted of three tiers of balconies, those on the ground floor running round to the proscenium on each side, three private boxes, two buffets and two smoking lounges. Prices varied from boxes at 15s. to balcony seats at 9d. and 6d. Dramatic and musical performances were given daily, and during the first five months the theatre was patronized by over a hundred thousand people. Many fine artistes performed at the theatre, including Henry Irving, Ellen Terry and Sarah Bernhardt.

Fig. 7.   Dated porch of the United Reform Church, Boscombe.

On the opposite side of Christchurch Road, facing the theatre, a large image of a devil can be seen leering down at passers-by. It was erected as a sign of protest by those who were horrified by the thought of 'bawdy' or 'improper' musical or dramatic performances coming to Boscombe. Efforts were made to prevent the building from opening, as it was the wish of some residents that a church be established there; and because the attempts were unsuccessful, the devil was erected. Underneath was inscribed 'The devil comes into his own' (this is no longer legible), and the date '1896'.

After the theatre had been closed for a time, it was re-opened on 27 February 1905 as a music-hall called the Boscombe Hippodrome. Music-hall artistes included Marie Lloyd, Dan Leno, Vesta Tilley, Hetty King, David Nixon and Eric Jones-Evans, a local celebrity. The Hippodrome was finally closed in 1956 to become the Royal Arcade Ballroom (now Tiffany's).

Chapter IX

WINTON

(Also Talbot Village, Moordown and Charminster)

WINTON, now a busy suburb of Bournemouth, was originally part of the liberty of Westover, within the Manor of Christchurch. It commenced as an area for artisans (similar to Boscombe, Springbourne and Pokesdown), with neatly planned workmen's cottages laid out on the east side of Wimborne Road, for those who worked in the district and also in Bournemouth.

Although the name 'Winton' was unknown until the mid 19th century, the following description of the heathland and moors, including Wallis Down (now Wallisdown) graphically portrays the lonely area:

> Inland the country was intersected by tracks of the carts in which peat, then almost the only fuel used, was taken to the outlying farms and here and there on some little hillock well away from the main road rose the sinister form of the gallows, the chains in which the bodies of those who had suffered on it had been hung still dangling from it and the ground beneath strewn with the blackened bones of earlier victims. In the summer a few sheep and oxen browsed upon the scanty herbage; their presence slightly relieving the desolation of the scene, but almost the only wild creatures were rabbits, hares and adders, the last so numerous than an antidote to the poison of their bite used to be kept in holes in the gates of farms ready for immediate application to the wound.[1]

The earliest known building was in Moordown – a small mud-and-thatch farmhouse erected in 1810 by Lewis Tregonwell, the founder of Bournemouth, on land purchased by him on the east side of Wimborne Road. The farm was renowned for its hospitality, which in its early days was extended to many free traders or smugglers. In the late 19th century it became known as 'Burt's Farm', David Burt living there in 1878 and George Burt, a cowkeeper, from 1911. The farm existed until the late 1920s, although it was by then surrounded by buildings and houses. The site was eventually occupied by the Moordown Branch of the Parkstone & Bournemouth Co-Operative Society, and today this very small shop is used by the Society as a store (it is situated on the corner of Coronation Street).

Development of the district was mainly due to the progressive outlook of the Misses Georgina Charlotte and Marianne Talbot, who were wealthy 19th-century philanthropists. The two sisters were well travelled and cultured, and lived in Grosvenor Square. Shortly before 1850 the family left London for the newly developed watering town of Bournemouth, where they lived at Hinton Wood House on the East Cliff (now demolished and replaced by a block of flats).

As a result of the great poverty then prevailing, crowds of peasants, including women and children, used to stand under their windows calling 'Give us work; give us work; we are starving'. In their bitter anger, sticks and stones were sometimes hurled at the house. One of the daughters, Georgina, whose social conscience had been stirred through reading a German book of Zschokke's (in English called *The Goldmakers Village*), decided to try to ameliorate the conditions of these poor people. She rented land on the moors from Sir George Gervis (the Lord of the Manor) and Mr. William Driver (one of the original freeholders) in order to provide agricultural work for some of the poor unemployed. Mr. David Tuck, a farmer, was put in charge of the scheme, which proved highly successful. People gladly travelled from miles around to obtain work there.

The idea of a self-supporting village community arose from this trial venture. In about 1850 a tract of land of 465 acres was purchased, 150 acres of which were reserved with grazing rights for the animals of farm workers and cottagers. The estate included six farms and 16 cottages, another being added in 1872 for the organist of St. Mark's Church, and was under the control of the landlord and trustees. Well constructed artisan cottages were erected, detached and of a high quality, each on one acre of land, including its own garden. There were three bedrooms, two living rooms, a large kitchen, a well and a pigsty. Rents were low, ranging from 4s. to 7s. per week, with no extra taxes or charges for repairs.

The village was designed for those who were prepared to work to maintain themselves and their families. No lodgers were permitted and no trade was allowed, except for the sale of poultry, eggs and bacon. If they became wealthy they were expected to leave the village to make way for other poor families. Although the operations of the venture were not based on charity but on hard work, all fear of the 'hated' workhouse was removed. The foundation of the village was based on the precepts 'Love God, Keep the Commandments and Honour the Queen'. Initially there were problems, however, as some of the women were lax and uncontrolled in their behaviour, whilst surrounding gentry and clergy had little sympathy with the idea of improving the lower classes.

In 1862 seven attractive almshouses designed by Christopher Crabbe Creeke were constructed of Portland stone, and endowed by the founder for the benefit of the old and infirm of the labouring classes, thus providing them with peace and security in their old age. There were flower gardens in front of the houses and vegetable gardens at the back, and also an ornamental well. Pigsties and a space for poultry were provided for those whose health permitted them to maintain such animals. Occupiers were allowed 6s. per week, two tons of coal and the attendance of a doctor. Burial fees and the setting up of headstones were provided. There were 18 rules; inmates had to be of good character, to assist their neighbours in times of sickness and not to quarrel with them. It was forbidden to hang out clothes or place other offensive matter in front of the almshouses. A deed of settlement of 1862 stated that the almshouses were for married or single men, and preference would be given to agricultural labourers with no means of support other than parish relief. For some strange reason, 'no one from Hampshire was to be admitted'.

A village school was erected in 1862 and endowed 1863, and consisted of a spacious schoolroom that measured 56 ft. 8 ins. by 14 ft. It commenced with 68 children who were to be instructed in reading, writing, arithmetic and religious instruction, with needlework for the girls. A deed of settlement of 1883 granted the sum of £66 'so long as the portrait of Georgina Charlotte Talbot shall be hung in the schoolroom and the inscription kept'. The provisions of the school were changed with the passing of the Education Act of 1944 when the school became grant-aided, but the beautiful portrait still has its place of honour in the school. A lodging was provided for the schoolmaster and his family, which has since been incorporated into the extended building.

The first headmaster was Samuel Kerley, who was appointed by Miss Talbot. The first log book commenced in October 1877 and records an area accommodation for 128 children and cubic accommodation for 232 children. The headmaster went on to say that when he took charge of the school in 1877 he found it in the charge of an uncertificated teacher, that it was not provided with a log book or admission register, and that none of the 128 children then attending knew their multiplication tables!

The school has been known by many names, including Talbot Village School, Talbot Village Mixed, Talbot Village Undenominational School, St. Mark's Aided School or simply St. Mark's, but it is still thought of by older inhabitants as Talbot Village School. Today its correct name is St. Mark's Church of England Primary School.

By 1870 St. Mark's Church, which was built of Portland and Purbeck stone at a cost of £5,000, had been practically completed. (A new porch added in 1969 cost as much as the original building.)

An early guide to Bournemouth describes the church:

> Forming a very prominent feature in the landscape; its situation in the comparatively open table land rendering it conspicuous in all directions. It is a small but exceedingly chaste building in early decorated style, consisting of a nave, north and south transepts and chancel with a very handsome tower, built in the most massive manner, 75 ft. high at the West end. The masonry is of hammer-dressed grey stone, from Swanage and Stalbridge. The seats are of open benches made of pitch pine, the roof being of the same material . . .[2]

Unfortunately Georgina died shortly before the consecration of the church and was the first to be buried in the spacious churchyard. An inscription around the fine Ionic Memorial Cross reads;

> She came of an ancient race and possessed in herself that nobility of mind which delighted in the happiness of her fellow creatures. . . . In the neighbourhood of this village she passed 25 years of blameless life giving up time and fortune to bettering the conditions of the poorer classes, seeking to minister to their temporal and spiritual welfare, and erecting habitations suitable to their position in life, herself enjoying a peaceful and happy existence in doing good, awaiting the end.

After the death of Georgina, her sister Marianne arranged for the completion of the church and added, as gifts, a gracefully proportioned pulpit, an ancient font procured at Rome by their father, Sir George Talbot, an organ and the church furniture, including two Chippendale chairs which came from the Talbot family home.

For many years Marianne was able to continue the policy adopted by her sister, which also permitted public access to the beautiful Talbot woods. Even today anyone can stroll along the paths in Talbot Village and enjoy the magnificent and secluded woodland scenery. When Marianne died on 3 November 1885, another memorial cross was erected in the churchyard, the inscription extolling her kind and affectionate nature, her exquisite taste in art and literature, her love of beauty and goodness which endeared her through her long and excellent life to her many friends.

Most of the farms have long since disappeared in the development of urban sprawl. Much of the land belonging to Talbot Village Farm is now occupied by the recently built Dorset Institute of Advanced Education. Slades Farm (formerly Talbot Farm) is subject to a preservation order, the land behind it having been developed as part of a housing estate, with a school and special housing for the elderly. Thus the aims of these two remarkable ladies are perpetuated, whilst Talbot Village remains as a sanctuary of beauty and peacefulness off a busy main road and growing industrial area.

As a result of the Christchurch Inclosure Act of 1802, land in the Winton and Moordown areas was purchased mainly by the Earl of Malmesbury and William Driver; the latter, a speculator, resold it to Rev. George Brice, who, like the Earl of Malmesbury, was interested in farming. Other parcels of land, including nearby Redhill, were later sold to the local authority.

The commissioners appointed under this Act had the duty of converting rough tracks across the heath into roads, which produced the road leading from the Decoy Pond (then known as Muscliff Road, and sometimes called the Richmond Hill Road), past Rush Corner (now Cemetery Junction), to the small artisan and farming community, eventually becoming the main road into Winton and continuing on to Wimborne. Heath and moorland surrounded the community, including Wallis Down, Moor Down, Red Hill, Wither Moor, Malmesbury Plantation and Poors Common (now Meyrick Park).

After the Misses Talbot had developed their own estate, they purchased land along the main road (i.e. Wimborne Road) where they built four-square artisans' cottages and public wells for the supply of water. Many of the cottages were occupied by their woodmen and keepers. The Talbots were of Scottish descent, of which they were very proud. They named the new settlement 'Winton' after their kinsman, the Earl of Winton (formerly the Earl of Eglinton). Roads were also named after Scottish towns and personalities.

As building work progressed, more labourers were attracted to the area, leading to a further demand for more houses. The brickmaking industry increased, as did that of excavating gravel and clay. The slopes and hollows which the latter caused formed the present roads of Calvin, Cranmer, Luther and other roads between Winton and Charminster. There were brick kilns on Abbot Road Hill, then known as Claypit Common. White clay was much in evidence in the district, and many of the early cottages were built of this distinctive material, typical ones having decorative bands of contrasting red and white bricks. These cottages were built mainly during the 1890s for £240 and could be rented for 4s. 6d. to 5s. 6d. per week.

By 1878 the population was over fourteen hundred, although it was still described as a hamlet in the parish of Holdenhurst. From 1875 it had its own branch post office, which was situated at the corner of Post Office Road (now Castle Road) and Winton Road.

Adjoining Winton was the mainly agricultural community of Moor Down (Moordown), comprising groups of cottages mainly in the areas of Nursery Road, Malvern Road (formerly Victoria Road) and Rose Garden (the oldest parts of Moordown). There was also an inn, a chapel and some older cottages scattered on the slopes of a hill near Moordown Farm. The farm, which became known as Charminster Farm and then Hunt's Farm, is now a built-up housing area in Charminster; the names of Huntfield and Hunt Vale Roads on the West Way Estate commemorate the occupancy of the farm by William Hunt and then by his son, Charles Meaden Hunt.

Spiritual and educational development in several outlying communities was due to the pioneering zeal and concern of the first vicar of St. Peter's Church, Rev. Morden Bennett. Soon after he had established the first church school in Bourne Mouth, he turned his attention to the poor and spiritually neglected area of Moordown, where artisans and agricultural workers were separated from the parish church by two miles

65

of open country and heathland and, therefore, were deprived of the church's ministrations. In order that religious services could be held, a mission was commenced in a farm cottage in 1851, which served the needs of the hamlets of Moordown, Redhill and Muscliff.

In 1853 Sir George Tapps-Gervis gave Morden Bennett a plot of land along Wimborne Road, which was to be used to provide a permanent chapel school. Funds were soon obtained for its erection from the vicar's generous congregation, and the building was dedicated to St. John in the Wilderness. The chapel became the first of several commissions undertaken by the distinguished ecclesiastical architect, George Edmund Street, who was introduced to Morden Bennett at that time, and who was to become one of his close friends.

The following notice was issued by the vicar:

Moordown, in the Parish of Holdenhurst, Hants, comprises a tract of heathland on which many poor families are settled. . . . It is proposed, under the sanction of the Vicar, on this spot to erect a schoolroom, which the Bishop has consented to license for an occasional service. It is hoped that the privileges of the Church being thus brought near to these poor people, may serve, by God's blessing, to improve their spiritual and moral condition, or may at least afford consolation to the aged and infirm.[3]

The chapel school, completed in 1854, was small and plain. According to Mrs. Lands the interior was plain to the point of poverty and hardly devised to afford consolation to the aged and infirm.[4] In 1865 £150 was spent on enlarging the building to provide more accommodation for the increased number of residents coming to the area. The extension soon proved inadequate and a new church was proposed. On 6 August 1873 the foundation stone was laid by the Earl of Malmesbury, who, by disposing of much of his land in the area for house building, did much to encourage the development and continued growth of Winton and Moordown. An appeal for church funds made by Morden Bennett was generously answered by his wealthy parishioners. The new and present-day St. John's was finished and consecrated in 1874. A new parish was created, comprising Moordown, Winton, Redhill and Muscliff, partly from the parish of Holdenhurst and partly from St. Peter's, Bournemouth.

The original St. John in the Wilderness survives today amidst shops and other buildings on the crowded main road as the showroom of Willis (Bournemouth) Ltd., and it is still called 'Old St. John's Buildings'. In 1878 a new school of St. John the Baptist, accommodating 225 pupils, was opened for girls, whilst Old St. John's was used for boys only. In 1892 a further Church of England school was built in Bemister Road for 300 children.

Other churches were built in the locality, including a Mission Hall for the Congregationalists in 1869 in the 'Pro Bono Publico' Hall at the top west side of Peter's Hill. Peter's Hill was said to have been so named because St. Peter's Church could be seen from its slopes, and also because an old man called 'Peter' had a stall there for several years.

In 1890 the following extract appeared in the Parish Magazine:[5]

Perhaps there is no other such place in the world as Winton, in all events it would be difficult to find one. Some of its characteristics it may no longer retain. We mean the beauty of its golden flowers in May and its purple heather in August. Much of this wild, natural beauty has already succumbed. But picturesque as are the gorse and the heather and beautiful as are the glimpses of the Stour Valley, with St. Catherine's Hill in the distance and grateful is the shade of the Winton Pines in the summer and their shelter in winter, it must be confessed that Winton's unique attraction consists not in these natural beauties . . . but in the affable style, disposition and arrangements of the working peoples houses, such as in the newer parts of the settlement. It would be difficult to find any other place where so much care has been taken to study from a business point of view the precise wants and wishes of our working people as regards their homes. . . . Winton is neither country nor town but seems to take practical hints from both . . . the houses themselves are certainly not without their attractiveness nor is the general view of Peters Hill looking south otherwise than picturesque. In the way of improvement there is of course a great deal to be done. The high road requires to be levelled. . . . The drainage is still primitive, the lighting though admirable depends on voluntary enterprise. . . . The fire engine like the water cart is conspicuous by its absence. Lastly we are, it is to be supposed, so orderly that we only require, or at least only get, the services of one resident policeman.

Nearby Charminster consisted mainly of brickfields, claypits and wasteland. There were small groups of cottages in the area of Malvern Road (between Wimborne Road and Charminster Avenue), and the older Strouden and Moordown (later Charminster and Hunt's) Farms. Charminster Road was then a narrow country lane. Around the 'Fiveways' (the meeting place of five roads) were more gravel excavations, occasional gypsy camps and the mysterious 'Indian Hut', said to have been inhabited 'by a dark or tramp-like gentleman'.[6] Most of the brick and gravel fields were owned by Mr. Mark Loader, a road builder, who introduced the steam engine into the district to carry his loads of bricks. From his brick works came the white bricks which characterised many houses in that locality.

On the passing of the Local Government Act of 1894, Winton was established as a parish council, an earlier attempt in 1892 by Bournemouth to include Winton in its newly formed municipal borough having failed.[7] It was hoped that improved drainage, better roads and the acquisition of public grounds for children would result from this status. The new parish was divided into three wards, east, west and Moordown. By the following year it was realized that the Council's powers were still inadequate to carry out essential work, and the need for urban powers was discussed.

In 1896, however, an application was made by the borough of Bournemouth to extend its boundary by the inclusion of 300 acres of Winton's most valuable land, in the area of Talbot Village. This was strongly opposed by the parish, which were quite willing to be incorporated into Bournemouth on the condition that the borough would take in the whole of the east and west wards. (Moordown was omitted, as it was indicated that this mainly agricultural district did not wish to be incorporated.)

At a meeting on 18 February 1897, a memorial was drawn up stating that the parish of Winton, with a population of about 6,000 and a rateable value of £16,000, was mainly populated by artisans and workmen who were employed in the borough of Bournemouth. The proposal to appropriate 240 acres in Talbot Woods and 60 acres on the eastern side of Wimborne Road, the most valuable parts of their parish, would place the Council in a difficult position to govern a denuded and poorer area. It was requested that Bournemouth should take over the whole of the east and west wards.

As Bournemouth was unwilling to take in the entire area of Winton excluding Moordown, an application was made in November 1897 for urban status for the three wards. This was opposed by Moordown, which wished to become a separate parish. In September 1898 urban status was granted to the whole of Winton (i.e. the three wards) by Hampshire County Council and the Local Government Board. A clerk was appointed at £50 p.a., a medical officer at £35 p.a. (in February 1899 this was increased to £40), the posts of surveyor and inspector of nuisances was combined at £140 p.a., whilst the rate collector was to be paid $2\frac{1}{2}$ per cent commission on the amount collected.

The lack of water supply in Moordown was one of the matters discussed by the Council in August 1899. At this meeting it was decided to accept the offer of Mr. Hunt (who was Vice-Chairman of the Council) to lend the Council a 244-gallon cistern, and to arrange for the surveyor to employ a horse and cart to carry water through the roads of Moordown. At other meetings there was discussion as to whether the Council should be responsible for collecting household refuse and emptying cesspools. As the cost of purchasing dustcarts, three horses, a van, and rental of stables would be almost £600, it was considered that the disposal of refuse should be undertaken by the occupiers.

Although urban status had been obtained, it was still felt by the Council that it would be more beneficial to all concerned if Winton could be incorporated into Bournemouth, especially as their interests were so closely linked. In April 1900 Bournemouth obtained complete independence from the County Council by becoming a County Borough, and the following year it was extended to include the whole of Winton, including Moordown. Pokesdown and Southbourne were also incorporated at the same time.

Chapter X

SELF-GOVERNMENT

PRIOR TO 1856 Bournemouth had no form of municipal government; estates were developed by individual landowners, and credit has always been given to these enterprising and farsighted planners. As the population slowly increased (there were still only 695 inhabitants in 1851), problems of water supply, sanitation, lighting, and the chaotic condition of roads all became increasingly urgent. Powers of local administration were required to carry out the essential work; it was also realized that the needs of a future developing town could no longer be determined by the predominantly rural village of Holdenhurst.

In the words of Mate and Riddle:

Prior to 1856, the residents of Bournemouth had less of the privileges of local self-government than the meanest village in the land now possesses. The smallest area now, at least, has its Parish Meeting, with opportunity, at all events for the ventilation of public grievance; Bournemouth before 1856 had not even that. Householders had the right to attend the Vestries at Holdenhurst or Christchurch; but the exercise of this privilege, meant a journey . . . and could not be counted as of much, if any value.[1]

The first step towards control of local affairs was taken when a Local Act was applied for, the aim of which was to improve Bournemouth.

The Bill, which received the Royal Assent on 14 July 1856, became known as the 'Bournemouth Improvement Act, 1856', the effect of which was to slowly change a picturesque little watering place into a new town. The Act provided for improved paving, sewering, draining, lighting and cleansing; it also empowered the provision of a new pier (see chapter VI), an amenity so popular with many residents and visitors, which had to be completed within five years of the passing of the Act. A restricted area of administration was defined as 'within the circle of the radius of a mile whereof the centre is the front door of the Belle Vue Hotel', being the extent of the marine village of Bourne. The new district also comprised part of the ecclesiastical district of St. Peter's Church, which somewhat complicated matters as portions of the area were included in the ancient Holdenhurst parish and other portions in Christchurch. The entire area comprised 1,140 acres.

Other provisions of the Act included the election and appointment of 13 commissioners, of whom the lord of the manor and his nominee were permanent members. Qualification for membership of the Board was by owning property of an annual value of £30 for those who lived in the designated area or not more than a mile outside it. The original Board comprised Messrs. Bayly, Clapcott Dean, Kerley, Ledgard (Chairman from 1856 to 57) Packe, Robson, Shettle, Tuck, John Tregonwell, Thompson and

Winter. A rate not exceeding 3s. in the pound was authorized, as was borrowing up to £5,000 for the erection of a pier and £5,000 for other purposes.

Mr. Thomas Kingdon became the first Clerk at a salary of £26 p.a., for which he was required to attend all meetings of the commissioners, their committees, and to keep all minutes and accounts.

The first Surveyor and Inspector of Nuisances was Mr. Christopher Crabbe Creeke, whose many duties included planning, improving by surfacing and gravelling the muddy, unmade roads, and producing a detailed map of the district. For this work he was paid £50 p.a., which was increased in 1868 to £150, out of which he was expected to pay a foreman and an inspector. Appreciation of his pioneering skill and ability was shown by a portrait and bust of him which used to be in the Town Hall council chamber; and which was inscribed 'Christopher Crabbe Creeke. First Surveyor. 1820–1886'.

Until the end of 1857 meetings were held at the *Belle Vue* Hotel, after which rooms were rented at Mr. Creeke's villa, Lainston Villa (at £20 p.a.) at the corner of Exeter Lane and at present one of the sites of the Hants. and Dorset Bus Co. Here meetings took place until January 1875, when the first Town Hall was erected in Town Hall Avenue, on the former site of the Ashley Villas (now the Criterion Arcade). In 1892 improved Corporation premises were leased in Yelverton Road. In 1921 the *Mont Dore* Hotel was converted into the present-day Town Hall.

An article in the *Poole Herald* of 31 May 1856 stated: 'No doubt Bournemouth will now have good water, good sewerage, proper footpaths, and a pier which will give visitors a delightful promenade', and on 31 July of the same year we read: 'Bournemouth now that it ceases to be so emphatically retired has become intensely dull . . . it must not now be considered simply for invalided and the convalescent'. It was further remarked that a pier would be an immense advantage and would answer the constant question of 'where shall we go?'

In June 1858 Bournemouth's first newspaper, the *Visitors Directory*, was published, first as a small four-page sheet, issued fortnightly, and then, as it proved to be successful, it was enlarged and appeared weekly. Bournemouth's main services still necessitated a journey to Christchurch. Births and deaths had to be registered in Christchurch. The relieving officers, board of guardians, parish doctor, public vaccinator, coroner, court and police work and parliamentary elections were all situated there. One of the earliest advertisements in the new *Directory* was from Mr. Attewell, a hairdresser and cutter of Christchurch, who announced that he would attend Bournemouth every Tuesday and Friday.

The board of commissioners eagerly set to work, despite the fact that they were faced with financial problems requiring them to borrow until the collection of the first rates. The first Bournemouth rate book of 1857 showed a rate of 1s. in the pound, which produced £282 13s. The following year the rate was 3s. in the pound, which produced £592 10s. 9d.

After negotiations with the Gervis Estate, land was soon transferred to the commissioners, including Westover Gardens, which was improved by paths and flowerbeds and also the construction of a central walk, then known as Invalids Walk, which led up to the *Bath* Hotel. Today's more appropriate name of 'Pine Walk' was given to the pathway after World War I. Development also took place in the Bourne Valley below the Bridge, then referred to as 'Holdenhurst Bridge' (now the Square). Meadowland on either side of the Bourne Stream consisted of bogs and mire and was only suitable for horses and cattle, until costly draining had been completed by the commissioners in 1873. The fields then became transformed into the attractive Lower Pleasure Gardens. Through the generosity of Mr. George Durrant the commissioners were able to purchase part of the Branksome Estate, known as Coy Pond Meadow, which was above the Bridge, at £3 an acre. This area was converted into the equally attractive Upper Pleasure Gardens.

The first road to be improved and gravelled was Westover Road, the main residential road, the labourers employed being paid about 12s. per week in 1857. Work then continued in the direction of Gervis Place, the Bridge, Commercial Road, Richmond Hill and other nearby roads.

The Lansdowne, where six important road junctions meet, probably owes its name to the famous Lansdowne Crescent in Bath, and can be said to be the second in importance to the Square. Its beginnings date from about 1863, when the Lansdowne villas were erected between Old Christchurch Road and Holdenhurst Road. Six years later, Lansdowne Crescent, the *Lansdowne* Hotel (one of the oldest remaining hotels) and Lansdowne House (which in 1891 became the Hotel Metropole, and in 1943 was destroyed by enemy action) were all constructed. Where Jacey House now stands (Bath Hill corner of the Lansdowne) was formerly the *Queen* Hotel, built on the site of an early villa known as 'Hilfield'. The *Imperial* Hotel, with its wide corridors and spacious bedrooms, once stood near the corner of Meyrick Road, also on the site of a villa (today it is the *Crest* Motor Hotel), whilst Bournemouth and Poole College of Further Education and the Dorset County Library, on the corner of Meyrick and Christchurch Roads, were built in the grounds of a villa known as 'Peachley'.

One of the oldest shopping areas was in Commercial Road, but in 1863 six modern and larger shops, with accommodation above, were erected by Henry Joy, a carpenter, builder and an astute business man. These splendid buildings (at the beginning of Old Christchurch Road and near the *Tregonwell Arms*) were named 'Southbourne Terrace'.

Gervis Arcade, or Bournemouth Arcade, as it is usually referred to, was also built by Henry Joy, who had visualized a modern arcade that would become a popular shopping precinct. The Arcade, which was commenced in 1866, was adversely criticized and became known as 'Joy's Folly', especially as it took seven years to complete. Until 1872 the structure resembled an avenue, lacking a roof until that year. After being glazed in the following year, the work was finally completed. It was thought by many that the venture would be a complete failure, and in 1868 a shop with accommodation in the Arcade could actually be rented for £40 p.a.

The high-class departmental store formerly called Bright's and now known as Dingle's, is well known to residents and visitors to Bournemouth. Less well known is the fact that a small needlework shop, opened in 1871 in the Arcade, belonged to Mr. Frederick Bright, who had been forced to return from missionary work in India to this country because of poor health. His son, Percy May Bright, a respected and active citizen, was elected Mayor from 1929 to 31.

One of the main reasons for the strong objections to Joy's project, although it was in the interests of progress, meant the destruction of a popular beauty spot known as Church Glen. One guide-book stated that it would spoil one of the most picturesque spots in Bournemouth.[2] The pretty glen was crossed by a charming rustic bridge, built of rough fir poles, and covered with ivy and other climbing plants. About 20 ft. below the bridge was a tiny brook which flowed from the direction of the Lansdowne, behind parts of Old Christchurch Road and into the Bourne stream. The bridge had been erected in 1853 by Mr. Thomas Shettle, an original member of the Board and Chairman of the Commissioners from 1861–64, for the benefit of his tenants in Old Christchurch Road; a fee of one halfpenny was charged for its use by other members of the public. In 1884 an arcade of similar style was constructed by Mr. Joy in Westbourne, at a cost of £18,000.

Despite continued opposition, a railway station was erected in Bournemouth in 1870. As a result, a population of 1,707 in 1861 increased to 5,896 in 1871. Gas lighting was introduced in 1864 and the first town crier, Francis Elgar, a retired naval stoker, was appointed in 1865. As he swung his heavy bell, each announcement was preceded by the phrase 'this is to give notice', and concluded with 'God save the Queen'.

Improved means of travel, combined with the passing of the Bank Holiday Act in 1871, meant that more people were coming to Bournemouth for the pleasure of a holiday by the sea and not merely for health reasons. The select, upper-class resort, catering for wealthy invalids, was slowly changing its character. During Bank Holidays the beaches were crowded; there were Punch and Judy shows, stalls, swings and games for the amusement of the crowds. These lively activities contrasted with the 'dullness' of Bournemouth during most of the year.

By 1875, the thriving town was still mainly residential. Great thickets of pines flourished in areas which were to become expensive and highly rated business quarters. There were still no business premises in Richmond Hill and only a few shops along Old Christchurch Road. An Ordnance Survey map of 1870[3] shows the sites of several fine Victorian villas of that period that have long since disappeared, but whose names are retained in present-day roads and buildings. These include Yelverton Villa, Verulam Villas, Granville Cottages (commemorating Dr. Granville who praised the new area of the Bourne in his book *Spas of England, 1841*), Palmerston Lodge, Dalkeith Villa (for many years a hotel, now practically demolished, except for the façade which is to be preserved) and Ashley Villas. Near Trinity Church, Old Christchurch Road (which was mainly destroyed by fire in 1979) was Wooton Lodge, Glen Fern and The Firs. Gervis Villa and Bourne Villa stood on land that is now part of a shopping complex adjoining Dingle's.

Due to the efforts of various landowners, including Mr. C. A. King, Robert Kerley and Chas. William Packe on the west side, and Sir Henry Drummond Wolff on the east side, estates were slowly being developed for building purposes outside the commissioners' boundary.

By 1876 Boscombe, together with a track of pine woods between Boscombe Chine and Derby Road known as Seventy Acres, had been incorporated into Bournemouth, as had Springbourne. Strong opposition from Boscombe, which applied to the L.G. Board for the formation of an urban sanitary district which would include Boscombe and Springbourne, was unsuccessful. After a L.G. inquiry in the same year, annexation of the area by Bournemouth was agreed. The new area was allowed to have three members on the Board, and differential rating concessions. Messrs. Joy, Cunningham and Toogood were elected from six candidates, one of whom received only six votes.

The first postmaster was Mr. George Fox. In 1832 he rented the *Tregonwell Arms* from Mrs. Tregonwell, and five years later was able to purchase the inn. In 1837 he bought the surrounding ground, known as Beckford Estate, for £560. The estate consisted of land extending to the Square and up Richmond Hill to Windsor Cottages (now the site of the Sacred Heart Roman Catholic Church). The inn, with tea gardens and stables at the rear, was very popular with summer visitors, and also, in its earlier days, with smugglers.

By 1839 the first post office was established at the inn with Mr. Fox as 'Receiver' for the large sum of £4 per annum. Services, by horse omnibus, commenced between Bournemouth and Poole, first with a morning delivery at 9 a.m. and an evening collection at 5.15 p.m. In 1855 this was extended to deliveries at 6.30 a.m. and 5 p.m. with a collection at 7 p.m. It was reported that it was not at all unusual for the small number of letters then received to be spread out and sorted in the bar.[4] In the first issue of the *Postal Guide, 1856* Bournemouth was shown as a sub-office under Poole.

As the postal service grew there were frequent changes of address. In 1848 Mr. Fox moved to an adjoining house, Beckford House (now the site of the National Westminster Bank by the corner of Richmond Hill), when he also became a stationer, bookseller and part-time taxidermist. He was probably one of the earliest tradesmen in Bournemouth. The third post office was established in Mr. J. Bell's grocery shop (on the present site of Woolworth's in Commercial Road), when Miss Bell became the postmistress and money orders were first issued. At that time there was one postman serving the area, who was paid 11s. per week (this was later increased to 15s.), and who in 1858 was delivering approximately 2,600 letters weekly.

The next post office was installed in a building adjoining the newly constructed Southbourne Terrace, when Mr. Fox again became the postmaster in 1863. The following year it received the distinction of becoming a head office, and the number of postmen had risen to about five, with 5,000 letters being posted weekly.

A further move in 1870 took the head post office into Mr. Joy's fine arcade. Work was in the charge of Mr. W. Dunn who, despite an increased volume of mail, managed with the assistance of one young boy. An urgent telegram sometimes involved closing the office so that the message could be delivered! By 1875, however, the staff was increased to one inspector and six postmen, the latter still being paid 15s. a week. When Mr. Dunn retired in 1899 there were 60 clerks, 102 postmen and 46 telegraph boys.

The first branch office was opened in Boscombe in 1871, and soon there were branches in Commercial Road, Lansdowne, Westbourne, Pokesdown, Springbourne and Winton, some remaining open until 9 p.m. on weekdays. Collections were at 10.30 a.m., 12 noon, 9 p.m. and deliveries at 7 a.m., 1.30 p.m. and 6.15 p.m., with one delivery and one collection on Sundays.

Postal services continued to be developed when, in 1883, there was another move into a handsome classical-style building near St. Peter's Church (on the site occupied by Dingle's, formerly J. J. Allens), which cost about £2,500. This remained the chief post office until 1896, when it was transferred to its present place in Post Office Road (then Beckford Road) and was opened with ceremony by the Mayor of Bournemouth.

The oldest letterbox in Bournemouth is no longer in use and stands outside Russell-Cotes Museum, protected by railings. A plaque above it is inscribed 'Bournemouth's first letter box, used by Gladstone, Disraeli and Irving'. Formerly it stood at the corner of Bath Road. Another Victorian box which is still in use is a tall, hexagonal one at the corner of Meyrick and Grove Roads. It was probably built c. 1866 and is the only one of this type in the town.

The old *Tregonwell Arms* was occupied by several tenants after Mr. Fox left the inn in 1848. Property values were increasing, and it was sold in 1863 together with the site of Southbourne Terrace for £3,000, which by 1877 had increased to £6,500 for the same site. When its licence was not renewed it was taken over by the Bournemouth Blue Ribbon Gospel Temperance Union in 1884 and became a coffee house, having been opened by the Countess of Cottenham in February of that year. The days of the picturesque inn were over; its rustic style no longer conformed with the modern buildings growing around it. A new roadway was planned called Beckford, now Post Office Road, which would cut through the site of the inn. Its demolition in 1885 was regretted by many people, including the *Observer and Chronicle* of 21 February 1885:

> The old Tregonwell Arms, Bournemouth, is at last being pulled down and by some its demolition seems to be regarded as almost an act of sacrilege. Though not an ancient historical building it has been regarded locally with a kind of veneration, partly from the fact that it was one of the oldest houses in Bournemouth, and partly because its retired position and ivy-mantled porch gave it an air of respectable old age that was in contrast to the more modern buildings which have grown up around it. . . . Times have greatly changed in Bournemouth since then, but though the old order of things has passed away and the town has attained a popularity such as was never dreamed of in those early days, there are, as we have said, many who will feel that in losing sight of the old Tregonwell they have parted as it were with an old and familiar friend.

Although the Sydenham's Royal Marine Library had been established in the *Belle Vue* Hotel since 1840, whilst from about 1855 concerts, meetings and church services, were held in the small Assembly Rooms adjoining, very little thought had been given to the provision of entertainment in the sedate district. What an achievement it has been that Bournemouth developed as a foremost music centre with a reputation that has extended throughout the world. It also became the first British municipality to establish a permanent orchestra with the engagement of Dan Godfrey Junr. in 1893, its population then being about forty thousand.

Prior to its inception, an Italian military band visited Bournemouth in 1876 on completion of an engagement in Bath. Their original intention was to remain for the winter of that year, but their popularity was such that Bournemouth residents gladly contributed to their support by public subscriptions to enable them to stay. Impressed by the pleasure given by this band, the Council formed the first Corporation Military Band in 1892. The band was conducted by Signor E. Bertini and consisted of 21 members, most of whom had served with the Royal Italian Band and wore military uniform, as they had been in the Italian Army. The band continued until May 1893, when two performances were given daily on Bournemouth Pier.

In an attempt to overcome the continued criticisms of dullness, a Bournemouth Winter Gardens Co. was formed in 1875 to erect a larger building than the Assembly Rooms. The site purchased was the Cranborne Gardens, formerly a favourite part of Mr. Tregonwell's estate, and later owned by Robert Kerley, who died in 1872. Since 1862 the Gardens had been used for the then fashionable sport of archery.

After the success of the Crystal Palace Exhibition in 1851, large, glass-covered buildings were demanded by many progressive seaside resorts. The main purpose of the Bournemouth Winter Gardens was, as its name implies, to provide a large greenhouse and covered winter garden, where concerts, exhibitions and displays of art and craft work could also be held, the design of the building being put in the hands of Messrs. Fletcher, Lowndes and Co., London, Horticultural Builders. The idea of the Gardens also arose from the great popularity of the Southbourne Winter Gardens, opened in 1874.

Before the completion of the building a roller-skating rink was formed in the grounds which was opened with ceremony in 1876 to the accompaniment of music by the

Fourth Hampshire A.V. Band. After dark the lively scene was illuminated by torch lights.

The magnificent glass structure was completed the following year. Its roof was supported by rectangular steel columns with elaborate Victorian-style brackets. Colourful vine leaves hung from the roof trusses, whilst a floor space of 2,000 sq. ft. with seating accommodation for 800 was embellished with exotic plants and tall, graceful palms. The building, which cost £12,000, was opened by Sir H. Drummond Wolff, M.P. for the borough of Christchurch, accompanied by Mr. T. J. Hankinson, Chairman of the Commissioners, on 16 January 1877.

Unfortunately the Winter Gardens were not a success, and they closed later that year. A second, unsuccessful attempt to get the project off the ground was made in February 1884, when it was reopened as a circus and as a commercial exhibition. After this failure the building remained closed until its conversion to a concert hall in 1893.

Bournemouth Municipal Orchestra was started in the summer of that year, after the Council had taken over the lease of the Winter Gardens. Following the advice of Mr. James Druitt Junr., the Town Clerk, and Mr. Henry Newlyn, the Mayor, the Council contacted Lieut. Dan Godfrey, the well-known band leader of the Grenadier Guards, with a view to setting up an orchestra. Mr. Godfrey suggested that his son, Dan Godfrey Junr., who was also a conductor, should be offered the post of Musical Director. The musical fame of the little town commenced with the engagement of Dan Godfrey Junr. in 1893, with a military band of 30 players. The debt owed to his skill and musical genius can never be underestimated. Besides playing as a military band on the pier, some of the players doubled and were able to form a string classical orchestra which played inside the Winter Gardens Pavilion.

The opening performance on 22 May 1893 was an enormous success. Five thousand people attended and enjoyed a programme of popular music which included ballet Music from Schubert's 'Rosamunde', and selections from Gilbert and Sullivan's 'Gondoliers'.

An early problem facing the commissioners was the replacement of the old wooden pier, which had been damaged beyond repair in the disastrous gales of 1867 and 1876. Abortive attempts had been made by the Promenade Pier Co., a private company, who had obtained a provisional order to erect a pier within two years and to buy out the commissioners' interests in the old pier. As no action had been taken on the expiry of the period granted by the Board of Trade, the commissioners decided that they must act speedily. A temporary landing stage was constructed in 1877 for use by steamers in the summer season.

In a guide to Bournemouth of 1878, Hankinson wrote concerning the proposed new pier; 'We can only hope that no fatal or cheeseparing economy will restrain them [the commissioners] from erecting a structure worthy of the town'. Authority was obtained for an amount not exceeding £40,000; estimates were submitted and the one accepted was for approximately £20,000, which was criticised by some leading residents as a gross extravagance and a burden on the rates.

Work commenced, however, and on 11 August 1880 the pier was opened with great ceremony by Sir Francis Wyatt Truscott, the Lord Mayor of London, who then described Bournemouth as 'the garden city of the south'. The new pier was constructed of iron, and was about 838 ft. long and 35 ft. wide for the first 650 ft., and about 110 ft. wide for the remainder. Later it was extended at the sea end, making a total length of about 1,000 ft. A clock for the tower at the pier entrance was donated by Mr. Horace

Davey, M.P. for Christchurch (including Bournemouth) in 1882. A few years later covered shelters had been erected, together with a bandstand and improved landing stage at the end of the pier. Although visitors were slowly being attracted to the town for pleasure and enjoyment of the new pier and not just for health reasons, there were still complaints of dullness.

In 1881, in an article entitled 'On the south coast', Charles Wood wrote that whilst Bournemouth was a beautiful and romantically-placed town, it was also melancholy due to the invalids 'who make the fortune of Bournemouth . . . but people usually go there in search of health, not gaiety; there is scarcely even a pastime'. He continued that people usually had the pier to themselves 'as visitors are mainly too delicate to venture there'.[5] An article in *Blackwood's Magazine* in 1883 stated that Bournemouth took 'depressing views of life . . . dances and light concerts are discouraged and dissipation is said to take the shape of bazaars and social meetings for charitable objects'.[6]

Even as late as 1891 Harry Furniss wrote:

> Life at Bournemouth is passed chiefly in Invalids Walk, on the sea shore, in bath chairs, in the saddle, in church and chapel. . . . It really seems as if the powers that be had resolved that the valley of the Bourne must henceforth do penance in sack cloth presumably for the plunderings and piratical peccadilloes of its former inhabitants'. He continued, 'of course it must be remembered that the place exists chiefly for the invalid . . . for the valetudinarian to whom expense is no object, a perfect palace has been erected: Mont Dore.[7]

Although various people expressed the pessimistic view that the pier would never pay, that it could destroy privacy and attract a cheap type of day tripper, it became a much-appreciated attraction. In its first year receipts totalled £2,225, and by 1890 this sum was increased to £5,101, which was most satisfying to the commissioners.

Another initially unsuccessful attempt to provide entertainment was made in 1882, when a Theatre Royal was erected on the site of a large, stately villa known as 'Albert House', which had been demolished in 1879. Despite sumptuous private boxes, dress circles, stalls, a balcony, an enormous foyer and a refreshment room, poor attendances resulted in its closure five years later. The few occasions when the theatre was packed, including two lectures by Oscar Wilde in 1883, were insufficient to keep it open.

On 22 August 1887 the building was re-opened as Bournemouth's second Town Hall. After extensive alterations and improvements the building again became a theatre, and it was re-opened on 28 July 1892, when the Town Hall moved to Yelverton Road, where it remained until it finally moved to its present site in the former *Mont Dore* Hotel in 1921.

For the first time the theatre became exceedingly popular, and its many performances comprised grand and light opera, drama and musical plays. Some of the outstanding actors who played there were Fred Terry, Frank Benson and his wife, Julia Neilson, Irene Vanburgh, Godfrey Tearle and Matheson Lang. Members of the D'Oyly Carte and Carl Rosa Opera Companies performed lilting shows such as 'The Merry Widow', 'Count of Luxembourg' and 'The Quaker Girl'.

In 1943, while in use as a services club under the control of Bournemouth War Services Organisation, the theatre was damaged by fire and was closed until 1949, when it emerged as the New Royal Theatre. After a further closure in 1957, it became an opera house for a short time in 1959. Its days as a theatre were numbered, and since 1962 it has been used as a cinema, a bingo hall and a social club.

The idea of a Pleasure Garden pagoda had been envisaged by Benjamin Ferrey as early as 1836, but as a result of many unfruitful schemes the present-day Pavilion was not constructed until 1929.

In 1876 a lease had been granted to the Council by Sir George Meyrick of the Lower Pleasure Gardens, which included the erection of a pavilion; this authority was also inserted in the Improvement Act of 1892. Although a competition was held for the design of a building to cost about £5,000, no action was taken because of opposition from many factions.

The idea continued to be advocated among the more far-sighted pioneers of Bournemouth's development, including Hankinson, Newlyn and particularly Russell-Cotes, who, through the press and at Council meetings, was continually urging the necessity of a seaside pavilion. The idea was also popular with visitors to Bournemouth, and would have helped to overcome their complaints of its dullness.

By 1902 there were further abortive attempts to secure the freehold of the *Belle Vue* Hotel (part of the site required for the new pavilion). A poll held to secure the support of the ratepayers was also defeated, as was a scheme to provide a pavilion on the Pier at a cost of £25,000.

The price was increasing all the time and in 1908 a scheme costing £45,000 was planned. As the *Belle Vue* Hotel had the only public bar on the sea front, it was important for the Council to obtain their licence, but strong opposition was voiced against the provision of licensed premises. By this time George V was on the throne, and the next project (at a cost of £60,000) was again defeated. In 1914 plans were shelved until the end of World War I.

Sir Merton Russell-Cotes died in 1921 and was succeeded as a champion and advocate of the pavilion by Alderman (later Sir) C. H. Cartwright. As a result of his efforts a further competition was held, the cost of the project then being estimated at about £100,000. The first prize of £300 was awarded to Messrs. Wyville Home and Shirley Kent of London, whose plan was accepted, with slight alterations.

A foundation stone was laid by Alderman Cartwright on 23 September 1925, almost a century after the project was first suggested by Ferrey. In a copper casket were buried bank notes; a silver crown dating from 1887, the year of Queen Victoria's golden jubilee; a florin of the same year; other coins, and also copies of the *Times*, the *Bournemouth Daily Echo*, the old *Bournemouth Guardian*, the *Radio Times*, the *Architect's Journal* for the Pavilion, and a history of the Bournemouth Municipal Orchestra published in 1914.

The old *Belle Vue* had been demolished in the winter of 1928 and its licence was transferred to the Pavilion, whilst Alderman Carter, whose endeavours were largely responsible for the successful conclusion of the protracted arrangements, was elected Mayor for the fifth time. The new municipal undertaking was opened by the Duke of Gloucester on 19 March 1929, when the stirring notes of Elgar's 'Land of Hope and Glory' were heard, followed by variety acts from Stanley Holloway, a Welsh prima donna, 'Nonsense on Wheels', and other musical items.

Chapter XI

MORE SELF-GOVERNMENT

IN 1882 the Municipal Corporation Act was passed, which allowed certain districts to apply for further powers of government and to become municipal boroughs with their own charters of incorporation.

At a meeting of the commissioners on 3 January 1882 Joseph Cutler proposed that Bournemouth should seek greater authority, which would enable the town to break away completely from the remaining controls exercised by the sprawling parishes of Holdenhurst and Christchurch, both of which received funds from Bournemouth for the maintenance of their poor.

The campaign for more independence lasted for eight years. Mr. Cutler was ably supported by Enoch White, a successful nurseryman and a prominent citizen. An association was created to promote incorporation, and on 1 July 1884 a petition for incorporation was made to the committee of the Privy Council. The petition was supported by 1,120 ratepayers and residents who felt that an increasing population, continuing development and prosperity necessitated greater administrative powers and improved status. Opposition was voiced from 934 residents who feared that this action was premature, and as a result the petition was rejected in November of that year.

As Bournemouth had extended its boundaries for the second time in August 1884 by the inclusion of Westbourne, Malmesbury Park, Freemantle and land between Sea Road and the Shelley Estate at Boscombe Manor (thus increasing its acreage from 1,140 to 2,414 acres), it was felt that a second application should be made.

Westbourne, in particular, was slowly growing from a wild, heathland area, where there were about six houses in 1860, to a development district. This was mainly due to the expansion of three estates on the west side of the Bourne. These had been purchased on the death of Miss Bruce, the owner of the extensive Branksome Estate, which stretched from the sea front along Poole Road to Talbot Woods.

The Alum Cliff Estate was purchased by Mr. R. Kerley for building plots. Branksome Dene, a fine Victorian mansion, was the first villa on the site and was erected in 1860. It was originally owned by Mr. C. A. King, and later by Sir Ernest Cassel, grandfather of Edwina Ashley Mountbatten, and also by Lord Wimborne of Canford. In 1951 Branksome Dene, considerably enlarged, became a Jewish convalescent home. Today this listed building, which still stands in a secluded woodland area, is being renovated and restored by its present owners, the Royal Masonic Benevolent Institution, as a home for retired Masons and their families.

There were also the Consolidated Land Society and the Branksome Tower Estate.

78

The latter, which is situated just outside the Bournemouth boundary, was purchased by Mr. C. W. Packe, M.P., who in 1855 built the picturesque Branksome Towers (now a block of flats) in the attractive tree-clad area known as Branksome Park. The Avenue, Poole, was then a private road leading to Branksome Towers. At its entrance was an attractive lodge (this was demolished for road widening in 1974 – see chapter XVIII) and iron gates to prevent tresspassers intruding into the delightful area surrounded by pine trees. The iron gates became known as County Gates because they marked the boundary between Hampshire and Dorset until, in 1974, Bournemouth became part of Dorset. The actual gates disappeared many years ago. The small pedestrian gate, however, has been removed and rebuilt in Pinewood Road, off Tower Road. Today, blocked by fencing and barbed wire, it has been described as 'the gateway that leads nowhere'. Now an enormous roundabout leads the stream of traffic into the Avenue, which is faced by towering office blocks.

By 1876 more houses and shops had been built, including the *Westbourne* Hotel; and a few years later Henry Joy, the builder of the Arcade in Bournemouth, who was then living at Seamoor House, Westbourne, erected a similar type of arcade there. (Seamoor House is now demolished, but its former existence is reflected in the name of Seamoor Road, formerly Crescent Road.)

The second application to become a municipal borough was presented in 1886, and was supported by 2,768 residents representing a rateable value of £85,230; weaker opposition was voiced by 413 residents, representing a rateable value of £32,859. The application was again rejected by the Privy Council on 26 March 1887. A third appeal resulted in a local inquiry in Bournemouth in November 1888, followed by an additional inquiry regarding suggested wards. The charter was finally approved, and received royal assent on 23 July 1890. This was the first really vital Local Government Act passed in Bournemouth to give the town greater power and authority. The board of commissioners was replaced by a council of elected councillors and aldermen, together with the creation of wards and the appointment of a Town Clerk and Borough Treasurer.

A holiday was proclaimed in Bournemouth on 27 August 1890, when the long-awaited Charter would be received from London. There was rejoicing and celebrations, and a great welcome awaited the delegation bringing the Charter, who travelled in a special coach on the London & South-Western Railway: from the East (later Central) Station they rode in an open carriage. There was a joyful procession with tableaux and eight bands. At the gaily decorated pier entrance the charter of incorporation was read out by Mr. James Druitt, the legal adviser to the commissioners.

On 1 November 1890 municipal elections were held for the appointment of 18 councillors, three of whom were to serve in each of six wards, who were elected for three years. Twelve of those elected had previously been commissioners, thus ensuring continuity of policy. Six aldermen were also elected for a period of six years. Mr. James Druitt Junr., who had been Clerk to the Commissioners since 1877, became the first Town Clerk in the new borough, thus receiving recognition of and appreciation for his long and helpful service to the town.

A system of secret ballot was introduced for the first time. In the early days of the commissioners open and plural voting had taken place; later, polling papers were taken to those qualified to vote, i.e. ratepayers and owners of property. After incorporation a system of ballot with elections in each ward was initiated which was open to all men and women living in that ward.

79

Fig. 8. County Gates, Pinewood Road, Bournemouth.

Mr. T. J. Hankinson, Chairman of the Commissioners, became the first Mayor, and his outstanding assistance and advice was thus duly rewarded. This highly-respected businessman came to Bournemouth in 1858 for health reasons and was soon known as a successful stationer, publisher and estate agent. Adjoining his home, Victoria House, he formed a popular library called the Victoria Library. In 1875 his business was transferred to the foot of Richmond Hill, and from 1876 to 1892 a series of local guide-books were published by him.

A mace and mayoral badge, engraved with the name of the first Mayor, were presented to the council in March 1891 by Mr. (later Sir) Merton Russell-Cotes and his wife (see chapter XVIII), and an 18-carat gold chain was paid for and presented by members of the council and the Town Clerk.

By charter the new authority was allowed to have its own armorial bearings. Lack of any history at first caused a problem, but as the area of Bournemouth was once a royal demesne of King Edward the Confessor, the College of Heralds decided that the arms of that monarch should form the basis of the Shield which would consist of a 'gold cross fleurie'. The first and fourth quarters are gold and show parts of the cross in azure, whilst reversal occurs in the second and third quarters. In the first and fourth quarters is a lion rampant holding a rose, representing the many battles of the Middle Ages. On the second quarter are six martlets or sand martins, and on the third, four salmons, thus linking the natural life of the district with its new crest. Besides being a royal emblem, the rose was the emblem of the county of Hampshire, in which Bournemouth was situated. Over all is a pine tree, under the branches of which are four more roses. Below the shield is the motto *Pulchritudo et Salubritas*, or 'beauty and health'.

Rapid development took place during the nine years of municipal government: more

Fig. 9. Bournemouth's coat of arms.

81

land was acquired and developed for use as public parks, including Meyrick Park, which was named in honour of its donors; a gift of 76 acres from the Talbot Estate enlarged the borough; agreement was entered into with the Dean Estate whereby a large tract of land called Horseshoe Common would be preserved as open space and parkland, and Seafield and Redhill Commons were purchased by the Corporation. Schemes for the improvement of Bournemouth included the Undercliff Drive, the Winter Gardens, the municipal orchestra and the provision of public libraries.

Although criticisms of dullness and lack of interest in Bournemouth continued, as has been mentioned Sydenham's Royal Marine Library had been established at the *Belle Vue* as early as 1840, and from about 1855 concerts took place in the nearby Assembly Rooms; in addition, from about 1859 to 1875 there was Hankinson's popular Victoria Library in the Square.

The idea of a free, public library received the usual opposition, and at a public meeting of ratepayers held in July 1885 the proposal was defeated. There were 749 votes in its favour, 914 against and 1,665 abstentions. However, after the passage of the Public Libraries Act in 1892, a second and favourable poll was held. People were slowly beginning to realize the importance of public libraries to a developing town.

In June 1894 Mr. Charles Riddle was appointed as the first Borough Librarian. The first library was opened by the Mayor, Merton Russell-Cotes, at 6 Cumnor Terrace (named after Joseph Cutler's house, 'Cumnor') in Old Christchurch Road, as was a reading room at Boscombe. By 1898 mobile libraries visited areas on the outskirts of the borough, and in the following year more branch libraries were set up in temporary buildings at Boscombe, Springbourne and Westbourne. By 1901 the Cumnor Terrace library had been replaced by better premises at 2, Stanhope Gardens, Dean Park Road, and by 1913 the present Central Library had been opened at the Lansdowne. It was the second library in the country to operate under the 'open access' system, the first being Clerkenwell.

From these small beginnings grew the comprehensive library service of today.

Problems of cliff erosion existed in Bournemouth's early days even as they do today, but construction of the Undercliff Drive was discussed for several years until a competition was organized by the then commissioners. Twenty-nine entries were received on 1 September 1885, three of which were selected by the adjudicator, Sir Joseph Bazalgette, the Thames Embankment Engineer.

Although it was considered by the commissioners, and later by the council, that the Undercliff Drive would be an added attraction to both summer and winter visitors and would also protect the cliffs and prevent them crumbling, criticisms and opposition were sufficiently strong to prevent any further action. In addition there was disagreement between the two main landlords, Sir George Meyrick and W. Clappcott Dean, who between them owned land extending from the East Cliff to Alum Chine. An extremely heavy cliff fall in November 1896 caused residents to realize that cliff protection was essential.

In 1897 Sir George became interested in a private scheme in conjunction with Mr. Archibald Beckett, who had built the Royal Arcade, the Hippodrome and the *Salisbury Hotel* in Boscombe. The project comprised proposals for shops and an electric tramway along the front, and villas in the cliff sides. How fortunate it is for later residents and visitors that this idea was strongly opposed! It was finally decided that it was important for the council to carry out the work as soon as possible. Further negotiations took place with Sir George, who on 20 March 1903 leased his interests in the cliffs and foreshore to the Corporation for 999 years and gave the Corporation exclusive rights to build an Undercliff Drive, the construction of which was to be undertaken within 10 years, beginning with an experimental section from Bournemouth pier to Boscombe. The first section was declared open by Alderman J. A. Parsons, the Mayor, on 6 November 1907. It was a memorable day, and one of particular pleasure to Merton Russell-Cotes, a progressive townsman and a strong advocate of an Undercliff Drive. To honour the occasion he presented the town with his wonderful collection of works of art, which he had obtained on his travels throughout the world. At the same time his wife presented their residence, East Cliff Hall (now the Russell-Cotes Museum and Art Gallery), where these valuable items were housed, with the proviso that they kept possession until their deaths. (See chapter XVIII.)

Refreshment pavilions, shelters, and rentable beach huts were soon provided. A zig-zag path was constructed from the top of the East Cliffs to the Undercliff, and an electric lift that took passengers from the cliff end of Meyrick Road (the end of the first section) to the Undercliff Drive was declared open by Lady Meyrick on 16 April 1908. Work commenced on an Undercliff Drive west of the pier, when a second electric lift was opened on the West Cliffs.

Local administration was further improved with the passage of the Local Government Act of 1894, which allowed small towns to become urban districts and country areas to become rural districts, with their own councils. Rural districts were further subdivided into parishes, thus allowing Winton and Pokesdown to achieve first parish status and then that of urban districts. Bournemouth was constituted a civil parish; prior to that period Christchurch and Holdenhurst had been the two centres for all parochial business.

This was a period of *ad hoc* authorities and overlapping boards; local government in Bournemouth was also complicated by the fact that there were differing controls, including the Town Council, the Board of Guardians and the Burial Board. Responsibility was shared between the County Council, Hampshire and the Bournemouth Municipal Borough, the former being responsible for main roads, asylums, technical and secondary education and other matters. The town was dissatisfied with its proportion of representation in the County Council, and felt that the answer was to be found in increased independence and the simplification of existing boards.

On 28 July 1898 Councillor C. Mate moved that steps be taken to secure complete autonomy and self-government, and that the council should make application to become a county borough with its own Court of Quarter Sessions and Commission of Peace. As the result of a petition to the Local Government Board and the Privy Council, increased status was granted on 1 April 1900. In the following year the borough was again extended by the inclusion of Winton, Moordown, Pokesdown, Southbourne and Richmond Park, which were formerly in the parish of Holdenhurst: it then comprised 5,850 acres, with a population of 59,762. A new council of 33 members was elected, three of whom served in each ward, the number of wards having been increased to 11. There were also 11 aldermen and the mayor.

Further extensions took place in 1914, when areas between the Charminster and Holdenhurst Roads and Castle Lane were included. In 1931 the parishes of Kinson and Holdenhurst (despite their opposition) were incorporated into the Borough, thus adding a further 4,627 acres.

Hengistbury Head, that great mound of antiquity of which Bournemouth is justly proud, was then owned by Gordon Selfridge, who had grandiose plans for constructing an immense, 300-roomed castle on the headland. Fortunately for posterity he was unable to carry out this scheme; instead, on 6 May 1930, he sold the headland to the Corporation for £25,250, and the land was then added to the borough. The latter then comprised 11,627.3 acres; the liberty of Westover, including the parish of Holdenhurst, was now part of the self-governing county borough. What an achievement! Heath and wasteland had been transformed to a fine, modern, residential coastal resort within a century!

After the end of World War II town planning became of major importance. Various schemes were mooted for the incorporation of smaller authorities into larger ones, thereby reducing the number of smaller local areas in the interests of better town planning.

In 1946 Bournemouth put forward a plan that would amalgamate Christchurch, Poole and Bournemouth under one single authority. This scheme was violently opposed by both Poole and Christchurch, and the new town of Bournemouth was likened to an octopus, whose tentacles were ready to envelop others. However, with the disbandment of the Boundary Commission in 1949 the project came to an end.

Local government reorganisation, which had been discussed over a period of many years, finally became law in 1974, with the result that the County Borough of Bournemouth, Hampshire, became part of a boundary extension into Dorset, and its status was reduced to that of a borough under the County Council of Dorset at Dorchester. The reorganisation was regretted by many county boroughs, including Bournemouth, where there had been hopes that the scheme would propose the incorporation of smaller, rural areas into the county boroughs, rather than *vice versa*.

1. Memorial to Charles E. Smith, who was accidentally killed while shooting rabbits on Hengistbury Head. Due to cliff erosion the monument was twice moved and is now in St. James' churchyard, Pokesdown.

2. Thatched cottages, Iford, 1896.

3. Kinson church, sometimes known as 'the smugglers' church'.

4. 'Smugglers at Bourne Mouth', photo by R. Day of a painting by Henry Perlee Parker (1795-1873) formerly in the *Tregonwell Arms*. The central figure is believed to be 'Old Gulliver', i.e. Isaac Gulliver.

6. The Mansion, the first house in Bournemouth, now part of the *Royal Exeter* Hotel.

5. Lewis Tregonwell (1758-1832), the founder of Bournemouth.

7. The *Tregonwell Arms* in 1883. Originally the *Tapps Arms*, it was a favourite meeting-place for smugglers.

8. Sir George Ivison Tapps, 1st Bart. and Lord of the Manor.

9. Miss Georgina Talbot, philanthropist and founder of Talbot Village.

11. Sir George Eliott Meyrick Tapps-Gervis, 3rd Bart.

10. Lady Tapps-Gervis, wife of the 3rd Bart.

12. The *Belle Vue* Hotel, library and baths, 1856.

13. The *Bath* Hotel (today the *Royal Bath* Hotel) in 1845.

14. St. Peter's Church, from an engraving published *c.*1860.

15. The *Mont Dore* Hotel (now the Town Hall), *c.*1886, from an original print.

16.   Southbourne pier in 1894. The pier was constructed between 1881 and 1888, and demolished in 1907.

17.   Boscombe Spa, 1876.

18.   The *Ragged Cat* inn, Boscombe, *c.*1860. The *Palmerston* Hotel now stands on this site.

19.   Rustic Bridge, 1855, from an engraving by Philip Brannon. The bridge was erected by Thomas Shettle in 1853 for the benefit of his tenants.

20. Bournemouth pier approach in 1899.

21.   Bournemouth pier approach, *c*. 1890.

22.   The Square, Bournemouth, in 1909, with the *Empress* Hotel at the corner of Richmond Hill and Old Christchurch Road.

23. (*top*) The first office of Fox & Son, 1889.

24. (*centre*) The old Winter Gardens, Bournemouth, *c.*1898.

25. (*right*) The original part of Stourfield House, Southbourne, which is now Douglas House (a long-stay hospital).

26. Sir Merton and Lady Russell-Cotes in 1909.

27. The Russell-Cotes Museum and Art Gallery, Bournemouth.

28. The original Fancy Fair, founded by John Elmes Beale in 1881.

29. An early Beale's van, *c.*1924.

30. John Elmes Beale and Mrs. Beale (original portraits in Beale's Department Stores).

31. Percy Bysshe Shelley.

32. The original part of
Shelley Park, formerly
Boscombe Manor.

33. Skerryvore, the Bournemouth home of Robert
Louis Stevenson from 1885
to 1887.

34. Lillie Langtry, as depicted in 'Three Heads of Lillie', by Frank Miles.

35. The *Langtry Manor* Hotel (formerly *Manor Heath* Hotel), which was built by the Prince of Wales (later Edward VII) for Lillie Langtry in 1877.

36. Cliff Cottage, West Cliff, Bournemouth in 1863; Charles Darwin stayed here in 1862. Until early in 1981 this was the site of the *Regent Palace* Hotel.

37. Guglielmo Marconi shortly after his arrival in England in 1896, with his apparatus for 'telegraphy without wires'.

38. The Hon. Charles Stewart Rolls in his plane, 1910.

HON. C. S. ROLLS'S

CONQUEST OF THE CHANNEL,
2ND June, 1910.

RETURN JOURNEY DONE
WITHOUT LANDING.

Start from Dover . . . . . . 6.30 p.m.
Over Sangatte, France . . . 7.15 p.m.
Return to Dover . . . . . . 8.0 p.m.

39. Tuckton House, Saxonbury Road, Bournemouth (now demolished).

40. The printing works in Iford Lane, Tuckton, where the forbidden works of Tolstoy were printed between 1898 and 1908.

41. St. Stephen's Church, Bournemouth, built between 1881 and 1908 as a memorial church to Rev. A. Morden Bennett.

42. Punshon Memorial Methodist Church, Bournemouth, built in 1958.

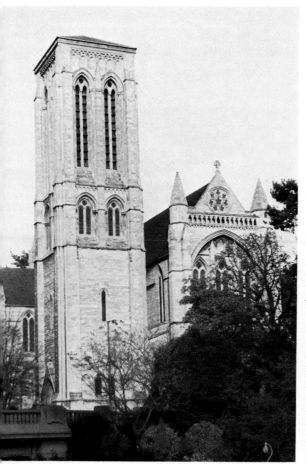

Chapter XII

THE DEVELOPMENT OF SERVICES

Education

Education in Bournemouth was originally provided by voluntary enterprise and two religious societies. The National Society was responsible for establishing Church of England schools, while the British and Foreign Society was responsible for nonconformist schools, the two bodies being concerned that many children were unable to read the Bible.

Rev. Morden Bennett, that great church leader, educationalist and active participant in the life of the community, soon appreciated the need for a church school in Bournemouth, even though in 1846 its population was little more than six hundred. An appeal for donations resulted in the construction of St. Peter's, the first purpose-built elementary national school in the marine village, which was opened in 1850 on land adjoining the church. The school, with extensions, satisfied the needs of the area until 1936, by which time the building and its equipment had become out-of-date. The character of the centre of the town had changed from being mainly residentail and rural to an area of business premises. The school was therefore demolished, to be replaced by more offices and shops.

The lack of church and educational facilities for those living in poor and outlying districts was Morden Bennett's next concern. Through his efforts the Moordown Chapel School was established in 1854 (see chapter IX), and Holy Trinity School (now St. Paul's Primary[1]), was opened in 1869 on its present site near the busy Holdenhurst Road, which was then regarded as being on the outskirts of the town. Other national schools of that period included St. Michael's, which was opened in Orchard Street in 1877 and transferred to West Hill Road in 1878, St. Clement's, Springbourne (1880), and St. John's, Boscombe (1893).

At the same time, British or Free Church schools were founded, the first being the Lansdowne British School, which commenced in 1858 in a building off Commercial Road, followed by the erection of new premises in 1875 at the corner of Madeira (then Oxford) Road. The school continued until 1935, when, due to lack of numbers, it was closed. It is now part of the Police Station. Nearby schools included Mrs. Balston's Infant School, Spring Road, Springbourne (1877–1915), and Boscombe British School, Gladstone Road (1879). Today the latter is part of the Centre for Community Arts.

The main subjects taught in the elementary schools were reading, writing and arithmetic (known as the three 'Rs'), with the addition of nature study, scripture, possibly a little history, and sewing for the girls. Classes were large and there was much rote learning.

The Education Act of 1870 established board schools in areas where the voluntary system was inadequate. Morden Bennett was firmly opposed to the introduction of board schools, as he feared that parents might be tempted to remove their children from the church schools; and because of his views there was no State education in Bournemouth until the 20th century.

Until 1877 the few Catholic children in the district received education at one of the Windsor cottages, now the site of the Oratory of the Sacred Heart. In 1877 a Catholic school was established at Blenheim House, Lansdowne Road, by Lady Georgina Fullerton, and two years later it was transferred to Avenue Road. In January 1880 a better site, consisting of two cottages, was obtained at Yelverton Road: it was given through the generosity of Lady Fullerton, and became known as St. Walburga's Roman Catholic School. (The school is now demolished, and the site is occupied by the showrooms of the Southern Electricity Board, the present school being situated in Malvern Road.)

It is not surprising that, due to the balmy climate and health-giving properties claimed by the area, a number of private schools opened with the aim of giving a more exclusive education than that provided by the elementary schools, mainly for the middle and upper classes. Among these was the Exeter House Collegiate School for Boys (1858–76), the headmaster of which was Rev. J. H. Wanklyn. It was considered to be a first-class preparatory school and the principal school of a higher grade character. Later it was sold to Mr. H. Newlyn, who transformed the house into one of the foremost hotels in the town: it was first known as *Newlyn's Family* Hotel, and then as the *Royal Exeter* Hotel (its present name).

More schools were opened after the Acts of 1870 and 1876, which made school attendance compulsory; by 1885 there were 28 private schools and by 1890 the number had increased to 40. Some of them had a short life, being mainly speculative ventures, but others were developed on high school and preparatory lines.

Rivalry soon developed among some of the private schools, which competed with each other by offering a more extensive range of subjects, including music, art and languages. An advertisement[2] for St. Margaret's Hall, West Cliff, stressed language teaching and vocal and instrumental music instruction, specifying that the school was 'exclusive to the daughters of those in a good social position'. Bournemouth Commercial School, which was established in 1865 in Avenue Road, was 'highly recommended by the resident gentry and others', while Knole Hall College, Knyveton Road, was a 'refined home where girls are trained to be worthy and self-reliant members of Society'.

Cranleigh Ladies' School started in Old Christchurch Road, opposite the Holy Trinity Church, and in 1883 moved to Bradbourne Road, near the Triangle, but shortly afterwards it had to be sold. Fortunately for posterity, it was purchased by Miss Mary Broad and her friend, Miss Thresher, when it was reopened in 1886 with 30 girls as the Bournemouth High School. Their aim was to provide a first-class liberal education with a good religious basis equal to that of the great public schools. By 1888 larger premises were required and a house was obtained in the newly-made Norwich Avenue, near to the West Station, which was then a little country station. After Miss Thresher left, Miss Broad found that the financial responsibility entailed in making progressive additions to the school was too much for one person, and in 1898 she handed over the buildings and contents to a body of governors in trust for a girls' school. By 1935 the reputation of the continually expanding school was well established, and in that year it moved to its present site among the pine trees of Talbot Woods, adopting the name of Talbot Heath School. Having been established as a direct grant school, it has now become one of the leading independent girls' schools in the area. Another leading school is Wentworth Milton Mount (see chapter VIII).

In 1865 a well-known preparatory school called the Private Gentlemen's School was established at Ascham House and Woodcote, in Gervis Road. In 1903 the buildings were offered to the town as a central school, but because of strong opposition from the residents no action was taken. The need for a municipal high school for girls had been urged for some years. It was not until 1918 that these premises were adapted to become the Bournemouth Girls' School. (For five years previously they had shared the accommodation of the nearby Municipal College.) The school commenced with 160 pupils, and fees were made as low as possible, ranging from one and a half to three guineas, which compared favourably with private schools, whose fees ranged from seven and a half to 18 guineas per annum. It was not until 1960 that the school was transferred from the two Victorian houses to its present, modern premises in Castle Lane West.

Although there were several good preparatory schools in Bournemouth, there was no boys' high school. This was rectified in 1901, when a Municipal Grammar and Technical School for Boys was opened in Portchester Road: in 1939 the school was transferred to East Way. The school was then occupied by Porchester Boys' Secondary School, which now has additional new premises in Harewood Avenue.

The demand for education beyond the elementary stage was shown by the popularity of early technical schools, which were established by voluntary agencies assisted by a grant and fees. By 1889 there was a science and art School at Poole Hill, Bournemouth West, and also at Drummond Road, Boscombe, where classes for pupil teachers were also held. In 1901 a third art and technical school was opened at the corner of Christchurch and Hannington Roads, Pokesdown (this is now a children's clinic). Eagerness to attend the classes soon resulted in overcrowding, which was overcome by amalgamation with the newly-built Municipal College, Lansdowne, in 1913.

The Education Act of 1944 introduced the 'eleven plus' selection examination, which determined whether a child went to a grammar school or to a secondary modern; a more extensive curriculum replaced the '3 Rs', and all State education became free. As there was only one grammar school for boys and one for girls in Bournemouth, which resulted in a shortage of grammar school places, G.C.E. courses were introduced in secondary modern schools from 1953. There was, however, some dissatisfaction among parents with a system which deprived many children of the opportunity of a grammar school education.

An Act of 1965 abolished eleven plus selection: however, Bournemouth decided to retain the system that it had been using, but with computerized selection based on school tests, maintaining that this was the best system for Bournemouth children. Bournemouth became the first authority to reject a Government request for the submission of plans concerning the re-organization of secondary education on comprehensive lines.

On 1 April 1974 Bournemouth Education Authority, which had been in existence for 70 years, became part of the Dorset Education Authority.

The Fire Service

The development that led to today's efficient fire service can be likened to the evolution of the steam engine to Concorde. There was no fire service at all in Bournemouth until 1870, although piped water had been available from 1866. Questions concerning the acquisition of a fire engine had been raised at meetings of the board of commissioners by Joseph Cutler, who pointed out that when a property was burning perhaps something should be done. Shortly afterwards a serious fire occurred at Hampstead House on Richmond Hill, the home of Dr. Falls, who was a prominent doctor and member of the board. Despite the existence of water mains there was no apparatus, and a large crowd stood by helplessly, watching the house burn. A bucket chain from the River Bourne was of little avail, while fire-engines from Poole and Christchurch arrived too late to be of real assistance.

As a result Mr. McWilliam was appointed the first captain of a volunteer fire brigade. He was authorized to purchase a hose and reel costing £67 13s. 6d., and a fire-engine at £65. Belts, axes and hose wrenches were obtained to equip 20 superintendents, while 50 labourer fireman operated the manual fire-engine. This volunteer fire service of public-spirited men became the forerunner of a great municipal organization. Attendance at practices was compulsory, absence or lateness being punishable by a fine of 3d. Subscriptions were requested from the general public.

Until 1902 appliances were horse-drawn, which meant that horses were usually hired from job masters, and when a fire occurred they could be engaged on other work. Eventually two pairs of horses were purchased for fire work only. Problems of communication remained, as is shown by a telegram received by the Bournemouth brigade: 'FIRE AT THROOP STRAW RICK OTHERS NEAR – HUNT Farmer'. The telegram took 20 minutes to arrive, and one wonders what happened to the rick in the meantime!

Fire stations had by then been built at West Hill, Boscombe and at Holdenhurst Road. Stables were provided at the back of the latter, which has been greatly extended, and which is the only original fire station still standing in Bournemouth today. A feature of the Holdenhurst station is the beautiful frieze that extends along three sides of the interior of the original part, showing the development of fire-fighting from buckets and squirts to the steam fire-engine, which was the most advanced piece of equipment when the frieze was completed. Mechanization and improvements continued, but on the whole the service continued to be manned by volunteers.

In 1938 the first professional Chief Officer was appointed, and his first task was to recruit more volunteers to form the Auxiliary and Emergency Fire Service. Besides being available in Bournemouth, they rendered valiant service in blitzed areas. In 1941 a National Fire Service was established, but shortly after the end of World War II County Councils and County Boroughs were made Fire Authorities, and the hours of duty were reduced to about sixty per week! Thus in a period of about eight-five years a highly trained, efficient force had emerged from humble beginnings.

The Police Force

As the result of a permissive Act of Parliament, the Hampshire Constabulary was formed in December 1839. Bournemouth, which was then a small watering place in Holdenhurst parish, had no police until 1856, and any police duties required were carried out by the village constabulary from Holdenhurst. From 1856 there was one policeman stationed at Bournemouth, P. C. Smith, who received from 17s. to 21s. per week. By 1862 Bournemouth had two constables and one sergeant, Sergeant Coles, who was paid 23s. per week.

A police station was built in Oxford Road (now Madeira Road) in 1869 as part of the Ringwood Police Division. When there was trouble in the area, extra police were drafted in. On one occasion in 1879 assistance was given to preserve the peace, and the police were instructed to pack their uniforms in a carpet bag to disguise the fact that they were policemen; on arrival at the police station they could change. Refreshments were provided in the form of three-quarters of a pound of cold meat, one and a half pounds of bread and two pints of beer.

Bournemouth was growing rapidly, especially after the opening of its first railway station in 1870, and in 1882 Joseph Cutler advocated the establishment of a police force that would be independent of the county: it was over sixty-five years, however, before this happened.

Police stations were erected at Pokesdown, Springbourne, Moordown and Westbourne, while the total police strength increased from 14 in 1884 to 44 in 1892. In the following year an instruction was issued that all members of the Hampshire Constabulary could wear white linen collars, 'which were to be kept scrupulously clean'.[3] Among the cases dealt with in July 1893, the *Bournemouth Observer* and the visitors' list record those of Mr. Butterworth, who was fined £1 or 10 days' imprisonment for refusing to take his dog off the pier; Luke Holden, who was fined £1 for bathing on an unauthorized part of the beach, and Walter Walliken, who was given one month's hard labour for sleeping out.

The need for increased mobility led to the provision of bicycles for some policemen in about 1896. Seven days' annual leave was granted to constables and sergeants, and 10 days' for higher ranks. A pay revision meant that constables received an annual salary of between £54 15s. and £73, and superintendents between £130 and £152. By about 1910 police strength had grown to over eighty, and beats were still on foot, cycle or horseback, two mounted men being stationed in Bournemouth. Several other police stations had by then been constructed as communication and mobility were still limited. More traffic duties resulted from the passing of the Motor Car Act in 1903, when speed traps were instituted, by means of a stop watch, to catch those reckless enough to exceed the limit of 20 miles per hour!

Proposals for the borough's autonomy were still discussed, as dissatisfaction was felt over the payment of £5,000 a year to the county, which was considered to be higher than the amounts exacted from other similar boroughs. By 1942 Bournemouth County Borough was the largest one in England to be policed by a county constabulary, but it was not until 1948 that, with Home Office approval, its own borough police force was created. A dinner of rejoicing was held in the Pavilion to mark the separation.

Progress and improvements continued to be made with the addition of motor cars and more motor cycles, the introduction of police dogs and better police-training methods. As a result of World War II women were accepted into the force and have played an important part since then.

Weaknesses in police forces operating over a small area, resulting in corruption and bribery, caused Roy Jenkins, when Home Secretary, to advocate a reduction in the number of police forces by amalgamating them with larger ones. As a result, in 1967 Bournemouth was amalgamated with Dorset County Council, but it still retained more power than it had had when it was a minor part of Hampshire County Council.

The earliest form of public transport service in Bournemouth was provided by the Emerald coaches, which from 1840 called at Bournemouth at 12 noon and 3 p.m. every day on their journeys between Southampton, Poole, Dorchester and Weymouth. After the *Bath* Hotel opened in 1838 a private coach service operated between the hotel and Holmsley (Christchurch) and Hamworthy (Poole), the nearest railway stations, and by about 1850 there were more horse-drawn omnibuses travelling daily between these stations.

Despite the growth of the railway age, which popularized many coastal resorts, the residents of Bournemouth were quite satisfied with their existing methods of travel, and opposed any suggestions of a noisy railway which would disturb the tranquility of the town and lower its tone. It was not until 1870 that Bournemouth East (now Central) Station was opened. (See chapter VI.)

The first coach service to be established in Bournemouth itself was provided by Henry Laidlaw, who traded under the lively name of 'Tally Ho', and who conducted a local service between the centre of Bournemouth and its station, as well as undertaking other journeys. The former hotel in Old Christchurch Road, *Dalkeith*, was originally his home: as he came from Dalkeith in Scotland, he gave that name to the hotel. Attached to the house were his livery stables. (The building is now being demolished, and only the Victorian façade, which is of historical importance, will remain.)

By the 1880s several regular horse-drawn omnibuses operated throughout the Bournemouth area, the stables for the Boscombe to Westbourne service being situated at Pokesdown, by the *New Bell* inn. Between 1899 and 1902 an open eight-seater motor wagonette service also ran between Pokesdown and Westbourne.

A family business commenced by Thomas Elliott in 1880 as the Royal Blue Coach Operators, is today known as the National Express Coach Service. The firm started with a handsome four-in-hand stage-coach travelling between Bournemouth and Holmsley, and later used horse-drawn buses and charabancs. At one time the firm had over two hundred horses, which were stabled at the Royal Blue Mews in Norwich Avenue. After 1911 the Royal Blue coaches became motorised, but unfortunately in that year Thomas Elliott was kicked by one of his beloved horses and died of the injuries: the business was, however, carried on by his son. The centenary of the firm was celebrated in 1980 with a four-in-hand coach ride from Holmsley to Bournemouth, its original route, followed by other festivities at the *Royal Bath* Hotel.

Between 1881 and 1899 proposals to construct tramlines between Bournemouth and Poole were strongly opposed by the Bournemouth Council on the grounds that the streets were too narrow and that tramlines would be detrimental to their appearance. By 1901, however, the Poole and District Electric Traction Company had established a tram route from Poole, but it had to terminate at the County Gates, Westbourne, the boundary between Bournemouth and Poole. The fare was only 3d. Eventually Bournemouth decided that it would prefer to run its own tram routes within its own borough. After a long period of litigation between the Company and the council concerning extensions of routes and powers, a Bournemouth tram service was installed between Pokesdown and the Lansdowne, later extending to other areas. The inauguration of the tram service was attended by John Elmes Beale, the 12th Mayor of Bournemouth, and the first tram passenger.

Through the Bournemouth Corporation Tramways Act of 1903, control was given to Bournemouth Corporation to operate all tram services between Christchurch and

Poole, and Bournemouth thus became the first municipality to have tramways in two other towns. The route, the longest in the south of England outside London, was inaugurated with a series of gaily-decorated cars; the maximum fare was 6d. Everyone was horrified when, in 1908, a serious accident occurred. The brakes of a tram failed and its normal speed of 8 m.p.h. was said to have increased to 70 m.p.h. It became derailed and crashed into the garden of Fairlight Glen in Avenue Road. Seven passengers were killed and 26 were injured.

Although the tram service was much appreciated, due to strong opposition it was not allowed to run on Sundays. In 1910, during the Bournemouth Centenary festivities, a prize-winning float bore the notice '1810 – No Sunday Trams. 1910 – Still no Sunday trams!' It was not until 1913 that a poll of ratepayers voted in favour of a Sunday afternoon service, which commenced at 2 p.m.

The slow-moving trams had several elegant features, including smart cloth-covered seats which the conductor, on pain of a serious reprimand, had to reverse during rainy weather. This prevented wet raincoats from damaging the upholstery. An ingenious system of spring flaps in the upstairs seats enabled passengers to sit on dry seats even during heavy rain periods. The open-topped double-deckers were said to be pleasant in the summer but cold and blowy in the winter, when they swayed on their two lines like a ship at sea.

In 1933 an experimental trolley-bus service commenced between County Gates, Westbourne and the Square in Bournemouth, and by 1936 this was extended throughout the town. Continual improvements in coach and engine design have resulted in today's modern fleet of Corporation buses. As for the trams, the last one left Christchurch in 1936, carrying the mayors of Christchurch and Bournemouth and other councillors, who then returned on the first trolley-bus. The trams were sold: some were bought by other authorities, whilst others were used as garden sheds, caravans and even as dog kennels!

The clock tower in the centre of Bournemouth Square will be remembered by some older residents as being all that remains of a tram shelter that used to be there, while another old tram depot opposite Pokesdown Station, looking somewhat dilapidated, is now a second-hand mart. At the Transport Museum in Mallard Road a collection of old trams and buses can be seen, while a horse-drawn omnibus found in the New Forest is in the process of being restored.

Sailing has always been a popular feature of coastal resorts and the purpose of the first Bournmouth jetty, which was built in 1856, was to provide easier facilities for this.

While some steamships called occasionally at Bournemouth, it was usually necessary to journey either to Swanage or Poole in order to go on a sea trip. It was a great day, therefore, when the *Heather Bell*, the first regular steamship, sailed from Bournemouth Pier in 1871: she often left the pier accompanied by music from the Bournemouth Promenade Band. The service was discontinued in 1876, but the *Heather Bell* was soon succeeded by other vessels including *Criterion*, *Lord Elgin* (with its magnificent saloon), *Windsor Castle*, and *Brodick Castle*. There was an hourly service between Bournemouth and Swanage, with excursions as far as the Channel Islands and France; no passports or landing permits were then required. At one time competition was so keen that it was possible to sail to the Isle of Wight and return for only $4^1/_2$d.

Chapter XIII

PARLIAMENTARY REPRESENTATION

CHRISTCHURCH, that ancient and venerable town whose Priory has dominated its borough and outskirts since Norman times, is sometimes referred to as 'the mother town of Bournemouth'. For many years before Bournemouth even existed, Christchurch was sending Members of Parliament to Westminster. As long ago as 1307 the mayor and burgesses were summoned to send two members to Carlisle, where a parliament was then to be held. On the grounds of poverty and the problems of a long and difficult journey, they managed to excuse themselves.

The earliest record of their parliamentary representation dates from when they were again requested to send two Members to Parliament, which by that time met at Westminster. Thenceforth two Members were returned at varying intervals, as at certain periods no Parliament was called by the king, or it was only summoned for a short period to raise additional money.

Christchurch was originally one of many pocket boroughs: by 1639 it was accepted that the Lord of the Manor of the Honour nominated one Member, and recommended the election of the second to privileged burgesses. Christchurch was then known as a close borough, and voting was restricted to the mayor and about twenty-four members of the Corporation, who had to agree that no expenses of representation would fall on the borough. This was a time of bribery; seats were bought and sold for vast sums and even advertised in the newspapers. Some areas, such as Old Sarum in Wiltshire, consisted of uninhabited land yet were able to send two Members to Parliament up to 1830, while developing new towns in the north, such as Manchester, Liverpool and Birmingham had no Members.

In order to prevent the king from indefinitely retaining a Parliament that pleased him, the Triennial Act was passed in 1694, which was substituted in 1714 by the Septennial Act: in 1911 the length of Parliament was decreased to five years, as currently obtains. No salary was paid until 1911, and up to that time government had remained mainly in the hands of wealthy landowners. Despite the lack of democracy (a concept that was practically unknown then), many outstanding and talented men represented Christchurch, which included the area of the liberty of Westover.

In 1708 the manor of the honour of Christchurch was purchased by Peter Mews, who became the borough's Member between 1710 and 1724. Due to a series of quarrels he lost control of the town, after which the owners of Hurn Court became very influential. From 1661 Hurn Court was owned by different members of the Hooper family. Edward Hooper, the last of the family, was Member between 1735 and 1760.

On his death in 1795 the estate was left to his cousin, James Harris, Lord Malmesbury, who was Member between 1761 and 1788. George Rose, who became Secretary of the Treasury in 1782, successfully ousted the Hurn connection by buying the votes of 14 burgesses and acquiring one seat for himself and the other for his son. The Rose family controlled Christchurch seats until the Reform Act of 1832.

By the beginning of the 19th century the Whigs had started to rebel against the systems of patronage and corruption. A Reform Bill was introduced by them in March 1831 that was strongly opposed by the Tories, who defeated the Bill by eight votes. Parliament was immediately dissolved, and reform processions paraded through the streets. The Whigs were re-elected with a majority of 136, but a second Reform Bill was rejected by the House of Lords in October. Riots occurred in many areas, and angry demonstrations took place in the big towns. A third Bill was passed by the Commons in December 1831 and was again rejected by the House of Lords. In order to avoid further disturbances and another dissolution of Parliament, William IV was advised to create about fifty peers to ensure the passage of the Bill through the House of Lords. The Lords, realizing that they could not delay the Bill any longer, unwillingly consented to it, and the Bill became law in 1832, followed by public rejoicing and illuminations. A large procession took place in Christchurch and a public dinner was held to celebrate the great event.

Under the Act borough seats were redistributed and many rotten boroughs were disenfranchised. Boroughs with a population of less than two thousand would have no M.P., while those of less than four thousand would have only one. The old borough of Christchurch then had a population of 1,599. In order to be able to elect one Member a new borough was formed, which included the chapelry of Holdenhurst and almost all the old parish of Christchurch. In the boroughs, male householders whose property was of a rateable value of at least £10 were allowed the vote, but their names had to appear on an electoral register.

Elections were now open to the middle classes, but in Christchurch landowners were still elected. Sir George W. Tapps-Gervis of Hinton Admiral became the first representative after the Reform Act, and he was elected again in 1835, when he had become Lord of the Manor of the Honour of Christchurch. The first contested election on the new register occurred in 1837 when Sir George decided not to stand again. Bitter and scurrilous attacks were made against the Tory and Whig candidates, resulting in the election – by a majority of 11 – of Sir George Rose, who had previously represented the town when it was a pocket borough.

In 1844 Captain Edward A. Harris, R.N., brother and heir presumptive of Lord Malmesbury was elected, followed by Admiral John E. Walcott, R.N., who was the Member from 1852 to 1868. Walcott was mainly concerned with Navy matters, and in 1858 he commented on the still unfinished statue of Nelson. He voted against many suggested reforms and opposed the repeal of paper duties, which caused newspapers to be too expensive for most people. Locally he was generous and popular, contributing as he did to the Priory Church and St. James's Church, Pokesdown. Although Walcott was re-elected in 1865, he was for the first time opposed by another candidate, the Liberal, Edmund Haviland-Burke. This was the first election in which there was a polling station at Bournemouth, and it marked the beginning of party speeches and manifestos. Walcott was always greatly respected for his good works for the local community, and when he died in 1868 a window was erected in St. James's Church in memory of this long-serving M.P.

In 1867 and 1884 further Reform Acts were passed, enfranchising more working-class men and agricultural labourers.

Haviland-Burke, an advocate of free trade and voting by ballot, contested the seat against Sir Henry Drummond Wolff and this time he was successful, gaining a majority of 51 votes. This was the last election before the Ballot Act of 1872, after which all voting was conducted by secret ballot. The importance of political parties, together with the necessity of obtaining members to give support, was slowly gathering strength. The Christchurch Conservative Club was founded in 1881 with Sir George Meyrick as President and Lord Malmesbury as one of its Vice-Presidents. The first Liberal Club was opened in Boscombe in 1882, when, at fortnightly debates, subjects such as 'The Abolition of the House of Lords' and 'The Admission of Atheists to Parliament' were discussed.

Owing to illness, Burke felt unable to contest the next election in 1874. Another Liberal candidate, Clement Millward, Q.C., was put forward to contest the seat against Sir Henry Drummond Wolff. In order to regain a Conservative victory, Sir Henry purchased Boscombe Towers from Lord Malmesbury in 1868, where he developed the Boscombe Spa Estate. In his 'Rambling Recollections' he commented that 'the Borough of Christchurch was a peculiar one. It covered an area of between 30 and 40 square miles, and comprised a large variety of interests. There was the building interest at Bournemouth. There were also fishermen and agriculturists; and, to meet the requirements of this large population, the laundry interest had great developments.' Sir Henry, a former diplomat, proved to be a popular man; he was an able speaker who attended many Tory dinners, and he gave liberally to local causes and hospital funds. He was elected by a majority of 371 votes.

In 1880 Sir Henry became M.P. for Portsmouth, while the Christchurch vacancy was won by a second Liberal, Mr. Horace Davey, Q.C., who later became the Solicitor General, then a Judge and finally a Peer. Davey was an active and progressive Member who supported several reforms, including the 1884 Reform Act, the reform of municipal government and the granting of limited powers to Ireland. His association with Bournemouth was commemorated by the pier clock, which he presented to the town in 1880. In 1885 he was defeated by Charles E. Baring Young, who was succeeded by Major K. R. Balfour, Arthur Acland Allen and Henry Page Croft respectively.

By the end of the 19th century the party system was fully developed in Christchurch, as it was elsewhere; the petty squabbles and bribery belonged to the past, and thenceforth people began to vote for the party rather than for the individual.

When the Representation of the People Act was passed in 1918, Bournemouth became a constituency in its own right and was known as the parliamentary borough of Bournemouth. Its first M.P. was Henry Page Croft (first Baronet of Knole from 1924), who had represented Christchurch since 1910. Mr. Croft was an active Tariff Reformer and Protectionist, and many lively and rowdy meetings took place in select Bournemouth when keen free-traders were present in his audiences. At one meeting in Winton he was attacked and had to be given police protection.

Mr. Croft's main estate was Croft Castle in Hereford, but he was able to purchase Knole House, Boscombe, a fine Tudor-style mansion situated on a steep incline, after it was vacated by Mr. Edmund Christy (see chapter VIII). There he spent many happy years enjoying its terraced gardens and five acres of secluded woodland. He remained the Member of Parliament for Bournemouth until 1940, when he was succeeded by Sir Leonard Lyle, Bt. (1940–45), who in his turn was replaced by Brendan Bracken in 1945.

As a result of the Representation of People Act of 1948 Bournemouth was divided into two constituencies, namely Bournemouth West, and Bournemouth East and Christchurch, both of which returned one Member; whereas Bournemouth had previously been part of the Christchurch constituency, the older constituency thus became part of the newly-created one.

In 1952 Nigel Nicolson was elected Conservative Member of Parliament for Bournemouth East, and a constitutional issue arose which, besides causing bitterness and anger, had a divisive affect on many Conservative M.P.s. Was a Member intended to act entirely as a delegate of his constituency?

Nigel Nicolson felt that the views he conscientiously held should precede the views of his party. Soon some of his speeches were horrifying the retired businessmen and hotel proprietors of the area, especially when, at a meeting of the Primrose League in Bournemouth, he advised supporters not to hate those in opposition and in particular Aneurin Bevan, who was then regarded by some as a dangerous character. Although Nicolson was strongly opposed to capital punishment, he compromised and voted with his party on this issue. But on the Suez question, when military forces were sent in to occupy the Canal zone in 1956, he felt he could not support the Government. At a crowded and stormy meeting at Selwyn Hall, Boscombe, he made a speech in which he criticized the action of the Government; as a result, a motion of no confidence was passed by the constituency committee and a new prospective candidate was chosen. An awkward period followed when the area possessed a prospective candidate, Major Friend, as well as a candidate in office who was unwilling to resign. Even more dramatic events ensued. It was found that the prospective candidate had been in contact with the League of Empire Loyalists, a right-wing organization disapproved of by the Conservative Party, and he was obliged to resign. Randolph Churchill offered himself as an alternative candidate, but was declined. Finally, Nicolson suggested that the controversy could be solved by a postal ballot of all members of the local Conservative Association as to whether they wished Nicolson to remain as their M.P. or not. This was the only primary election in British political history, and it aroused much excitement. After a three-week campaign Nicolson lost the election by 91 votes; there were 3,671 for him and 3,762 against him. He was succeeded by Mr. John Cordle, who retained the seat for Bournemouth East until 1977, when he resigned owing to accusations of involvement in the Poulson corruption case.

Fortunately Bournemouth West has had no such complications. From 1950 it was represented by the Hon. Robert Edward P. Gascoyne-Cecil, Viscount Cranborne and from 1954 onwards by John Eden (later Sir John Eden).

Under the Parliamentary Constituencies Order of 1970 the areas covered by these two constituencies were revised, and Bournemouth West then comprised Westbourne, West and East Cliffs, Central, Kinson North, Kinson South, Winton and Redhill Park wards; Bournemouth East comprised Boscombe West, Boscombe East, West Southbourne, Southbourne, King's Park, Queen's Park, Moordown South and Moordown North wards.

Chapter XIV

HOSPITALS AND SANATORIA

THE VIEWS OF eminent physicians including Dr. Granville, Sir James Clarke (physician to Queen Victoria), Dr. Aitken of Poole and others concerning the warmth and equability of Bournemouth's climate, together with the health-giving pines and other curative qualities, established it as a winter residence for invalids, particularly consumptives and those with chest complaints. Thus Bournemouth became an invalid's paradise, but it was depressing for those visitors who began to come for sea-bathing and a change of air in pleasant surroundings. Bath chairs, respirators and sputum-flasks were a familiar sight.

Recognizing the advantages of Bournemouth for chest complaints, the governors of Brompton Hospital decided to establish a sanatorium for consumptive patients who had good prospects of a cure. To obtain money, bazaars and concerts were held at Boscombe Manor and other large houses, while an amateur dramatic performance was held at Campden House, Kensington, at which Charles Dickens presided. The building, which cost about £15,000 and was known as the National Sanatorium for Consumption and Diseases of the Chest, was erected on land generously given by one of the town's great benefactors, Mr. George Durrant. It was situated between St. Stephen's Road and Bourne Avenue (then Sanatorium Road), and was surrounded by pine woods, shrubs and flowers. The sanatorium consisted of a long, low series of buildings, with many windows looking towards the south. Patients came from every county in England, justifying the name 'National'. A popular parade from Westover Gardens to the *Royal Bath* Hotel was known as Invalids Walk (today it is called Pine Walk).

Shortly after it opened on 2 October 1855, the London body found themselves financially incapable of maintaining the new sanatorium and it was threatened with closure. Through the generosity of Mr. Charles Lavington Pannel of Guildford, who took over the property and vested it in a number of trustees, it soon established a reputation as the principal provincial consumption sanatorium. In 1863 a new wing was added, and in 1865 a chapel was erected. Further extensions were added later. A local advertisement in 1895 requested a resident medical officer, and offered an annual salary of £80, including board, lodging and washing.

Today the Royal National Hospital, part of the East Dorset Group of Hospitals, specializes in chest treatment and dermatology.

The 'invalid's paradise' soon became a centre for convalescent homes, in particular for consumptive cases. The foundation stone for the Hahnemann[1] Convalescent Home and Homoeopathic Dispensary was laid on 4 January 1878 by Earl Cairns, the Lord

96

Chancellor, and the building was opened by him on 3 June the following year. (In a case in the entrance hall is the silver trowel used by Earl Cairns, inscribed with his name and the date 1878.) Land on the West Cliff was granted for a period of 999 years by W. Clapcott Dean at a nominal ground rent.

The home was established for consumptive patients, particularly labourers, artisans, and persons of small means, who were in the early stages of the illness and who had a reasonable possibility of restoration or improved health. It also accepted cases from hospitals and dispensaries who required rest and medical supervision. Homoeopathic medicines were prescribed and made up on the premises. Today the Hahnemann Home is part of the Bournemouth Royal National and Royal Victoria hospital service and accepts convalescing patients from hospitals in the east Dorset area.

The Firs Home, Trinity Road, dealt with advanced cases of consumption who were not curable at the Sanatorium. It was founded by Rev. S. R. Waddelow, acting chaplain to the Sanatorium, and was also for the benefit of invalids in poor circumstances. The home was financed by voluntary subscriptions. For many years The Firs was a popular and much appreciated maternity home, and was part of the Bournemouth hospital service.

After the break-up of the Stourfield House estate in 1893 (see chapter VII, Pokesdown), the house became a private nursing home known as The Home Sanatorium, for the treatment of consumption. During World War I it was taken over by the British Legion as a sanatorium for servicemen suffering from tuberculosis, and after the War it was used for civilians again. The Home was fortunate in its medical superintendent from 1908 to 1923, Dr. John Esslemont, who was greatly appreciated for his work in both caring for patients and also endeavouring to discover both preventative and curative methods. Unfortunately, he himself became afflicted with the disease, but he carried on with his work as long as he was able. Dr. Esslemont was a profoundly religious person and a strong advocate of a National Health Service.

After World War II The Home was taken over by the British T.B. Association, and in 1958 it became known as Douglas House and was part of the hospital service. Care and attention is today given to long-stay elderly patients.

The Herbert Convalescent Home, Alumhurst Road (today the Herbert Psychological Day Centre) was built as a memorial to Lord Sidney Herbert of Lea (1810–61), M.P. for Wiltshire from 1832, and Secretary of War 1852–55, who was greatly concerned with Army administration, improved sanitation and better health conditions. He was a close friend of Florence Nightingale of Embley Park, near Romsey, and as Secretary of War he asked her to go out to Scutari to nurse during the Crimean War. After Herbert's death at Wilton House, near Salisbury (his death was said to have been caused by work and strain due to the Crimean War), it was decided by his many friends and admirers that a memorial to him should be established in the form of a seaside convalescent home for the benefit of the poor and the weak.

An extract from a report issued by the Committee of Subscribers to the Herbert Memorial Fund in September 1867 stated:

A commodious and handsome edifice has risen within the last two years at Bournemouth, on a noble site facing the sea, upon a sandy cliff, where the patients will possess the advantages of a pure and healthy air, the quiet of the country and the convenience of a town close at hand.

The design of the building was furnished by a lady who was specially qualified to form a judgment of the best mode of treating the sick and whose fond regard for Lord Herbert induced her to devote her care to his subject even in the hours of suffering and sickness. In this design of Miss Nightingale, the arrangements, instead of being concentrated in one block, as is the case generally in hospitals, provide for the patients in detached wings joined to the centre building by corridors . . .

Florence Nightingale, although by then bedridden, was greatly interested in the plans and construction of the home; every window was designed so that it would catch the sun and all rooms had to be light and airy. She expected to be consulted at all stages and wrote numerous letters stating her exact requirements. The building was constructed with Purbeck stone, in Gothic style, with a short spire and italianate stucco chimneys. In the porch tower is a statue of St. Elizabeth holding a rose, and the fine clock tower in a diamond shaped frame containing a handsome, ornamental two-faced clock, with an interior and an exterior side, was presented by Lady Herbert in Memory of her husband. The words 'Herbert Home' with the date of its foundation were carved in large letters on two stones prepared for the purpose in the front of the building.

On 14 September 1865 there was an elaborate stone-laying ceremony, the first stone being laid by the 15-year-old Earl of Pembroke, who was accompanied by his mother; a local procession, headed by the clergy and choir of St. Peter's Church, marched and sang psalms as they walked towards the new site. Afterwards there was lunch in the Cranborne Gardens, which had been lent for the occasion by Mr. R. Kerley.

Besides two other magnificent buildings, Branksome Dene (1860) and Branksome Towers (1855), Herbert Home was the only other building on the lonely heathland in the Westbourne district.

The home received half its patients from Salisbury Hospital, which was the founding hospital, and the remainder from other hospitals. During World War II soldiers and pilots from the Battle of Britain came for a welcome period of convalescence, many of whom had had skin grafts after burns and disfigurement caused by enemy bombs. From 1942 the home dealt with consumptive cases until 1967, when it became a day centre for disturbed cases and alcoholics.

In 1874 a convalescent home was also established at Blenheim House, Lansdowne Road, by Lady Georgina Fullerton for the sick and afflicted of all creeds. (Lady Georgina Fullerton, who was greatly appreciated for her kind and philanthropic work, came to Bournemouth in about 1844 when it was still a marine village. She was also a well-known writer of that period, and her novels include *Ellen Middleton* (1844), *A Will and a Way* (1881), and *Life of Elizabeth Lady Falkland* (1883). She lived at Ayrfield, St. Peter's Road, where she died on 19 January 1885.) Unfortunately the matron of the home became ill and it seemed as though the work carried out there would be ended. On hearing of the plight of the home, three Sisters of Mercy from the Great Ormond St. Hospital in London offered their services. They rented the premises formerly occupied by the Daughters of the Cross in Branksome Wood Road (see chapter XV), which they gradually transformed into St. Joseph's Convalescent Home. In 1888 the first mass was celebrated, two postulants entered the convent and the first ward was opened for eight patients.

Financial provision was gratefully received from Mrs. Blake, a cousin of the first Superior, who paid the first three years' rent for No. 11 Branksome Wood Road, and who in 1892 donated a further £2,000 in memory of her husband, enabling the purchase of the adjoining property, Ulverston Grange, as a home for male patients. The sum of £5,000 was donated by Mr. Fullerton in memory of his wife, who died in 1885, enabling the Sisters to buy No. 11 as a permanent home for women. In 1896 Baroness von Hugel (whose generosity was mainly responsible for Corpus Christi Church in Boscombe), obtained permission to dismantle the old iron church, which had served as the first church there, and paid for its transportation and re-erection at St. Joseph's. This remained as the chapel for Sisters and patients until the erection of the present one in 1959.

Prior to 1915 the Government provided no financial assistance for the sick. The only income available to the home came from annual bazaars and the salaries of some of the Sisters who taught at a school in Yelverton Road. Despite this, many patients were nursed who would otherwise have had to enter Poor Law Institutes. During the Boer War and World War I many wounded servicemen convalesced in the home, while during the mass unemployment of the 1920s and '30s many undernourished people were restored to health at St. Joseph's.

Since May 1968 several of the Sisters have given voluntary service to the local hospitals, which has been of spiritual benefit to the patients and also helpful to the nursing staff. Today St. Joseph's admits private and National Health Service Patients, and also treats patients from various benevolent funds.

Until the middle of the 19th century the Government did not consider that the health of the nation was their concern, despite frequent cholera outbreaks; refuse disposal, cleansing and water supply were dealt with by various *ad hoc* bodies. The need for social reform began to be realized by progressive-minded people, while the slow development of a public conscience resulted in a desire to help less fortunate members of the community. No free facilities existed in Bournemouth for the treatment of the poor, the nearest dispensaries being in Southampton or Dorchester, neither of which were very accessible for patients.

In 1852 Charles William Packe, a member of the board of commissioners and a prominent local citizen, purchased the Branksome Towers Estate and in 1855 built a fine, picturesque mansion for himself called Branksome Towers (it is now a block of flats). (See chapter XI.)

Mr. Packe was a philanthropist, greatly interested in social improvements and the welfare of the community. To him can be attributed the title 'Founder of Bournemouth's General Hospital Service'.[2] He felt that a public dispensary service was required to provide for the needs of poor agricultural workers and artisans in the area. In 1858 he arranged a meeting with a few friends, all active philanthropists and supporters of better health provision, at the home of Richard Stephens, Eastington House, in Cliffe Road, Bournemouth. This was followed by a public meeting in January of the following year, when a committee was formed under his chairmanship. Other members of the committee included Richard Stephens, Rev. A. M. Bennett, Dr. Burslem (Hon. Physician), Mr. Lacey of Poole and Mr. Falls as Hon. Surgeons, and others.

As a result the Bournemouth Public Dispensary was established on 15 October 1859 at 2 Granville Cottages, Yelverton Road, which was leased at £25 a year. Its aim was to give free medical and surgical advice to the poor of Bournemouth; visits by dispensary medical staff would be arranged when a patient was unable to attend the dispensary. The dispensary served an area of a 12-mile radius from the centre of Bournemouth and included Poole, Wimborne and Christchurch. It was estimated that an annual income of £150 would be required, which it was hoped would be met by donations and subscriptions from supporters. A donation of 50 guineas was made by Mr. Packe, the newly-elected chairman, who believed that the dispensary would be of great utility and a blessing to the neighbourhood. At the end of the first year 218 patients had received treatment, and in the first six months 620 seriously-ill patients had been visited in their homes. Patients with incomes of over £1 a week were not accepted, as the average weekly wage of agricultural workers in the area was then about 9s. Surgeons attending confinements charged £1 and in approved cases the dispensary paid 15s. of this.

As larger premises began to be required the dispensary was moved to more suitable accommodation in Madeira Vale, near the junction of Stafford and Lorne Park Roads, on land provided by Mr. R. Kerley at a cost of £200. The new building was designed by Mr. Peter Tuck and was opened on 18 May 1868 by the wife of Richard Stephens. (Mr. Stephens, the president of the committee, was a close friend and associate of Mr. Packe who died in November 1867.)

The new Dispensary and Cottage Hospital comprised two small wards for men and women, a laboratory and a consulting room, and dealt with accident cases. On the recommendation of the medical staff a Mr. and Mrs. Dacombe were appointed to assist at a joint salary of £12 per annum, plus the addition of one room for their accommodation. Nursing qualifications had been required, and their many duties included cleaning, supervising both in- and out-patients, and checking goods received from tradesmen. The committee and medical staff were motivated by religious and humanitarian principles, and were anxious that progress should be maintained.

By 1869 Dr. J. R. Thomson, Admiral Sir James Sulivan, Merton Russell-Cotes (see chapter XVIII) and others were stressing the need for a cottage hospital for infectious diseases. Obtaining land proved extremely difficult, as local landowners were unwilling to grant any parts of their estates for this purpose. By 1874, however, part of Boscombe allotments in the Shelley Road area was offered by Mr. Sharp for £55, and Mr. F. Moser offered two adjoining plots of land on the opposite side of the road for the sum of £20. As soon as the news of a proposed fever hospital became public, protests were immediately received from 60 landowners and local people who considered that it would be prejudicial to the interests of nearby inhabitants. Among the names was that of Mr. Moser, who must have been unaware of the purpose for which his land was required. When it was completed in January 1876 the building cost £1,310, and proved to be of a disagreeable yellowish colour due to a mistake in the cement mixing. Owing to a lack of funds and objections it was not possible to open the building for infectious diseases. This proved a major and expensive set-back for the members of the Bournemouth Dispensary and Cottage Hospital.

Fortunately, shortly afterwards the Boscombe dispensary committee was able to purchase the building, which was opened as the Boscombe, Pokesdown and Springbourne Infirmary, with 12 beds, where care was provided for local artisans who paid a small weekly sum through which treatment and medicine could be provided.

The Boscombe Dispensary had been established in 1876 over a shop at 4 Gervis Terrace, Christchurch Road, opposite the *Palmerston* Hotel in Boscombe.

The new Cottage Hospital and Provident Infirmary soon experienced financial difficulties as subscriptions were not always forthcoming. In January 1880 an advertisement was even inserted in a London newspaper for patients requiring treatment 'owing to the emptiness of the Infirmary at the present time',[3] while failure to meet a water account resulted in the water supply being cut off for a time.

Active among the supporters of the hospital were Sir Percy and Lady Shelley of Boscombe Manor, who raised funds by holding bazaars and putting on plays and other performances, often assisted by devoted helpers: but even after 20 years there was still a debt of over £1,000, and an income that failed to cover annual expenditure.

As the Golden Jubilee of Queen Victoria approached, it was suggested that a new hospital should be constructed to meet the needs of people living in west Bournemouth. By December 1886 a fund committee was set up to provide a general hospital and dispensary with at least twenty beds for medical and surgical cases. Dr. Thomson, who was so active in improving the administration and growth of the health service, became its chairman. Donations were received, land was generously given by Mr. Clapcott Dean in Poole Road, and plans were approved for a hospital at a cost of £6,000.

On 21 June 1887, the Golden Jubilee of the Queen, a foundation stone was laid by Mr. E. W. Rebbeck, Chairman of the Improvement Commissioners, to the accompaniment of the town band. By permission of the Queen the hospital was named the 'Royal Victoria Hospital', Westbourne. The hospital was officially opened by the Prince of Wales (later Edward VII) on 16 January 1890 as the town's memorial to the Jubilee, and the day was celebrated as a public holiday. A west wing was opened by the Duke of Connaught in 1892 and a children's ward by the Duchess of Argyll on 17 January 1903. At about this time the Duke of Argyll wrote to Lord Malmesbury of Heron Court, saying that he found it very pleasant to see the wonderful advance in prosperity and importance made by the forest city of our southern sea.

The work of the original Bournemouth Dispensary and Cottage Hospital was finished and its assets were handed over to the new hospital, but the services of the Boscombe Cottage Hospital were still available. The latter had become too small, and as a result certain patients had to be refused owing to shortage of beds. A new site was required, and by 1898 land fronting Ashley Road, Boscombe was purchased from the Bournemouth Gas & Water Company for £1,500. Here additional wards could be provided, while the old cottage hospital was to become an out-patients' department. Mr. Godwin Pratt became the hospital's first paid secretary, at a salary of 20 guineas per annum; a nurse-matron was appointed at £40, and two fully qualified nurses at £25 per annum.

By 1900 the first block of the new extensions was opened by Miss Wills who, together with Sir Frederick and Lady Wills, had contributed £3,000 towards building costs. The new general hospital was entirely dependent on voluntary contributions, and visits to outpatients in their own homes ceased. By 1904, owing to shortage of accommodation, some patients had to be refused admission and a long waiting list commenced. The need for new wards, an administration block, an isolation ward and other departments became increasingly urgent. New extensions were eventually opened by Princess Alexandra in 1909, and by 1921 the Royal Victoria Hospital, Westbourne, and the Royal Boscombe and West Hants. Hospital were amalgamated under the title of the Royal Victoria and West Hants. Hospital, resulting in a period of further growth, expansion and more specialization.

During World War I arrangements were made for the treatment of war casualties, and tents were erected in the grounds at Shelley Road for 100 wounded soldiers who were admitted from overseas. Altogether a total of 10,738 military patients were treated in the hospital.

In 1927 a large house in Windham Road, Springbourne, was rented to provide extra accommodation for the nursing staff at Boscombe Hospital. A donation of £12,000 was received from Mr. Walter Clarke towards the erection of a nurses' home in Shelley Road, and due to his generosity it was possible to build and open the hostel by 1922. Mr. Clarke donated a further gift of £250 towards the building fund and arranged for the removal of the original Boscombe Cottage Hospital adjacent to the new hostel, replacing it with a beautiful garden of flowering shrubs.

Further new extensions were opened in 1932 by Prince George, the Duke of Kent,

101

which included a new out-patients' department and private pay wards. By the end of the first year 460 patients had been admitted to the latter, which considerably helped the hospital's ailing financial position in the years of poverty after the War: plans could thus be made for additional operating theatre accommodation. A board-room was erected in memory of Mr. A. H. Vernon, F.R.C.S., whose administrative ability and progressive outlook, together with those of Dr. Thomson and other dedicated people, largely contributed to the successful development of the hospital service in the Bournemouth area. (A bronze memorial tablet was erected to the memory of Dr. Thomson in Westbourne Hospital in 1926.)

The hospital service, the small beginnings of which were due to the pioneering activities of those who had wished to provide better health care for the poor, was to witness radical changes after the last World War.

In November 1946 a new era commenced when a National Health Service Act was passed by the Government to provide a comprehensive health service without direct payment by the patient. The National Health Service, besides effecting improved physical and mental health for all, reduced the anxiety caused by financial problems arising from illness. In order to control the new hospital service the country was divided into regions, and the Bournemouth hospitals became part of the Bournemouth and East Dorset Hospital Management Committee Group. The years since 1946 have been a period of continuous growth and expansion, with more laboratories, operating theatres and wards, and better amenities for patients and staff.

Chapter XV

A PERIOD OF RELIGIOUS GROWTH

RELIGION PLAYED A GREAT PART in the lives of the Victorians; it is not surprising, therefore, that as the marine village expanded into a sedate watering resort there was an accompanying growth in church building. The visiting population soon considerably exceeded the number of permanent inhabitants, so that initially small churches often had to be reconstructed on a larger and more commodious scale. Most of the Victorian churches were built in a mock-Gothic style that was considered appropriate for places of worship by many architects of that period, including Pugin, Ferrey, George Street, Norman Shaw, Seddon and Tulloch.

While it is not possible to give detailed descriptions of all the churches in Bournemouth, it is hoped that the main churches with backgrounds that are of historical interest are covered in this chapter, or in previous chapters dealing with particular areas.

The development of St. Peter's, the first church in the marine village, from its commencement in 1838 in two cottages to the elegant building and landmark of today, reflects the growth of the district into a well-known seaside resort (see chapter V). From an ecclesiastical point of view it is referred to as the mother church of Bournemouth, as well as being its civic church. The old Saxon church in Holdenhurst and, later, the present one, St. John the Evangelist's Church (constructed in 1834) were also both regarded as the mother church of Bournemouth, in the sense that Bournemouth grew out of the parish of Holdenhurst.

Of the churches not already described, a record of the historical backgrounds of the following seems relevant to this chapter.

Congregationalism, which developed from groups of Protestant dissenters, grew in Bournemouth and the area as a result of the pioneer work and co-operation of ministers and members of the Poole and Christchurch churches, which had existed since 1662 and 1660 respectively, and which were strong and flourishing churches when Bournemouth was merely heathland.

Pokesdown Congregational (now United Reformed) Church, founded in 1820 in a thatched cottage, was the oldest Free Church in that area and then the only church between Poole and Christchurch. It was started by Dr. Daniel Gunn, a fervent preacher from Christchurch Congregational Church, for the benefit of villagers living in the vicinity of Stourfield House and Pokesdown Farm (see chapter VII).

Due to the activity of visiting preachers and followers of Dr. Gunn in the Hampshire area, it was decided to commence services in Bournemouth. From July 1848 prayer meetings were held on Tuesday evenings, and a few months later they were extended to two weekly Sunday services in a house in Poole Road. From October 1849 services took place in a small chapel in Orchard Street erected by Mr. Hapgood, one of the first church members. By 1850 there was a Sunday school and also a day school, which developed into the Lansdowne British School, one of the earliest Free Church schools.

When a larger church became necessary, its present site on one of the most commanding positions in the town was donated as a gift by Mr. G. Durrant, who owned land in the area of the Lower Gardens. Although he was a member of the Established Church, his kindly action showed his generosity and his sympathy for the problems of other denominations. Subscriptions were requested, and when the sum of £1,200 had been reached work commenced on the new church, which was designed by Mr. C. Crabbe Creeke in a Gothic style. On 4 July 1854 a foundation stone was laid by Mr. G. O. Aldridge, a layman of Christchurch Congregational Church and one of the first deacons of the Richmond Hill Congregational (now United Reformed) Church.

Rejoicing was soon replaced by trouble when the title to the land was assailed; work on the building had to stop and a law suit resulted. There were also difficulties in obtaining a pastor; unfortunately there was unhappiness when a Presbyterian minister was appointed, and when he resigned after four months in office he took a third of the congregation with him. When work on the church recommenced, its unfinished roof was destroyed by a great storm. But friends were at hand and many donations were received, including one from Rev. Morden Bennett.

After five years of problems the church was finally completed, on 8 March 1859 and the title to the land was officially established. The 10 years that followed were years of peace and growth. In Holdenhurst Road a mission hall costing £400 was erected, which in 1878 developed into the East Cliff Church, while several other churches in the area were established and fostered by the mother church.

After their first Congregational minister, Rev. Hurry, left in 1869 for health reasons, the church underwent another period of friction and unhappiness due to a second unfortunate choice of minister. Peace and prosperity was restored with the appointment of Rev. W. Jackson in 1873, and Rev. J. Ossian Davies in 1888. The latter was an eloquent Welsh preacher whose fervour and faith inspired a new spirit in the Free Churches of the town, and whose lectures were requested all over the country.

A larger church was again required, and on 24 November 1891 the present one was opened on the site of its predecessor. It was designed in late Gothic style by Messrs. Lawson & Donkin at a cost of about £12,000.

In 1898 Dr. J. D. Jones was appointed, whose sincerity and compelling manner made him much loved by all. Visitors came from far and wide to hear 'Jones of Bournemouth', and in the holiday season long queues formed outside the church, while his writings and books were circulated to many parts of the world. Due to his vision and enterprise as an educationalist the Bournemouth Collegiate School was founded in 1899 (see chapter VIII). Dr. Jones was always active in promoting the welfare of the town, and was on the Education Committee, a Governor of secondary schools, the Chairman of the Collegiate School and a member of the Library Committee for over thirty-five years.

In 1937, after 39 years, the strain of managing a large church, coupled with the loss of several members of his family, caused him to retire from the ministry. A farewell dinner was held at the Pavilion, when moving tributes were paid from one speaker after another, including the Earl of Malmesbury, the Bishop of Winchester, the Mayor,

Councillor T. Rebbecks and many others. Dr. Jones's happiness was complete when he was made a Companion of Honour, thus receiving national recognition of his work. He was also presented with the Freedom of the Borough, marking the town's appreciation of his long public service. On the silver casket was a bas-relief of the Richmond Hill Church.

During World War II crowded services were held in the church until in 1941 it was bombed and damaged. While it was under repair worship continued at the Pavilion, when more people than ever attended. The church, along with others, welcomed and cared for serving men stationed in Bournemouth, and from the beginning of 1943 about a thousand Canadian soldiers held their weekly church parade at Richmond Hill.

Many well known Bournemouth names have been associated with the growth and development of the church, including the Beales, Mooring Aldridges, Brights, Hankinsons, over seven mayors and many others, so that its religious teaching has always been closely associated with the town in which it is situated.

Another of the early churches constructed in the marine village was St. Andrew's Presbyterian (now United Reformed) Church, originally referred to as the 'Scotch Church'. An unattractive building of galvanized iron was erected in 1857 at the foot of Richmond Hill by Rev. H. McMillan, who, like so many others, had come to Bournemouth because of ill-health. The church could hold 320 people and its structure cost £700, most of which was raised through the efforts of Rev. McMillan, who remained with the church for 27 years. In 1872 the iron building was demolished, and the foundation stone for a new church was laid by the Earl of Kintore in March of that year. The handsome stone structure was still small, being 60 ft. by 37 ft., and cost £4,000, including a schoolroom and vestry.

Rev. Rodger of Wolverhampton became the pastor in 1885 and was a devoted and faithful preacher for 25 years. Due to his able preaching the church became overcrowded, and in 1886 land was acquired in Exeter Road, where the third and present church stands. The church, which was built in Gothic style with Purbeck stone, had a spire of 140 ft. and cost about £12,000, including the site, Session House and schoolroom. The appreciation of land value meant that £7,000 was received for the small area of the previous church.

The commencement of Methodism in Bournemouth was due to the initiative of far-sighted members of the Poole circuit, who in November 1859 rented simple quarters over some workshops in Orchard Street. Contemporary records show that the people were too poor even to entertain visiting ministers from Poole, who usually ate their lunch on the beach. An early account book of the period states that a sum of 16s. 4d. was received in one quarter.

When this room became too small better accommodation was hired at the Belle Vue Assembly Rooms, when a congregation of 200 people attended. It was obvious there was need for a Methodist church in the town. Land was purchased in Old Christchurch Road adjoining the *Tregonwell Arms*, where a small temporary building was opened in 1866.

By 1883 the congregation had become too large for the church and a new site was acquired on Richmond Hill, the opening ceremony of the splendid Gothic-type building taking place on 30 June 1886. The new church was named the Punshon Memorial Church in memory of Rev. Dr. W. Morley Punshon, a preacher of vision and wisdom who was highly esteemed both in his own church and elsewhere. In 1875 he became Overseas Missionary Secretary, a position he held until his death in 1881. The church

105

soon became exceedingly popular with holidaymakers from all parts of the country. Dr. Morley Punshon was deeply concerned that his church should play its part in the development of more coastal churches, and to this end he raised the sum of £10,000 from his lectures and contributions, from which grants were made to other holiday resorts.

The church continued to be the headquarters of Wesleyan Methodism until it was demolished by an enemy bomb on 23 May 1943, one hour after morning worship. After a long period of worshipping in temporary buildings, a site was obtained in Exeter Road, and on 17 December 1958 the new church was dedicated by Rev. Leslie Weatherhead, the former President of the Methodist Conference. The architect, Mr. Ronald Sims, was honoured by the award of a bronze medal from the Royal Institute of British Architects for his elegant, modern church. It was the first example of a break from the traditional Gothic-style churches in Bournemouth, with its outstanding tower of brick and glass rising 60 ft. above the ground, which rises to a slender spire surmounted by an alloy cross 132 ft. above the ground. The church still continues to take a special interest in the many holidaymakers who come to Bournemouth today.

The need for a second Anglican church arose owing to a difference of opinion between those who supported the Tracterian service of St. Peter's Church and those who wished for a more Evangelical service.

It was even reported in the Bournemouth *Visitors Directory* of 7 December 1867 that families were deterred from coming to the town, despite its ideal climate, because they were unable to worship according to their own beliefs. Harmony was restored among differing opinions when the parish of Holy Trinity was created by Order in Council of 4 November 1867. John Tregonwell (the son of the founder of Bournemouth) and four other trustees guaranteed a £3,000 endowment for a living and site in Madeira Vale facing Old Christchurch Road, on land given by Robert Kerley, churchwarden of St. Peter's from 1856 to 1857.

A temporary brick church dedicated to the Holy Trinity, 60 ft. long and 35 ft. wide, and capable of holding 300 people, was opened for worship on 1 December 1867, the foundation stone having been laid about three months previously by Mrs. John Tregonwell.

It was soon realized that a larger and more permanent church was required, and in June 1868 a foundation was laid by the famous Earl of Shaftesbury. In September the following year the church was consecrated by Bishop Ryan. The architect was Mr. Charles Ferguson of Carlisle, who had spent considerable time in north Italy studying the Lombardo-Gothic churches, otherwise known as Italian Romanesque. The style was described as a masterpiece of architecture by a writer of that period, who regretted that people unfamiliar with the style failed to appreciate it.

The first vicar of Holy Trinity was Rev. Philip F. Eliot, whose achievements and energy were considerable. As well as being mainly responsible for the building of the first and second churches, and additions such as the transept, porch and tower, he also provided the cost of building St. Paul's Parish School and the major part of the teachers' salaries. In 1891 Rev. Eliot was appointed as private chaplain and spiritual advisor to Queen Victoria. The new parish was active in supporting education in the town, as well as the development of hospitals and sanatoria, and also donated sums to the poor for boots and shoes.

Many important people were attracted to the new church, including the King and Queen of Sweden. Sometimes as many as five Cabinet Ministers were seen in the church when they were visiting Earl Cairns, brother-in-law of the vicar, who was Lord Chancellor between 1868 and 1888, as well as being a distinguished lawyer and philanthropist. In 1865 Admiral Sulivan, who had sailed on the *Beagle* under the command of Captain Robert Fitzroy, retired to Bournemouth, and was actively associated with the church and the development of the town. The *Beagle* was depicted on one of the windows of the north transept. Another distinguished parishioner was Dr. J. R. Thomson, who, as has been noted was made a Freeman of the Borough, and who also became president of the B.M.A.

Many outstanding vicars have been associated with Holy Trinity, including Rev. A. S. Blunt from 1906; Rev. Pechey, a poet and hymn-writer, from 1912, who for long and faithful service was made an Honorary Canon of Westminster; and Rev. W. Marshall Selwyn from 1929, whose powerful preaching attracted great crowds to the church, so that those without pew sittings had to queue for their seats. The name of the latter's father is commemorated in Selwyn Hall, Boscombe. From 1942 Rev. Wade (the father of Virginia Wade, the tennis star) was vicar, and in 1947 he was succeeded by Rev. F. Bussby, now Canon of Winchester.

In the 1950s people began to find it difficult to live in the large Victorian villas of their parents; many moved to outlying parts of the town, and a number of villas became guest-houses, offices and flats. The congregation decreased in number, and from 1973 it was no longer used as a church. It was let for medieval banquets, and unfortunately the whole building, except for the square brick tower, was destroyed by fire in the winter of 1978 – a sad ending indeed to a fine church and an early part of the town's history.

By 1866 Rev. Morden Bennett, the first vicar of St. Peter's, who was so active in the religious and educational development of Bournemouth, realised that a church and school were required on the west side of the town. Land was secured in the area of the present St. Michael's Road, where the *Devon Towers* Hotel stands. George Street was commissioned to build the new church, which was called St. Michael's and All Angels. The edifice was 70 ft. long and 47 ft. wide, built with Purbeck stone and timber, and fashioned like a medieval French barn with its roof reaching almost to the ground. The church was consecrated in December 1866 by Rev. H. Powys, the Bishop of Sodor and Man.

Although Morden Bennett was pleased with the small, temporary church, he immediately began to work for a larger and more permanent one. George Durrant, a great benefactor, donated a sum of £500, as well as land on Poole Road. When £3,000 had been raised, a new parish was formed from part of St. Peter's. The architect for the new church was Norman Shaw, a pupil of Street's, and the foundation stone was laid by Morden Bennett on 4 August 1874. A nave was erected in 1876 at a cost of £12,500, a chancel in 1883 and a tower in 1901, all of which added to the splendour of the church, which was constructed in the Early English style. After the first part of the new church was completed the old 'barn' was demolished, to the regret of many residents, as the unusual building was the only one of that type designed by Street.

Land was generously given by Mr. Clapcott Dean, and a further gift of £2,000 from Mr. Durrant led to the building of schools in 1877.

St. Stephen's Church is often referred to as the Bennett Memorial Church, as it was built to honour and commemorate the memory of Rev. A. Morden Bennett, who died in 1880. As with so many other churches in Bournemouth, it started in a temporary building, which was consecrated by Dr. Harold Browne, the Bishop of Winchester, on

107

14 August 1881; a memorial stone for the permanent church was laid on the same day as it was the anniversay of Morden Bennett's birth. In his sermon the Bishop compared Morden Bennett with the ark builder, Noah, stating that the vicar would always be remembered as a great builder and organiser.

The church, like St. Peter's, was constructed over a period of years. The first part was completed four years after building commenced, when the nave was consecrated by Dr. Browne. It was designed by John Loughborough Pearson, one of the great 19th-century architects, who was responsible for Truro Cathedral, and in character the church is indeed like a cathedral in miniature. Its style is a transition of Early English to Geometrical Decorated. A massive tower that was built on in 1908 harmonizes with the rest of the church, but it has never been possible to add a spire that was included in the original design.

Morden Bennett's son, Rev. A. S. Bennett, was the first vicar, an office which he held until 1911. The church maintained the Oxford Movement or Tracterian revival so popular in Victorian times, while Rev. Bennett introduced services of a higher ritual than at St. Peter's.

On 15 March 1888 Prince Oscar, the second son of King Oscar II of Norway and Sweden, married Miss Ebba Munck of Fulkila here after a civil ceremony at the Registrar's Office in Christchurch. After their marriage he assumed the title of Prince Bernadotte and renounced his claim to the Swedish throne. His son was Count Folke Bernadotte, a United Nations envoy, who was assassinated in 1948.

Baptism developed in Zurich in 1525, but the first Baptist church in England was not established until 1612 in London.

By 1874 a few Baptists resided in Bournemouth, and they felt that their denomination should be represented in the town. Several problems had to be overcome, as their members were mainly scattered over a wide area. It was decided to build two chapels, one in Boscombe and one at the Lansdowne. Money was collected and soon contributions reached £1,200, which would practically pay for the cost of one chapel. Despite financial problems a foundation stone was laid in Boscombe on 1 October 1874, and the chapel was opened for worship in 1875.

While the chapel was under construction services were held at Heatherleigh, the home of Rev. H. C. Leonard, the first pastor, and also at the British and Foreign School in Lansdowne Road. A foundation stone was laid in Lansdowne Road by Sir Morton Peto in November 1875, and services commenced the following year with a membership of 30.

Several extensions have taken place to accommodate the growing congregation and also to make space for the many holiday visitors who attend the services.

In September 1870 several Sisters and nuns of the Congregation of the Cross from St. Quentin in northern France came to England, and they were received with great hospitality at the Convent of Mercy in Blandford Square, London. The Jesuit Fathers of the Society of Jesus encouraged them to make a foundation at Bournemouth, where Father Mann, S. J., and Lady Georgina Fullerton would endeavour to find them a suitable house.

When the Sisters first moved to Bournemouth they stayed at Astney Lodge in St. Stephen's Road; weekly meetings of Catholic ladies were soon held in the convent, where they all helped the poor of the district. On 28 October 1871 the Sisters moved to 'Mineham', which became the Convent of St. Joseph and also a convalescent home.

The Religious of the Cross found that the Bournemouth Convent was not situated centrally enough, and in 1886 they decided to make a foundation in Boscombe. Several acres of land were purchased near the sea and cliffs, and Dr. Vertue, the Bishop of Portsmouth, erected a small iron chapel purchased from Lord Petre, which was opened on 1 January 1888. It was called the Church of the Holy Cross and functioned both as a convent chapel and a parish church until the opening of Corpus Christi Church in 1896. It was served by Father de Lapasture, S. J., from Bournemouth, who became a familiar figure riding his tricycle or pushing it with a crowd of children clinging to him. On cold winter mornings he could be seen riding in a parishioner's brougham reading his office by candlelight.

The foundation for the new convent was blessed on 6 September 1888, and while the building was under construction the nuns, together with their pupils, lived in a large house (now demolished) at the junction of Parkwood and Darracott Roads in Boscombe. The convent, an immense, solid building, was built in Tudor style with an outer facing of Purbeck stone with Chilmark and Wardour stone dressing, although bricks were used for the interior; each final gable is surmounted by a stone cross.

An elementary school was soon opened in a nearby house, which served its purpose until a more permanent school could be obtained. Due to the generosity of a Mrs. James, ground was purchased adjoining the convent and presented to the nuns in May 1889.

By 1895 the convent had become too small for the growing school and another wing was added. The imposing main entrance was constructed at this time, surmounted by a handsome stone carving depicting the crest of the Order, a cross and anchor, with the words *O Crux Ave, Spes Unica* upheld on a shield by two angels. A boy's preparatory school was opened and by 1902 more dormitory provision and classrooms were provided for girl boarders. Twenty years later a beautiful chapel was erected to replace the original one. It was designed in Gothic style, using Purbeck and Chilmark stone to maintain uniformity with the convent.

Factors such as the size of the building, a dearth of religious vocations, and changes in the educational system have meant that the school and convent, with its history of effort and success, supported by clergy and laity, had to close in 1980, many of the pupils being transferred to St. Peter's Comprehensive School in Southborne.

Until 1861 the nearest Catholic church was St. Mary's at Poole. However, during the winter of that year a Mrs. Washington Hibbert from London stayed at the *Belle Vue* Hotel, where she formed a private oratory to which other Catholics in the area were welcomed. During the following two winters Lady Catherine Petre was able to continue this service. There was at that time only one resident Catholic in the resort. During the winter of 1865–66 Mr. Thomas Weld Blundell, who was staying at Walton House, Richmond Hill, had his own domestic chaplain, as did Lord Edward F. Howard of Glossop when he stayed the next winter at Brunstath on the East Cliff. When these services were not available, Catholics continued to travel to Poole. In 1868, due to the generosity of two Irish visitors, a bus was hired from the Square to Poole Church, leaving at 9.30 a.m. on Sunday mornings.

In 1869 the first public chapel and presbytery was opened by Fathers Brownhill and Eccles at Astney Lodge, St. Stephens Road: in 1870 this was replaced by a temporary wooden chapel for 90 worshippers. The small building was erected on land that had previously been occupied by Hampstead House, the home of Dr. Falls, which was burnt down in 1868. Prior to that the Windsor Cottages were situated there, the remaining one serving as a presbytery until 1896, when it was demolished to extend the church.

Although there were only about 30 Catholics in Bournemouth in 1871 the number began to increase considerably. To accommodate the growing number of worshippers the wooden chapel was replaced by the first Oratory of the Sacred Heart, which was commenced in 1873 and consecrated by Dr. Dannell, the Bishop of Southwark, on 5 February 1875. A larger church was soon required, and the foundation stone for this was laid in April 1896, the new portion being opened in 1900. Alterations were made to the original part to unite it with the new extension, and an early French Gothic style was adopted in both the old and the new parts.

During the latter part of the 19th century other Catholic churches were constructed at Boscombe, Westbourne, Winton and Richmond Park.

When the iron church (see Convent of the Cross) became too small the need for a larger one was met by Baroness Pauline von Hugel, the gifted daughter of an Austrian diplomat who, with the assistance of some friends, purchased a villa called Holyrood and two acres of land ajoining the convent grounds. On this land she built a fine church, for the use of the nuns and members of the community, which she presented to the Fathers of the Society of Jesus. The new church of Corpus Christi was commenced in 1895 and opened on 8 September 1896 by Bishop Vertue. The beautiful church was designed in Early English style with mellow red bricks and stone dressings, a 50 ft.-high nave and lancet windows.

Between 1932 and 1934 the church was enlarged to meet the needs of an increasing congregation, and one of its most outstanding features was the addition of a magnificent tower 108 ft. high surmounted by an 8 ft.-high iron cross. On the western side of the tower are two large windows containing richly-tinted old Norman glass.

When Corpus Christi became a parish in its own right in 1897, Father de Lapasture became the first parish priest. He resided at the Sacred Heart and drove over each morning in an old-fashioned brougham. After he died in 1923 a large pulpit was erected in his memory.

Baroness von Hugel died in 1901, aged 41, and was buried in the small parish cemetery at Stratton on the Fosse. A brass plaque in the church commemorates her great work.

Although there were Jewish people living in Poole by the 18th century, it was not until about 1900 that Bournemouth had any Jewish residents. A small Jewish community formed itself in the town centre and began to hold services in the Belle Vue Assembly Rooms, at the back of the *Belle Vue* Hotel, where the congregation met for six years.

The first three Jewish boarding houses were opened by 1905, and as the congregation increased it became desirous to obtain its own synagogue. Land was obtained in Wootton Gardens, off Old Christchurch Road, at a small ground rent from Sir George Meyrick, and in 1910 a foundation stone was laid by the Very Reverend Chief Rabbi Hermann Adler, and a second one by Mr. Albert Samuel, brother of Herbert Samuel, who later became Home Secretary and then High Commissioner for Palestine. The building accommodated 140 gentlemen downstairs and 120 ladies upstairs, in accordance with Hebrew custom, which requires that men and women should occupy different places in the synagogue. In 1922 a red-brick building was built adjacent to the synagogue in which Jewish children could enjoy social recreation and also attend Hebrew classes.

As more Jewish people were attracted to Bournemouth, a larger synagogue was required. In 1961 work commenced on an extension, which was re-consecrated in September 1962.

The main feature of the original synagogue, the ark, had stained-glass windows above it bearing the ten commandments, and this part was retained when the synagogue was reconstructed. The ark is set with a magnificent mosaic recess, into which are built motifs of columns with lions rampant. Above the ark a Hebrew phrase tells all worshippers to 'know before whom you stand', while a lamp is kept alight for 24 hours daily, as in the days of the temple. Also within the ark are the handwritten scrolls of the law comprising the five books of Moses.

Chapter XVI

WAR YEARS

THE SERENITY OF BOURNEMOUTH was barely disturbed by the rationing, queuing for food and billeting of soldiers of World War I; the same cannot, however, be said of the town during World War II.

Besides becoming a reception area for evacuees from Southampton, Portsmouth and London, many vital offices, including those of insurance and Government, were transferred to Bournemouth and established in some of the main hotels. In others, troops of various nationalities including Czechs, Americans and Canadians were accommodated.

In the *Royal Bath* Hotel there were Canadian, R.A.F., and other officers, and at the Bath Hill Flats there were R.A.F. sergeants. American soldiers were lodged at the *Palace Court* and *Ambassadors* Hotels, and American Red Cross in *Marsham Court* Hotel. More Americans were under canvas at nearby Bransgore and Holmsley. Troops were billeted in the College of Technology and also in Wentworth Mount Girls' School, the girls having been evacuated to Wales. After the evacuation of Dunkirk in 1940 French soldiers appeared for the first time, dirty, 'scruffy' and showing signs of the suffering they had undergone. Later the 'Desert Rats' came, tired and disshevelled, to rest, and then left for D-Day.

An Area Defence Ban was soon in force and very few civilian visitors were allowed into the town. The sea front was closed to all but the military, the beach bristled with barbed wire and other obstacles, while Army vehicles were positioned along the cliff tops to prevent any possible invasion. Gaps were cut in Boscombe and Bournemouth piers, which were stripped of most of their main planking. On Hengistbury Head, that great vantage point, there were tanks, tank trenches and a multitude of barbed wire.

Despite the inky black-out and the dark, tree-lined paths, cinemas were crowded with soldiers and civilians, weekly dances were given by the Americans, socials were held by church organizations and concerts continued in the Pavilion. The cinemas changed their programmes two or three times weekly, charging 6d., 9d. and 1s., and many famous stars appeared at the theatre. Rationing and shortages meant that people had the money but very little on which to spend it. If the audience was caught by air-raid warnings, impromptu music and films would continue; and if public transport was suspended, people walked home.

Although Bournemouth did not suffer the devastation of many of the major industrial towns, it did not escape bomb damage and suffering. The town was raided about fifty

112

times; 219 persons were killed, 75 premises were destroyed and others were so severely damaged that they had to be demolished. In all 2,271 bombs were dropped there.

The first air-raid took place on 3 July 1940, when a house in Cellar Farm Road, Southbourne was destroyed and 19 other properties nearby were damaged. In September 1940 there was a direct hit on the orphanage wing of the House of Bethany. Fortunately the orphanage had been closed and the children placed elsewhere, but the convent was damaged and several houses were made uninhabitable.

One of the most destructive raids occurred on 16 November 1940, when 53 people were killed and 2,321 properties were damaged after six parachute mines descended on parts of Westbourne. Christ Church, Westbourne, suffered a thousand pounds worth of damage. The Malmesbury Park area and Alma Road, Winton were badly devastated, and Alma Road elementary school was a maze of torn walls and twisted masonry. 'Skerryvore', formerly the home of Robert Louis Stevenson, was destroyed by a bomb, and a nearby house in Alum Chine Road had to be demolished. Soldiers were stationed in Skerryvore at the time, many of whom were killed, as were also about seventy people living in adjoining Robert Louis Stevenson Avenue.

On 23 May 1943 more serious damage was caused when bombs were dropped in 10 districts; the *Central* Hotel in Richmond Hill and the *Metropole* Hotel at the junction of the Holdenhurst and Christchurch Roads were both destroyed, and it is said that after the bombing of the latter an army of rats was seen wending its way up Holdenhurst Road! Beale's Departmental Store was completely burnt out after a direct hit from an H.E. bomb, followed by an explosion of its gas main. Allens (now part of Dingle's) was badly affected by the destruction of Beales when the wind blew flames in its direction. Wests Cinema (on the site of the Burlington Arcade) received a direct hit, and the Punshon Memorial Church, which was then in Richmond Hill, was extensively damaged. Many other churches, buildings, bus premises and houses were partially destroyed: there were 77 dead, and 3,481 buildings were seriously scarred.

After the raids thousands of enquiries were dealt with at the Administrative Centre in the Town Hall, including general ones, problems of ration and identity cards, billeting, war damage to property, and the removal of furniture. Many organizations were involved in giving help, including the Assistance Board, the Soldiers, Sailors and Air Force Association, the W.R.V.S., C.A.B. and others; rest centres were opened and 'Good Neighbour' and housewives' schemes operated for those who were bombed out. In the local *Echo* many letters of gratitude appeared in appreciation of the services of the police, N.F.S., Civil Defence, W.R.V.S., and others.

An interesting event took place from near the *Carlton* Hotel when a rehearsal for Normandy landings was staged in Bournemouth Bay, organized and watched by Field-Marshal Montgomery, General Eisenhower and other Allied commanders from the cliffs by the *Carlton*, where they were all then staying.

After the war Bournemouth was shabby and scarred, with widespread damage, ruined and unpainted buildings, loose scaffolding, shortage of houses for bombed families, derelict piers and the rusty remains of defence weapons on the shore and in the sea. The beach had partially disappeared; because of winds and heavy tides there was only a narrow strip of sand. The daunting task of restoring the former beauty of the town lay ahead.

113

Chapter XVII

THE GROWTH OF THE BOURNEMOUTH SYMPHONY ORCHESTRA

DURING THE 19th CENTURY Bournemouth was variously described as a 'garden city', 'paradise of pines', 'paradise for wealthy invalids' and a 'stately pleasure dome'. It was also considered to be elegant, genteel, moneyed, but stuffy and dull. That the fashionable invalid resort should emerge as a town whose musical reputation spread throughout the world is little more than miraculous.

The miracle was due to the appointment in 1893 of Dan Godfrey junior, the son of a famous and popular Victorian Grenadier Guards bandmaster. Godfrey's fights and arguments with the non-musical council over a period of 41 years are vividly described by G. Miller in his fascinating book *The Bournemouth Symphony Orchestra*. The fact that Godfrey remained in Bournemouth, facing unjust criticism and apathy, show his resolve that musical culture should be established in the new watering place. His pioneering work and determination made musical history.

From the moment Godfrey was engaged on a short-term contract of £95 per week, arguments commenced. Since there was already a small band playing on the pier, accusations of extravagance were made by some council members and residents. The claim of extravagance could hardly be justified, as under his contract Godfrey was to provide the uniforms, supply the music, and play three times daily from Whitsuntide to October both on the pier and in the Winter Gardens; out of his allowance he paid his 30 musicians from £2 5s. to £4 per week.

An admission charge of 3d. allowed the public to wander around the Gardens and listen to the band playing among a cluster of palms and pot plants. The opening night for concerts in the Winter Gardens took place on 22 May 1893, when an enthusiastic audience of 5,000 attended; how fortunate it was for posterity that the young conductor and bandmaster was unaware of the many years of struggle with the council that lay ahead.

As October (and the possible termination of the contract) approached, an event of great importance occurred. His famous father, Lieutenant Dan Godfrey, brought his Grenadier Band to Bournemouth, and the band and orchestra combined to play in a momentous performance. The enthusiasm created by this grand orchestra of nearly seventy instruments ensured Godfrey jun.'s future popularity, and as a result of the success of this concert he was able to persuade the council to renew the contract for the winter months, emphasizing the point that the wealthy visitors who came to Bournemouth in the winter expected high-class entertainment. For this period 25 double-handed musicians were allowed to play both in the Winter Gardens, and outdoors on the pier when the weather was suitable.

In 1895 Godfrey made his first move towards symphony music by announcing that classical concerts would be given each Thursday. On the pier he was seen with his band in uniform and pillbox hats playing popular band music. In the Winter Gardens he gradually introduced the music of Composers such as Beethoven and Mozart. Where possible he played new British music, and his zest and enthusiasm for performing British compositions remained with him throughout his life.

When money was required to improve the orchestra more criticisms were made, which always aroused the fighting spirit of young Godfrey. Through the press he eloquently defended both his actions and his orchestra, always stressing the importance of playing good music for residents and visitors.

In the autumn of 1895, despite a loss of £105, he managed to persuade the council to increase the orchestra to 33 players for the winter months, thus commencing the weekly symphony concerts which continued from that year except for a short period during the last World War . Despite half-empty houses he soon began playing symphony concerts twice weekly, on Mondays and Thursdays. Admission was 1s., and for an additional fee of 9d. an invalid could be wheeled in a Bath chair to a reserved place. a fee of 6d. was charged for other concerts.

Eventually, in 1896 he received a permanent appointment as Musical Director and also as General Manager of the Winter Gardens; however, the usual arguments took place. The new contract was for three years at £700 per annum, and the council was to take over the orchestra, which became the first Municipal Orchestra in the United Kingdom.

Godfrey's aim was always to increase the strength of his orchestra and encourage good music. In 1896, when he engaged Adelina Patti to sing, every seat for her recital was taken and people lined the streets for a glimpse of the world-famous singer. In January 1897 Sir August Manns, the most revered conductor in England, directed a concert of Schumann's D Minor Symphony and Schubert's C Major to a crowded audience. In a letter of praise the distinguished conductor gave credit to Godfrey for his orchestra and his musical services, artfully indicating that the orchestra needed to be strengthened by the addition of several more instruments. Godfrey, as was his wont, made the letter public, with the result that he soon received more instrumentalists.

As a concert hall the old Winter Gardens had many faults. It was broader than it was long, and its acoustics were so poor that quiet passages were often unheard and other passages were sometimes ruined by the sound of heavy rain on the glass dome; and the orchestra gallantly played seated among groups of ferns and hot-house plants. The players names for the immense glass pavilion were varied and included 'glasshouse', 'hothouse', 'greenhouse', 'conservatory', 'kitchen garden', and 'cucumber frame'.

Besides arranging symphony concerts and classical and popular music, Godfrey's many duties included staging variety shows with singers, dancers, comedians and even jugglers and ventriloquists, always with the orchestra in attendance. In between variety acts he would insert parts of a symphony, both to broaden the musical knowledge of his audience and also to allow his orchestra a small practice, as it was only allowed two hours' rehearsal time each week. To make his programmes more popular he encouraged audience participation in talent evenings for amateurs and request evenings. With the extra money thus earned he was able to engage additional musicians for special occasions, such as a Wagner concert and an outstanding performance when Edward German conducted his own music. By 1900, despite arguments about the cost of the orchestra and the choice of music and variety shows, he was able to introduce chamber music to the town.

Godfrey's advocacy of British music was an important feature of his concerts. Many famous musicians came to the Old Winter Gardens and conducted their own work, including Stanford, Coleridge-Taylor, Mackenzie, Elgar, Gustav Holst (who once cycled 110 miles from London to Bournemouth) and Hubert Parry. The latter was born in February 1848 in Bournemouth, when it was still a marine village. His mother died shortly afterwards and he was taken back to Higham Court, Gloucestershire, the family home, not returning until March 1900 when he conducted his English Symphony.

In 1910, to celebrate the anniversary of Bournemouth's first house, a great concert was staged where many British composers shared the conducting with Godfrey; and in the following year he was invited to perform a British concert at the Crystal Palace for the Festival of Empire, where he was fêted by composers and other distinguished people.

In 1911 he managed to persuade the council to create a separate military band for the pier, thus relieving his orchestra of that duty. Until the first cinema opened in 1912 Godfrey remained responsible for the administration of the Winter Gardens, the engagement of artistes and the organization of variety entertainments throughout the town. For 1s. audiences could enjoy the performances of Dan Leno, Vesta Tilley, Fay Compton, Clara Butt, Paderewski, Ellen Terry, George Robey and many more. Even Pavlova came and danced her famous Swan Lake.

Music was slowly becoming a daily part of life in Bournemouth, and anniversaries such as Burns Night, St. Andrew's Day, Trafalgar Day and others were celebrated with special programmes. Godfrey's business instincts were never dormant, and he always considered what types of programme would attract the crowds. His main aim, however, was to foster musical education and appreciation.

During World War I the growing town remained beautiful and secluded, 'a retreat for leisured classes',[1] where it was still almost possible to forget the existence of the War. Despite the fact that some members were called up, together with diminished attendance due to the dangers of blackout, the orchestra was one of the very few that continued playing. They proudly played patriotic music, British music and the music of our allies, Russia. When the Americans joined the War, the orchestra gave the first performance in England of the new Triumphal March by Glazounov, as well as playing the works of other American composers.

Unfortunately losses of over £6,000 were made during the War, and with the return of peace the financial problems of the orchestra recommenced. Although the population of Bournemouth had increased to 90,000, a new wave of apathy resulted in half-empty halls; and in an attempt to overcome this and to appease his critics, Godfrey replaced the Monday afternoon concerts with a series of lectures on the instruments of the orchestra, always with a principal player demonstrating his instrument, but attendance still remained poor.

By 1921 further losses caused the council to consider reducing the number of players. Godfrey desperately argued that the orchestra was at its minimum for symphony music: the council, undeterred, spoke of scrapping the orchestra altogether. Godfrey reluctantly agreed both to the disbandment of the military band, and also that his orchestra (which then comprised 41 players) would perform on the pier in addition to the Winter Gardens.

Supporters of the orchestra and musicians in general were horrified when they heard of the financial plight of the Municipal Orchestra, in particular Ethel Smythe, who had recently been created a Dame of the British Empire. Godfrey had played her work when other orchestras would not accept music by a woman composer, and now she showed her gratitude. If Dan Godfrey could receive a knighthood the importance of his efforts for Bournemouth would be appreciated. Through publicity efforts and her contacts with important people, including the Prime Minister, Lloyd George, a knighthood was eventually bestowed on Godfrey on his birthday, 3 June 1922, in recognition of his valuable services to British music. That night a delighted orchestra played 'For he's a jolly good fellow', while the Corporation, impressed by his popularity and elevated status, realized that they could not decimate this amazing orchestra. Praise for the work of Sir Dan Godfrey, this pioneer of British music, continued to be received from all quarters despite financial losses each year. Ecstatic reviews appeared in American papers extolling the watering place where 600 concerts were performed annually, and where prominent composers such as Sibelius, Casals, Sir Henry Wood and Elgar frequently directed their own music.

However, the Old Winter Gardens had become an anacronism in a growing modern town where department stores, cinemas and businesses had multiplied. A new pavilion was proposed, and Godfrey was happy to think that another of his ambitions – a modern concert hall with proper acoustics – was to be realized. The *Belle Vue* Hotel and Assembly Rooms were demolished to make way for the new building, a splendid edifice with bright colours everywhere, including a pale-blue vaulted ceiling embellished with golden stars; there was a modern stage, three restaurants, two bars and a ballroom. The magnificent structure was declared open by the Duke of Gloucester on 19 March 1929, and this was followed by a variety show that included a trick cyclist and comic sketches by Stanley Holloway.

To the great disappointment of Sir Dan his orchestra had only a minor role on the opening night, and again its activities were curtailed to a weekly symphony concert and a popular performance on Sundays. For the remainder of the week they played for stage shows, or in the bandstand in Pine Walk. Dwindling audiences resulted in the reduction of the orchestra to 31 members; a small military band was formed for outdoor work, which he could draw on to increase his orchestra to 44 for symphony concerts. Bitterly, Sir Dan realized that the orchestra was little more than a jobbing group.

In September 1934 he retired. His last performance took place on 30 September before a crowded audience at an emotional and sentimental concert. His last year had been a sad one, with the bitter disappointment of the Pavilion, the down-grading of the orchestra and the deaths of Elgar, Holst, Delius, all of whom were composers who had been associated with the orchestra. Over a period of 41 years Godfrey had conducted 2,000 symphony concerts, played 842 British works and brought 160 composers to Bournemouth to conduct their own music.

'The Glass House' remained deserted and was only used for occasional exhibitions and meetings. Before its demolition Sir Dan conducted the orchestra there for the last time in aid of charities for old people. The rain beat on the glass roof and most of the pot plants had gone, but the hall was crowded; the orchestra was joined by all its former members, who, as Haydn's 'Farewell' Symphony was played, each extinguished a nearby candle and left the platform. The final one was snuffed out by Sir Dan and darkness reigned. A month later the Old Winter Gardens was a shell, and an indoor bowling green was erected on its site.

1934 saw the appointment of a young man called Richard Austin as conductor. In order to increase audience attendances he re-organised the orchestra so that of the 46 players some would be available for outdoor duties and others for orchestral concerts; the word 'symphony' was no longer used, although classical music was interspersed with popular music. Performances were again increased and there were more concerts on the pier, a weekly concert in the Pavilion, morning concerts in the ballroom and a Sunday evening concert. After the start of World War II attendance was poor, and the council again discussed economies and retrenchment. The orchestra was reduced to 24 players, who were to work a shorter working week of 17 hours at a reduced salary of £4 per week. Austin promptly resigned.

Through the determination of local enthusiasts and redundant musicians, an independent body was formed which began to play symphonies in St. Peter's Hall to an audience of about four hundred on Monday lunchtimes and evenings, thus catering for war workers. The remainder of the Municipal Orchestra gave popular Sunday evening concerts under the control of Monty Birch, a long-standing member of Godfrey's orchestra. The drabness of wartime black nights, the evacuees, and the Government departments and servicemen stationed in Bournemouth meant that both concerts were well attended. Despite Bournemouth's cut-backs, it was still the only town in Britain to maintain a Municipal Orchestra at all during the War: indeed, profits were made during those years through the popularity of those two small orchestras, which were sometimes augmented by players in the Forces.

After the War a new, red-brick concert hall with a flat roof was constructed; its plain style was similar to that of the Memorial Theatre in Stratford-on-Avon, and like that theatre it had ideal acoustics. Rudolf Schwarz, an Austrian who had suffered greatly in German concentration camps, was appointed as Musical Director. Although the engagement of a foreigner was at first the subject of criticism, Schwartz soon became the idol of the people of Bournemouth and proved a great success. After the war-weary years a new audience emerged and music once more became popular. Nationwide publicity was received in 1948 when, after a memorable concert conducted by Sir Thomas Beecham before a crowded audience, the conductor praised the skill of the newly-formed orchestra. Schwarz continued Sir Dan's practice of introducing British composers, many of whom had been unknown to the Austrian when he first came to Bournemouth.

When Schwarz resigned in 1947 to become Musical Director of the Birmingham Symphony Orchestra, Charles Groves of the BBC Northern Orchestra was appointed. Due perhaps to an unfortunate strike and the fact that he was replacing an idolized conductor, Groves faced a changed musical climate. To his disappointment he found himself playing to half-empty concerts, while the council discussed the importance of the orchestra being self-supporting and not receiving subsidies from rates. Soon there were threats of closure or a reduced orchestra, and higher costs of living resulted in salary demands: losses thus continued.

In 1952 the council decided to disband the orchestra. This was a great blow to Groves, who had given up a secure post with the Northern Orchestra to come to Bournemouth. Publicity saved the day however. Fortunately, Barbirolli conducted the Hallé Orchestra at the Winter Gardens on the following night. In a speech to the crowded audience the famous conductor informed them that there would have been a revolution in Manchester if they tried to take his orchestra away from him. He added: 'You must see in the next few months that the concerts are given to full houses. By supporting the orchestra to the hilt you can show your council that you cannot do without it.'[2] Criticisms also came from Schwarz, Beecham and others, while the *News Chronicle* attacked the council for its parsimonious actions in disbanding a pioneer orchestra after 60 years. An appeal fund was set up by a newly-established Winter Gardens Society which, to its surprise, was well supported.

As a result the council reversed its decision, but the orchestra was expected to play in the Pavilion ballroom in the mornings, the bandstand in the afternoons, and to play symphony concerts in the evenings. Groves, whose energy and determination were considerable, also commenced monthly youth concerts. On Sundays he mixed classical music with light pieces, discussing them and acting as conductor and commentator at the same time. For the first time the council was agreeable to the orchestra travelling in the hope that more revenue would be earned.

Diminished audiences continued, and in 1953 one month's notice was given to the orchestra, and after 62 years of chequered history the Municipal Orchestra came to an end. Ironically, the last performance was on Easter Sunday, and the house was packed to capacity.

The Winter Gardens Society acted swiftly; meetings were held with arts councils, local authorities and supporters of the orchestra. It was proposed that a regional orchestra was established that would visit areas in the west of England, and that the Winter Gardens Society and other bodies would be responsible for costs. The council was in agreement; the organization of the orchestra was to be in the hands of a new body, the Western Orchestral Society Ltd., which changed its name from the Bournemouth Municipal Orchestra to the Bournemouth Symphony Orchestra.

After years of indifference Bournemouth residents began to take a pride in their historic orchestra and its great reputation.

In 1958 Groves received the Order of the British Empire in the Birthday Honours 'for services to British Music'. Those who knew him thought it should have also included, 'for artistic valour, boundless energy and insatiable appetite for hard work'.[3] After 10 years Groves decided to resign, but he will always be remembered as the man who saved the orchestra during its worst financial crisis.

When Silvestri was appointed in 1961 the glamour of an internationally famous Romanian conductor once more produced packed halls; the orchestra, besides playing in the west of England, also played in concerts abroad. In 1964 Schwarz and Silvestri shared the conducting of a mammoth tour throughout Europe, East Germany and Poland. The orchestra's recordings were heard worldwide, and a television debut was made in Winchester Cathedral. This dazzling era ended sadly with the death of Silvestri at the age of 55. He had loved Bournemouth, and appreciated its quiet beauty and musical traditions. He had requested that he be buried near the Winter Gardens and the sea which he loved so much, and his grave is close to that of Sir Dan Godfrey in the churchyard of St. Peter's. He left a collection of scores and tapes to the Western Orchestra Society, as well as establishing a fund for the orchestra's benefit.

Despite the petty-minded, commercial and unmusical attitude of the Bournemouth council, in the past, it should be said that financially it contributed more to music than any other town council in Britain.

Despite the appointment of further distinguished conductors such as Paavo Berglund up to 1979, and the present Principal Conductor, Uri Segal, 1980 was a year of acute financial difficulties similar to the crisis years between 1952 and 1954. An important event, however, occurred in the summer of 1980 with the formation of the Friends of the Bournemouth Orchestras, a group of music-lovers who, through special concerts and social events, are assisting greatly with fund-raising. Through their efforts, together with more public support and local authority contributions, it is to be hoped that the future of the internationally famous and historic Bournemouth Symphony Orchestra will not again be at risk.

Chapter XVIII

SIR MERTON RUSSELL-COTES AND OTHER PIONEERS OF BOURNEMOUTH

SIR MERTON RUSSELL-COTES was one of the outstanding pioneers of Bournemouth, a man of progressive ideas and a great benefactor to the adopted town that he admired so much. Today he is particulary remembered for the fine Russell-Cotes Art Gallery and Museum, previously East Cliff Hall, his former home, which, together with its many treasures, he and Lady Russell-Cotes donated to Bournemouth.

Russell-Cotes was born on 8 May 1835 in Staffordshire, and from earliest childhood he had been enamoured with pictures and beautiful *objets d'art*. His love of antiques and curios was further stimulated by the Great Exhibition of 1851.

After the death of his father he went to live in Glasgow with his sister and her husband, James McEwen, who became his guardian, and there he studied medicine. When he was 18 it was discovered that he had congestion of the lung, and on the advice of his doctor he spent a period in South America for the benefit of his health. Because of his great interest in foreign places he travelled throughout the world, usually in search of better health, and on these many journeys he was able to gratify his delight in collecting wonderful curios and paintings.

He was appointed Secretary to the Scottish Amicable Society in Dublin and also became the manager of the *Royal Hanover* Hotel, Glasgow. Recurring attacks of bronchitis resulted in his visiting resorts on the south coast, again on medical advice. One of these resorts was Bournemouth. There he met Mr. A. Briant, proprietor of the *Bath* Hotel, the first hotel built in Bournemouth. Mr. Briant wished to sell the hotel and suggested that Russell-Cotes purchased it as an investment. After consideration the latter took possession on Christmas Day 1876. One of the inducements to purchase was that he would be able to foster his love of art and his weakness for building and property development. He looked forward to the time when he could form an art gallery to house his many treasures, and also his loan collection of 250 paintings, which were borrowed by different galleries in the United Kingdom.

The Duke of Argyll happened to be staying at the hotel, and he advised Russell-Cotes to enlarge and improve the building, which he considered could become one of the most distinguished in the town. Plans to increase the size of the hotel by the addition of two new wings were prepared by Christopher Crabbe Creeke, the Town Surveyor, another progressive and active-minded resident (see chapter X). There was much unwelcome criticism, as some local people thought that the project was a rash and risky venture which was unlikely to succeed. However, the hotel, with the addition of the prefix *Royal* was re-opened on 11 August 1880 by Sir Frances Wyatt Truscott,

121

the Lord Mayor of London, who was in Bournemouth to open the new pier on the same day.

Soon the hotel was resplendent with priceless paintings by Turner, Corot, Edwin Long, Landseer and others, exquisite Chinese and Japanese curios, Dresden cabinets, old Worcester, and Sèvres china, all of which had been collected by Russell-Cotes on his many travels throughout the world. H. Furniss, on one of his numerous visits to Bournemouth, referred to the *Bath* Hotel as a 'home of luxury and a temple of art',[1] and marvelled at how the hotel, containing so many priceless treasures, could possibly pay its way. But Russell-Cotes, besides being wealthy, loved art and was happy to share his superb collection with others.

The *Royal Bath* soon boasted many famous and royal visitors, including Empress Eugenie, the Queen of Sweden, the King of Belgians, Edward VII (when he was Prince of Wales), Prince Oscar of Sweden and his bride, Paderewski, Henry Irving, Ellen Terry and many other celebrities. Disraeli actually used it as a meeting-place for Cabinet councils before the opening of Parliament in 1875. There was a special gallery for musicians, and two hotel coaches were available to transport visitors to and from Holmsley Station, which was then the nearest one to Bournemouth.

When the British Medical Association came to Bournemouth in 1890, Russell-Cotes generously contributed 200 guineas towards a guarantee fund in connection with their visit and gave a garden party in their honour; they were entertained by the Grenadier Guards under the conductorship of Lieut. Dan Godfrey senior, who also played at the visit of the Prince of Wales.

Russell-Cotes and Christopher Crabbe Creeke were elected members of the board of commissioners in 1883; both these far-sighted men had great faith in the successful development of Bournemouth and hoped that one day it would be pre-eminent as a health resort. They both realized the necessity of an Undercliff Drive as an essential amenity, for invalids would be able to take carriage drives by the sea, and a well-constructed drive would help to prevent erosion and cliff falls.

Besides frequently stressing the importance of an Undercliff Drive, Russell-Cotes considered that a pavilion close to the pier entrance was absolutely essential; he contended that unless there were more attractions to overcome the many complaints of Bournemouth's dullness, people would go to other places where these amenities were provided. Suggestions and counter-suggestions continued to be made for many years.

Russell-Cotes also spent time and energy working for a sanitary hospital. In this plan he was supported by the four or five doctors living in the town in about 1882, who considered that a hospital for infectious diseases was vital. There had already been some cases of infectious illnesses and if this news had become widespread people would have been deterred from coming to the town. Russell-Cotes obtained information and contacted the medical officers of other seaside resorts; he became the chief spokesman for the doctors as a member of the board of commissioners. But the idea of a fever hospital horrified people, and there was considerable opposition to his proposals. To his distress, he was abused, anonymous letters were sent to him and his effigy and those of other commissioners were burnt. It was suggested that the name 'sanitary hospital' might be less objectionable to residents than 'fever hospital', and this was the name eventually given to the hospital when it was built in 1885.

Due to the efforts and strain involved in urging the necessity of a hospital, Russell-Cotes became ill and on the recommendation of his doctor friends went abroad again to rest and recover his health. On his return to Bournemouth two years later the

Sanitary Hospital had been erected. (Today it is part of the considerably enlarged Royal Victoria Hospital in Gloucester Road, Boscombe for geriatric patients.)

When Bournemouth became a municipal borough in 1890 Russell-Cotes was delighted. To show his pleasure and in order to enhance the dignity of the town he and his wife presented a mace and mayoral badge, the loop consisting of 18-carat gold, richly ornamented and enamelled with the Hampshire rose. After donating them Russell-Cotes said he hoped that the motto *Pulchritudo et Salubritas*, which was engraved on the badge, would shine out in letters of gold and act as a talisman to make known the beauty and health of the most uniformly charming resort in the universe.

In 1891 he was invited to become Mayor, but as certain sections of the borough council opposed his Undercliff Drive scheme, he refused the honour. Further such invitations were refused in 1892 and 1893, but in the following year the council agreed to support his plans on the condition that he accept an appointment as a magistrate in addition to that of Mayor. Russel-Cotes described that year as the most active of his life.

To celebrate this eventful period and as a birthday present for his wife, Russell-Cotes commissioned the building of a magnificent hall on the East Cliff, facing the sea (now the Russell-Cotes Art Gallery and Museum). The hall was erected in a style which combined Italian Renaissance with Old Scottish Baronial, and besides being their home would accommodate the ever-increasing treasures he brought from Europe, Asia and the Far East.

After further delays and discussions the first section of the Undercliff Drive between Bournemouth Pier and Meyrick Road was commenced in January 1907. Tributes were showered on Russell-Cotes, who had advocated the scheme for so long. An article in the *Directory* of 9 November 1907 stated that he had preached an Undercliff Drive in season and out, and that now, due to his accomplishments, he would be more proud than ever of his beautiful Bournemouth. The *Bournemouth Observer* of 16 November 1907, expressing admiration and gratitude, states that 'probably no one has done more to enhance the prosperity of Bournemouth than Russell-Cotes'.

He showed his appreciation of this great achievement by donating his fine collection of souvenirs and *objets d'art* to his beloved town, while his wife presented their home, East Cliff Hall, as an art Gallery and museum in which to house the treasures permanently, together with a fund for their maintenance. For their generosity and unceasing work for the welfare of Bournemouth Mr. and Mrs. Russell-Cotes were made Honorary Freemen of the Borough in 1908, and in the following year a knighthood was bestowed on the worthy couple by King Edward VII.

On the occasion of their Diamond Wedding in 1920, more gifts were donated to the town. These included £8,000 in connection with a Russell-Cotes Nautical Training College at Parkstone, land, and a cheque for £3,000 for the Shaftesbury Society for Poor Children. A few years previously Lady Russell-Cotes had presented six houses to the Royal Victoria and West Hampshire Hospital and £500 to Dr. Barnardo's Home, as well as giving donations to other charitable institutions.

Lady Russell-Cotes died in April 1920, and her husband died in January the following year. Both were greatly mourned, and were buried in the Bournemouth Cemetery.

Today the Russell-Cotes Museum and Art Gallery displays a comprehensive collection of Victorian treasures in the sumptuous surroundings of an elegant home. About three-fifths of the contents came directly from Sir Merton's collection, while the remaining two-fifths have been donated since his death in 1921. Lady Russell-Cotes's drawing room, her boudoir (where she died), and other rooms retain the charming atmosphere of Victorian prosperity and reflect the couple's love of acquiring beautiful objects, which range from paintings, sculpture, ceramics, miniatures, and fine furniture to Japanese and Burmese carvings and temples.

In addition to the Russell-Cotes Museum there is the Rothesay Museum [formerly owned by Russell-Cotes]. Originally the fine Victorian house stood next to the *Royal Bath* Hotel, but early in 1971 it was demolished to provide a new car park and a flyover bridge. The new Rothesay Museum is now housed in a building on the opposite side of Bath Road. Here can be seen the Lucas Collection of early Italian paintings, pottery, porcelain, 17th-century furniture, Victorian pictures and bygones, a marine collection and prehistoric remains found in the area.

In October 1978 **Mr. Wilfred Beeching** and **Mrs. D. J. Beeching** of Manor Road, Bournemouth presented their own private collection of 260 typewriters to the council, and this now forms an additional attraction at the Rothesay Museum. The collection is the largest private one in the world and was formerly kept at Mr. Beeching's own museum in Stewart Road, Bournemouth.

Mr. Beeching had been collecting typewriters since 1946, and some of them he even found in dustbins. Included in this priceless collection are a typewriter used by Edgar Wallace and donated by his daughter, a Chinese machine, an 1873 Sholes and Glidden (the first commercially produced typewriter), a 1902 Blickensderfer (the first commercially-produced electric typewriter 'with a golf ball!'), and also a typewriter costing £1,000,000 that was produced by Lord Lascelles at his factory and was the only one of its kind made. In January 1980 the latest kind of typewriter was donated by Silver Reed International; it has an electro-mechanical keyboard that can be linked with a micro-processor, which controls the typewriting electronically.

Bournemouth is indeed grateful for the donation of this priceless collection, which was given on the condition that it would always be displayed. The town happily gave this undertaking.

John Elmes Beale (1848–1928) was a contemporary of Merton Russell-Cotes. He was actively connected with the development of Bournemouth, and was a staunch advocate of the need for an Undercliff Drive.

In 1906 J. E. Beale had the honour of becoming the first local Freeman of the Borough (he was preceded by Earl Roberts of Kandaham in 1902 on the conclusion of the South African war). Appreciation for his work on the council, particularly during his three years as Mayor and Chief Magistrate, was further shown by the presentation of a fine portrait of him in his mayoral robes, which now hangs in the Mayor's Parlour in the Town Hall. Two other paintings of Mr. and Mrs. Beale were also presented in recognition of their services, both of which are now well displayed in Beale's Stores.

John Elmes Beale was born in Weymouth on 6 December 1847. After business training in Manchester he returned to Weymouth in 1873, where he was employed as assistant to J. Russell, the draper, and worked from 8 a.m. to 9 p.m. It was during this period that he became an active member of the Wesleyan Church and a local circuit preacher in the nearby villages. In about 1881 he proposed a joint partnership to Mr. Russell, but as this did not materialize Mr. Beale looked for a new opening in the surrounding area. The place which most impressed him was the new town of Bournemouth (its population in 1881 was 16,859), which he considered had a great future. With £400 capital he purchased a small double-fronted shop, No. 3 St. Peter's Terrace (now part of Hinton Road), and even made his own fixtures and shelves. The Fancy

Fair, as it was known, sold numerous small items, such as tin buckets, wooden spades, toy boats and string bags, all of which were sold for a few pence, while some toys and tumblers imported from Germany and Japan until the outbreak of World War I only cost one penny! When shell boxes, mirrors and photo frames were added the maximum price rose to 2s. 11d., and even a complete train with rails could be purchased for 2s. 6d. From this small venture grew today's fashionable eight-storey Departmental Stores.

Five-shilling train excursions from London and Birmingham soon attracted large crowds, particularly at weekends. The popularity of the shop increased and larger premises were obtained by purchasing adjacent properties.

At about this time the first Father Christmas was introduced to parade in the shop and showrooms, and as we know he is still an important feature in stores today. Lighting was originally provided by gas 'fishtail' burners, which were replaced by electricity in 1895, and the building was heated by brass lamps containing about two quarts of paraffin. As the store-room was on the top floor, goods were passed along by means of a human chain of strong young men and women.

Mr. Beale also became a partner in a draper's and furnishing shop in Commercial Road, which was opened in 1889 by Mr. W. H. Okey, and arrangements were made whereby the sons of the two families obtained work experience in each other's shops. By 1920 Mr. Okey had sold his share in the business to the Beale family, and, as four of the Beale sons were then employed in the Company, its name was changed to Bealesons (Beale & Sons Ltd.), by which it is known today. Further extensions were made to the original Beale's, resulting in a new five-storey building in Old Christchurch Road complete with lifts and a magnificent restaurant.

The outbreak of World War I slowed down the growth of the business, as the importation of goods ceased; soon, however, new departments were developed which included stationery, ironmongery and wools. Fashions, furniture and furnishings only became a part of the modern structure after the original building was bombed in the last World War (see chapter XVI).

For many years J. Elmes Beale was also one of the church officers of the Richmond Hill United Reformed Church, and was appointed Deacon in 1896 and Treasurer in 1902. The renowned preacher Dr. J. D. Jones wrote most highly of him:

> ... by his business skill and absolute integrity he built up what has become the biggest business in the town ... his outstanding quality was that of real kindliness ... and care of the young people of the church. ... While perhaps the Church was his chief interest, Mr. Beale also took his share in civic life and for three successive years filled the office of Mayor and never had Bournemouth a Mayor and Mayoress more generous in their hospitality.[2]

In 1905 J. Bennett Beale joined his father as a deacon, and in 1937 he, too, was chosen for Mayor.

A tradition of service to the town has been established and maintained by successive members of the closely united Beale family, who since 1900 have served as mayors, magistrates and councillors. Devotion to the religious life of the town has also been maintained by members of the family, from John Elmes Beale to present-day Beales. Councillor Frank Beale, a former mayor, has been an elder of the Church for about twenty-six years, while his aunt, Mrs. Rita Beale, became one of the first lady elders.

Beale's Fashion Stores, well known throughout England, has remained an independent and mainly family-owned concern, and two of its present directors are descendants of its great founder, John Elmes Beale. This year (1981) marks 100 years of progress and growth, and celebrations include a replica bathing-machine procession followed by bathing off Bournemouth pier in Victorian costume. There are centenary sales, with the Dorchester Town Crier in attendance, a Victorian shop, tea-time piano serenades, and many other attractions. The distinguished portraits of John Elmes Beale and Mrs. Beale look down on the merry proceedings with satisfaction from their pride of place on one of the main staircases.

Bournemouth was fortunate in many of its early pioneers, some of whose descendants are still well known and respected members of the community. While it is not possible to refer to everyone connected with the history of Bournemouth, the author feels that reference should be made to the following, who have not been mentioned in previous chapters.

The name of Rebbecks, the local estate agents, is well known today. **William E. Rebbeck** of Cranborne (1803–1879) came to Bournemouth as bailiff to the Tregonwell Estate: he was, therefore, one of the earliest settlers in the little village of Bourne, and both he and his descendants were connected with the progress and development of the new town.

In 1845 he started in business as an estate agent and auctioneer, while continuing to manage the Tregonwell Estate. A triangular plot of land at the corner of Gervis Place and Old Christchurch Road was leased from Sir G. Gervis, the Lord of the Manor, for 99 years at £1 per annum, on which a one-storey building could be built. The picturesque building, with its iron railings and pretty garden, became known as 'Rebbeck's Corner', as it was occupied by successive members of the Rebbeck family. Adjoining was Bourne Villa and Gervis Villa, the latter being the home of Mr. W. E. Rebbeck. The business premises were enlarged twice before being demolished in May 1935, when Rebbecks moved to their present position in Exeter Road. (Their original site is now occupied by Lilley & Skinners.)

Interesting items concerning the management of the Tregonwell Estate are shown in an old account book dating from 1846–1884:

One week's pew rent	3s.
Paid beer at Belle Vue for shaking carpets at Mansion	3s.
Poor rate Holdenhurst parish	£7 16s. 5d.
Beer for mowing and haymaking	7s. 6d.
Paid Giles Sweetapple, molecatcher (one year)	£1 0s. 0d.
Cow at Parkstone pound	2s.
Advanced to thatcher for work on cottages at Moordown	8s. and 10s.

During the latter half of the 19th century the face of Bournemouth began to change as big estates (or parts of them) were sold for building purposes. Because Rebbecks were the only estate agents and auctioneers in Bournemouth for many years, many of these estates were handled by them, including the Moordown and Kinson estates, parts of Boscombe Manor, the Chewton Joy Estate (now Chewton Glen), Alum Chines and the Branksome Towers Estate, which was then the temporary residence of the Duke of Westminster: Lloyd George had stayed there, and many foreign ambassadors had been invited there as official guests of the Government.

After the sale of the Branksome Towers estate in 1892 Rebbecks acquired the historic entrance lodge as their Westbourne branch, which remained their office for over eighty years until it was demolished for road widening and the erection of huge office blocks in about 1974. Its demolition came as a shock to many local people, who were dismayed by the disappearance of an attractive landmark that had marked the boundary between Poole and Bournemouth, and which had once stood among acres of pine forest as part of Branksome Towers Estate.

The Rebbeck family also has a history of service to Bournemouth. Both W. E. Rebbeck, the founder of the business, and his son, E. Wise Rebbeck became chairmen as well as members of the board of commissioners, while in 1891 his son also became the second Mayor of the developing town. Colonel T. V. Rebbeck, who was the last member of the family to be associated with the firm, continued the tradition of civic service. He was a member of the council for several years and was also Mayor from 1936 to 1937; and his administrative capacity was as greatly appreciated as his sincerity and friendliness. After his death in 1942 the last family link with the firm was broken, but the name 'Rebbecks' still lives on as the well-known firm of Estate Agents.

Another old-established firm of Estate Agents in Bournemouth is Fox & Sons. The founder, **Anthony Stoddart Fox**, was born in London in 1838. He opened his first office in London in 1868, which was followed by another in Basingstoke; but these original ventures were mainly unsuccessful and he experienced periods of great poverty and hardship. It was not until the opening of the first office in Bournemouth in 1889, in part of a shop shared with a coach-builder, that he met with success. The premises were at 36 Holdenhurst Road, and by that time his sons had joined him in the business.

The business continued to improve, and in about 1892 larger premises were obtained at 4 Holdenhurst Road. After the development of the Lansdowne area the office was renumbered 15 Holdenhurst Road, and the whole of the Fox family lived over the premises. (These were closed in 1961 and the staff transferred to 44/52 Old Christchurch Road, their present offices.) The brothers were active Congregationalists, and were connected with the East Cliff and the Westbourne Congregational churches. They were serious and hard-working: monthly records of all the earnings had to be balanced to the last penny, but Sunday was observed as a day of rest whether work on the books had been completed or not.

The late 19th century was a period of road development and the gradual breaking up of many large estates. The auction side of the business increased, and the firm was soon involved in the sale of parts of several large estates, including that of Boscombe Manor to Mr. R. Sobey, parts of the Portman Estate, the estates of Earl of Leven and Melville in Talbot Woods and Winton, and the Cooper-Dean Estates at Iford and Littledown. Many of these sales took place in huge marquees erected on the site, and were preceded by a cold lunch with beer on tap.

In the 1890s the firm also specialized in letting large, furnished villas on the East Cliff to wealthy families, who stayed for two to six months at a 'high rental' of 10 guineas per week. These families arrived in their own carriages. Besides the coachmen, they brought with them a large number of domestic staff, including footmen and butlers, and also their own plate, silver and linen.

Until 1914 Bournemouth mainly catered for holiday visitors, but after World War I the building industry grew more and more important. In addition to the six or so builders who were already established, hundreds of builders' employees started on their own, buying single plots of land for about £200, and borrowing the 10% deposit. Development of the major estates continued and more roads were built.

The firm of Fox & Sons continued to grow by buying up or amalgamating with several smaller firms, including Hankinson & Sons, the second estate agents to open in the town. Today's large and respected firm has developed from very small beginnings, and has many branches throughout the south of England. Descendants of the original founder are still connected with the firm.

David Tuck, who was employed by the Gervis Estate, was probably the first builder and road-maker in the town. He built the first houses on the Gervis Estate as well as the first of the Westover Villas, and undertook building and roadwork in the area of the pier, Exeter Road, and on the East Cliff. Much of the construction work essential to the development of Bournemouth was carried out by David Tuck (who died in 1860) and his son Peter, who purchased land in the Springbourne area and was responsible for much of its development. They were assisted by their foreman, James McWilliam.

James McWilliam was related to the Tuck family by marriage, and succeeded to the Tucks' business, which became known as McWilliam & Son. After the creation of the board of commissioners in 1856 he became the first rate-collector at an annual salary of £5 for collecting the first rate of 1s. in the £, and £7 10s. for the second rate of 3s. in the £ (Mr. W. E. Rebbecks was the second collector from 1861 to 1866). In 1874 Mr. McWilliam was appointed Chairman of the Board of Commissioners, and also a councillor after Bournemouth became a borough. As his area, the Westover ward, included the poorer districts of Winton, he spent much time assisting the needy members of the community. One of the services rendered to the town by Mr. McWilliam was that of being the first captain of the volunteer fire brigade (see chapter XII).

Members of the **Mooring Aldridge** family, who originated from Christchurch and Winkton, were also connected with the early days of Bournemouth. Matthew Aldridge was mentioned in the Christchurch Award of 1805, and was buried in the churchyard of the United Reformed (then the Congregational) Church in Christchurch in 1806.

Mr. Henry Mooring Aldridge originally practised law in Poole, and opened a branch office in Commercial Road in about 1860, travelling twice weekly from Poole to his new office in Bournemouth. After purchasing a house in one of the first villas constructed in Westover Road, he built a better office at the rear of the building. Soon Mr. Haydon became a partner in the firm, which then became known as Mooring Aldridge & Haydon, its present name. The present offices in Hinton Road were built at the beginning of the 20th century.

His son, who was also called Henry Mooring Aldridge, lived in Swanage during the summer months and commuted daily from Swanage to Bournemouth by paddle steamer; the journey took about half an hour, a time which would be difficult to improve upon today by car and ferry. When no sailing could take place because of inclement weather, it was necessary to travel by train to Bournemouth via Wareham, a journey that could exceed one hour. There was no Sandbanks ferry at that time and no motor bus service. He was described by Dr. J. D. Jones, the pastor of Richmond Hill United Reformed Church, as 'a leading lawyer in the town and a Christian of the old Puritanical type'.[3]

Many of the Mooring Aldridges were actively connected with the beginnings of the Richmond Hill Church. Mr. G. Olive Aldridge, another relation, became a founder of the church, and he and Mr. M. H. Cox were appointed the first Deacons. Mr. G. O. Aldridge, who lived in Christchurch, used to ride over each Sunday in his gig.

The name Mooring Aldridge is still well known and respected in Bournemouth, quite apart from the fact that the family is connected with the town's oldest firm of Solicitors.

Robert Day (1822–1878) was Bournemouth's first photographer. His studio-hut adjoined the Scotch Church (St. Andrew's Presbyterian) at the foot of Richmond Hill. Many of his excellent photographs showing the early history of Bournemouth were purchased by Bournemouth Library (now Dorset County Library) from his son W. J. Day, who continued in the business.

Members and relations of the **McQueen** family have worshipped at St. Peter's Church for over a century. They include William John Palmer, who came to Bournemouth from Ringwood in 1864 and founded a wholesale and retail wine business that has only recently closed, and Charles W. Keep, who managed a group of shops known as Leverett, Frye & Keep. These shops were demolished in about 1913 to permit the erection of Bobby's departmental store (now Debenhams). Ian McQueen, a present member of the family, is both a well known solicitor in the town and also a writer of note. His books include *Bournemouth St. Peter's* and *Sherlock Holmes Detected*, amongst others. His wife has been a member of the local council since 1967.

The **Druitt** family, which has connections with Wimborne, London, Christchurch and Bournemouth, was originally very large, James Druitt senior having had 15 children. Among its members were solicitors, doctors and preachers, many of whom were great benefactors of both Bournemouth and Christchurch.

James Druitt senior (1816–1904) founded the well-established firm of Solicitors, J. & W. H. Druitt, Bournemouth, with which the family was connected until 1945, when its interests were sold. He held many honourable positions, including that of Town Clerk of Christchurch for many years, and was a councillor and Mayor five times between 1850 and 1896. After the appointment of the board of commissioners in Bournemouth James Druitt was their third clerk, from 1861 to 1877, when he was succeeded by his son, James Druitt junior, who held that post until 1890. When Bournemouth attained municipal borough status in 1890 James Druitt senior became its first Town Clerk; continuity of service was thus ensured, and official appreciation was shown for Mr. Druitt's services. Mr. Druitt junior also gave much service to the town, both as a councillor and as Mayor in 1914, as well as through his other valuable duties.

The family's former home was the present Christchurch Library, which was donated to the council, together with the Druitt Gardens, in about 1950.

Chapter XIX

THE SHELLEY CONNECTION

ALTHOUGH BOURNEMOUTH LACKS the background of its two distinguished neighbours, many literary and eminent people have been attracted to the district during the 170 years of its existence. Often they came in the latter part of their lives, usually in the hope of improving their health.

Of all such literary figures the Shelley family has had the longest connection. Sir Percy Florence Shelley, was the only surviving child of Percy Bysshe Shelley, the great poet, who was tragically drowned in the Gulf of Spezia in July 1822, and of Mary Wollstonecraft Shelley, the author of *Frankenstein* and other works. He was born in Florence on 12 November 1819, and succeeded to the title on the death of his grandfather, Sir Timothy Shelley, in 1844, inheriting the family estate at Field Place, Horsham, in Sussex. By that time the building had deteriorated and was damp. Neither his famous mother nor his wife, Jane (the widow of the Hon. Charles Robert St. John) found any pleasure in living there.

In 1849 Sir Percy bought land in the undeveloped area of Boscombe, hoping that the mild and balmy climate and its health-giving pines would benefit the health of both his mother and his wife. Land in Boscombe was cheap in those days, and was still separated from Bournemouth by dense pine woods and heath. The only building in that area was a small cottage known as Boscombe Cottage,[1] near Honeycombe Chine. From about 1801 it was occupied by Philip Norris and stood in 17 acres of ground. After the Inclosure Act of 1802 the estate was increased to over a hundred and fifty acres. Other occupiers included Richard Norris (1807–11), Robert Heathcote (1811–16), after whom Heathcote Road, Boscombe is named, James Dover (1819–40) and Major Stephenson, who was the last person to live there before Sir Percy moved in.

Boscombe Cottage has had many changes of name, including Boscombe Alcove[2] and Boscombe House, and when purchased by Sir Percy it was known as Boscombe Lodge. The house was considerably altered for Sir Percy by Christopher Crabbe Creeke, the first surveyor to the Bournemouth commissioners, and was renamed Boscombe Place,[3] probably after the Field Place estate. In 1873 it was further enlarged and given the more imposing title of Boscombe Manor.

Unfortunately Mary Wollstonecraft was never able to live in Boscombe. She died at her London home in Chester Square on 1 February 1851 after living for some time in a land of memories in which her beloved husband, Percy Bysshe Shelley, predominated.

Sir Percy Shelley lived at Boscombe Manor until his death in 1889, and Lady Shelley until her death 10 years later. During that time the house became famous as a centre

Fig. 10. Italianate doorway, San Remo Towers, Boscombe.

of culture, literature and drama. Sir Percy proved to be a much more stable person than his brilliant and emotional father. On his estate he lived the life of a wealthy country gentleman, and his many guests included Robert Louis Stevenson, Sir Henry Drummond Wolff, Sir Henry Irving, Sir Beerbohm Tree, old friends of Mary Shelley such as Trelawny, Leigh Hunt and Jefferson Hogg, Shelley's sisters, and others. In Boscombe Manor there was a specially-constructed theatre that seated 300 people, with a gallery and private box from which Lady Shelley could view the performance. It had a large, well-equipped stage and a drop-scene of Lerici, Italy, the last home of Percy Bysshe Shelley, which was painted by his son. Some of the plays were written by Sir Percy, and often both he and his wife performed in them; both were considered to be excellent actors. In a place of honour stood a bust of Sir Henry Irving, which was presented by the actor to Lady Shelley.

In a recess in Lady Shelley's boudoir was the Sanctum, a room which was kept sacred to the memory of Percy Bysshe and Mary Shelley. The room contained two cases of Shelley's manuscripts. Other relics included a miniature by Duc de Montpensier of Shelley holding a book of Sophocles, which, together with a book of Keats, was discovered in his coat pockets after he was drowned. In a glass case were locks of hair of dear friends such as Leigh Hunt, Byron, Edward Williams (who was drowned with

131

Shelley), Trelawny, and of Clara and 'Willmouse' (two of the children of Mary and the poet), and of Mary herself. Over the mantelpiece was a portrait of Mary Shelley; the ceiling was painted with stars under which, it is said, visiting children talked in whispers because of the many relics of the dead.

In a niche stood a life-size model of a monument by the well known sculptor Henry Weekes, which was commissioned by Sir Percy in memory of his parents. The fine original in white marble can be seen in Christchurch Priory, where it was placed after being rejected by Rev. Morden Bennett on the grounds that it could make his church a showplace.

After the death of Percy Bysshe Shelley his wife gradually created a Shelley legend by editing many of his works and letters, and removing from them and from her own journal any passages she considered unfavourable. This idealization was continued by Lady Shelley, who on the death of her mother-in-law established a cult of Shelley worshippers at Boscombe Manor. After consideration, Sir Percy and Lady Shelley decided that Thomas Jefferson Hogg, a friend of Shelley since his schooldays, would be the most suitable person to undertake a biography of the poet. When they read the first two of the four proposed volumes in 1858 they were horrified by what they considered to be a fantastic caricature of the poet, and immediately withdrew all their material from Hogg. In the following year Lady Shelley brought out her own Shelley Memorial, which contained some selected letters and biographical notes. Her deep attachment to the Shelley reputation and status caused her to destroy documents that she considered to be unsuitable for publication and unfavourable to Shelley; at the same time she acquired new material of which she approved. As a result of her researches she published four volumes in 1882 entitled *Shelley and Mary*, containing letters and documents that she considered would be of use for a history of the life of Shelley.

In 1886, 64 year after the death of the poet, an approved biography was published by Edward Dowden, a professor of English literature, which remained the standard work for many years.

In a large family vault in St. Peter's Churchyard the following members of the family are buried. **Mary Wollstonecraft Shelley**, who died in 1851, was the second wife of Percy Bysshe Shelley and the mother of Sir Percy Florence Shelley: she was the author of *Frankenstein* and other books. Her body was brought there from Chester Place, London, where she died. **William Godwin**, who died in 1836, a radical freethinker and philosopher, and the author of *Political Justice*; and **Mary Wollstonecraft Godwin**, who died in 1797, the author of *Vindication of the Rights of Women*, were also buried there. Originally William and Mary Godwin, the parents of Mary Wollstonecraft Shelley, were buried in St. Pancras Cemetery. After a Bill passed in Parliament authorizing the building of a railway through the churchyard, their bodies were brought to Bournemouth to be laid beside their daughter. **Sir Percy Shelley** (d. 1889) and **Lady Jane Shelley** (d. 1899) also rest in the family vault.

The heart of Percy Bysshe Shelley, snatched from the burning funeral pyre in Italy by Trelawny, was carefully kept at Boscombe Manor until the death of Sir Percy, when it is said to have been buried with him in the literary shrine in St. Peter's Churchyard.

After Lady Shelley's death in 1899 Boscombe Manor was inherited by the fifth Baron Abinger, a descendant of the Shelley family. Since then it has been owned by various people, and in 1937 it was purchased by Bournemouth Corporation for £37,000. During World War II it became an A.R.P. centre, after which it was used first by the business students of Bournemouth College of Technology, and latterly by the Department of Foundation Studies of the Bournemouth and Poole College of Art. Its present name is Shelley Park.

It seems fitting that when the Casa Magni Museum at San Terenzo, Lerici, had to be sold for financial reasons in 1979, the collected works were donated to the Russell-Cotes Museum in Bournemouth by Miss Margaret Brown, M.B.E., the former curator of the Lerici Museum. The new Casa Magni Shelley Museum is housed at Shelley Park, the home of the poet's son for 40 years. Here students and admirers of the works of Shelley and other romantic poets can come and browse in the reference library. Among the momentos are portraits of Shelley, Mary and their friends, Byron, Trelawny, Leigh Hunt, Jane and Edward Williams. There are models of Byron's magnificent boat, the *Bolivar*, and Shelley's smaller one, the *Ariel*, as well as sketches by Shelley, Mary, and Edward Williams, and many pictures and prints of the period.

Chapter XX

OTHER FAMOUS PEOPLE

SIR HENRY TAYLOR, who had been knighted for his outstanding work in the Colonial Office, came to Bournemouth in 1861 in the latter part of his life. He was by that time famous for his historical drama *Philip van Antevalde*, which was published in 1834, and his many literary and political friends included Wordsworth, Southey, Tennyson, Carlyle, Gladstone and Melbourne. At his home, 'The Roost', in Hinton Road (then a residential area), he welcomed many distinguished visitors, the most popular being Sir Percy and Lady Shelley, Mr. and Mrs. Robert Louis Stevenson, and Lady Taylor's cousin, Aubrey de Vere, an Irish poet.

He lived in Bournemouth for 25 years until his death on 27 March 1886. Like so many others at that time he was charmed by its delightful and unspoilt surroundings, and was soon writing that he considered Bournemouth to be 'the most beautiful beyond any sea-side place I have seen except the Riviera'.

Sir Henry was a strong supporter of the Tractarian movement. The eldest of his three daughters became the wife of Rev. C. Seymour Towle, who was vicar of St. Clements, Springbourne, from 1892 to 1908. The three daughters were all writers of repute, the youngest of whom, Una Taylor, gave a vivid account of life in Bournemouth in her book *Guests and Memories* (1925).

Charles Darwin's association with Bournemouth was a short one. On 31 August 1862 he rented a house there as one of his boys had scarlet fever. Unfortunately, on the journey Mrs. Darwin also caught the disease, and it became necessary to take two houses.

Darwin stayed at Cliff Cottage, an attractive thatched cottage built in 1810, but he found the inactivity there frustrating. Plaintively he wrote to his friend John Lubbock (Lord Avebury), 'I do nothing except look at a few flowers, and there are very few here, for the country is wonderfully barren'.[1] Later he wrote to his botanist friend, J. D. Hooker; 'This is nice but barren country and I can find nothing to look at. Even the brooks and ponds produce nothing. The country is like Patagonia. My wife is almost well thank God and soon home.'[2] Darwin was more than delighted when he and his family were able to return to Down House in Downe, Kent, at the end of September.

When he came to Bournemouth he was already famous, his great masterpiece *The Origin of the Species*, which revolutionized world thought and was the subject of many conflicting and heated views, having been published in 1859.

Until this year the site has been occupied by the *Regent Palace* Hotel, which is now demolished, along with other hotels, to make way for the controversial West Cliff Conference Centre.

Paul Verlaine, who was born in Metz, France, in 1844, enjoyed one of the few happy periods of his troubled life when he was in Bournemouth. Described as a genius by many writers, most of his life was ruined by alcoholism and dissipation.

Verlaine came to England in 1876 after serving a prison sentence in Belgium for wounding his former friend of bad influence, Rimbaud, with a revolver. As he was an unknown poet at that time, very few people were aware that he had recently left prison, so it was not necessary to change his name. He first taught for a short time at Stickney Grammar School in Lincolnshire as a French master, and then came to Bournemouth in June of the same year. He was appointed as tutor to Rev. Frederick Remington's small private school, 'St. Aloysius', which later became a part of the *Sandbourne* Hotel in Poole Road. In March 1877 the school moved to another, larger house, which was given the same name, but which was later renamed Villa Remington. (Today it is a block of flats known as 'Queenswood' at the corner of Queen and Surrey Roads.)

Verlaine stayed in Bournemouth until September 1877, and here he led a more peaceful existence, finding comfort through attendance at the newly-consecrated Oratory of the Sacred Heart at Richmond Hill. During his short stay he wrote two poems about Bournemouth in which he describes its calm and beauty. One is called 'La mer de Bournemouth', commencing 'La mer est plus belle', and the other is called 'Bournemouth' and begins 'Le long bois de sapins'. In translation the first verse of this reads:

> The long fir wood winds down to the shore,
>   The narrow wood of firs, laurels and pines,
> With the town around disguised as a village;
>   Chalets red here and there among the leafage
> And white villas of the watering-place.

On leaving Bournemouth he returned to Paris, where he succumbed to a life of debauchery again and where he died in poverty in 1896.

Emilie Charlotte le Breton, born in Jersey in October 1853, became one of London's most celebrated society ladies under her married name of Lillie Langtry.

Her Bournemouth connection commenced shortly after her phenomenal popularity and acceptance as a 'professional beauty', mainly as a result of sketches and reproductions made of her by the artist Frank Miles, when her exquisite features and amazing beauty reached a wider public. The celebrated portrait by Millais gave her the name of 'the Jersey Lily'.

Because of the continuing publicity and increasing adulation from the crowd the interest of the Prince of Wales (later Edward VII) was aroused. At his suggestion a meeting was arranged, with the well known consequences. Lillie became the first of his many mistresses to be accepted in public, and was even received at Court by Queen Victoria.

In order to meet in peace away from the ever-watchful eyes of crowded London, the Prince arranged for a personal retreat to be built in the newly-developed watering place of Bournemouth, in secluded grounds among tall pine trees and facing the sea which Lillie loved so much. The large, red-brick, red-tiled house, the upper part of which was in Tudor style with black beams, was called The Red House.

Lillie loved her new home, which had been built entirely to her requirements. Like her royal lover she had a great disregard for convention, and on the minstrels' gallery was carved the legend 'THEY SAY, WHAT SAY THEY? LET THEM SAY': on a beam in the palatial entrance hall is the hospitable greeting, 'AND YOURS TOO, MY FRIENDS'. On an outside wall near Edward's bedroom the words 'STET FORTUNA DOMUS' – 'may fortune attend those who dwell here' – were inscribed, and on an exterior wall near Lillie's suite, 'DULCE DOMUM' – 'a sweet home'. A foundation stone dated 1877 and bearing the initials E.L.L. was engraved on the east side of the building.

In the magnificent dining-room one senses the presence of royalty, frivolity and happiness. High up in a corner near the minstrels' gallery is a small hatch leading through to the first floor, through which Edward could inspect the guests before descending the staircase to dine. Hanging above the finely-carved mantelpiece of light oak, which also bears the initials E.L.L., is an original painting of Edward with his faithful hunting-dog by Heywood Hardy.

The Red House has been a hotel for about thirty years, being known firstly as the *Manor Heath* Hotel and today as the *Langtry Manor* Hotel. Edward's room, which has long since been divided into three small bedrooms, is in the process of being restored to its original state. Above a low false ceiling was revealed an original oak-beamed one. Also uncovered were the original ornately-carved wooden fireplace with mullion windows, inglenooks, and blue and gold tiles depicting Shakespearean scenes, which were chosen by Lillie for the room.

A feature of Lillie's room are the extremely wide doorways, specially designed to give ample space for the fashionable dresses worn then. With her diamond ring she scratched on a downstairs window the famous 'E.L.L.' and two hearts pierced by an arrow, together with the word 'Dora', Edward's pet name for her, and the date 1883.

It is thought that Lillie spent at least four years in Bournemouth, where she later built an adjoining house, known as 'Langtry House', for her mother. (This building has now been converted into flats.) Lillie (then Lady de Bathe) died at Villa de Lys in Monaco in February 1929 at the age of 72, still beautiful and a celebrity.

The story of Edward VII and Lillie has its place among royal love affairs of the past, while the *Langtry Manor* Hotel will remain for future generations of visitors as one of Bournemouth's listed buildings, worthy of historic preservation.

Robert Louis Stevenson, one of the great writers of the 19th century, was born in Edinburgh in 1850. He came to Bournemouth after many years abroad, in search of improved health and the alleviation of his tuberculosis.

Before settling in 1885 at 'Skerryvore' in Alum Chine Road, the family stayed at numerous places. These included the 'Iffley' Boarding House in West Cliff Road, the 'Firs' Boarding House in West Cliff Gardens, the 'Wensleydale', and 'Bonallie Towers', which was situated among the pine trees in Branksome Park.

Skerryvore, which had been given to Mrs. Stevenson by her father-in-law, was originally known as 'Sea View', but it was renamed by Stevenson to honour his father and the family firm, which had constructed the Skerryvore lighthouse off the Argyll coast. The attractive ivy-covered house, with its blue slate roof, adjoined Alum Chines and was surrounded by a mass of laurel bushes, gorse and rhododendrons.

Despite his illness Stevenson was happy in Bournemouth, and its wild heath and dark, thick pinewoods reminded him of his native Scotland. At Skerryvore he lived 'like a weevil in a biscuit': he welcomed a few special friends and limited his outside visits mainly to Boscombe Manor, the home of Sir Percy and Lady Shelley, and The Roost, Hinton Road, the home of Sir Henry Taylor.

In an article in the New York *Critic* of November 1887 William Archer refers to Bournemouth as a colony of health-hunters and the home of British invalidism and philistinism, but Skerryvore in its secluded position he finds most picturesque. With enthusiasm he vividly describes some of the main rooms. 'In the dining room, or Blue Room, are fine pieces of Sheraton furniture. Over the fireplace hangs an engraving of Turner's Bell Rock Lighthouse, built by Stevenson's grandfather. Among the many paintings are those of Shelley, Mary Shelley, photos of Sir Sidney Colvin, Keeper of Prints at the British Museum and of the late Sir Henry Taylor.' (Sir Henry Taylor died in 1886, two years after Stevenson's arrival.) Archer describes Stevenson as a fine, sensitive person with a pallid complexion who talked eagerly with a faint Scottish accent; his stooping shoulders indicated his continual suffering, which did not, however, diminish his indomitable spirit.[3]

Despite ill health, Stevenson's three years in Bournemouth were most fruitful. During that period he wrote several of his best known works, including *A Child's Garden of Verse* (1885), *More Arabian Nights* (1886), *The Strange Case of Dr. Jekyll and Mr. Hyde* (1866) and *Merry Men and Underwoods* (1867), which contains two poems about Skerryvore. *Dr. Jekyll and Mr. Hyde* was an immediate best-seller, and further enhanced his already well-established reputation. Within six months 40,000 copies were sold. It is thought that the bizarre plot originated from Stevenson's thoughts about the duality of man's nature, which probably resulted from a period of rebellion against the views of his stern presbyterian parents, some of which he considered hypocritical. He was also said to have been influenced by the life of William Brody in the 18th century, who was a respected councillor and business man during the day and a criminal at night.

On 21 August 1887 he left England for the last time for America, where he stayed in winter quarters for consumptives near the shores of Saranac Lake until April 1888. In that year, still searching for relief for his worsening condition, he settled in Samoa in the South Seas where he died suddenly in 1894 from a rupture of a blood vessel in the brain.

On his grave was inscribed his own epitaph:

> Here he lies where he longed to be;
> Home is the sailor, home from the sea,
> And the hunter home from the hill.

Unfortunately Skerryvore was almost destroyed by bomb damage in November 1940 and was demolished the following year, despite appeals for its restoration as a historic building.

Not far from Robert Louis Stevenson Avenue, Westbourne are the quiet, secluded memorial gardens, also named in memory of the famous writer. A small stone lighthouse stands in the centre of the gardens, in front of which is a plaque explaining that the model is a copy of the 'Skerryvore' lighthouse built by the Stevenson firm on the Argyll coast.

The brilliant artist **Aubrey Beardsley** came to Bournemouth in 1896 for health reasons. He lived first at Pier View, Boscombe, and then at a house called Muriel in Exeter Road, from where he was received into the Catholic Church on 31 March 1897. Beardsley's individualistic style of Art Nouveau often bordered on the fantastic. He was art editor of *The Yellow Book*, and also illustrated Oscar Wilde's *Salomé*, as well as *The Rape of the Lock*.

137

He left Bournemouth in April 1897 and died of tuberculosis in Mentone, France, on 16 March 1898.

Guglielmo Marconi was born in Bologna, Italy, on 25 April 1874, and came to England after his experiments with electro-magnetic waves and a system of wireless communication had been rejected by the Ministry of Posts and Telegraphy in Rome.

Following successful demonstrations in London and on Salisbury Plain he established the world's first permanent wireless station at Alum Bay on the Isle of Wight in November 1897 (this was dismantled in June 1900). A second radio station was established in February 1898 at the *Madeira* Hotel, Southcliff Road, Bournemouth, which is now part of the Court Royal Convalescent Home for Miners. After a disagreement with the manager he moved his equipment to a house nearby called Sandhills. A 125 ft.-mast was erected from which experiments were carried out on small vessels cruising between the Needles near the Isle of Wight and the mainland.

On 3 June 1898 Lord Kelvin, a famous scientist, had the privilege of sending the first paid radiogram, as he insisted on paying one shilling for each greeting he sent from the Isle of Wight to his friends at the receiving station in Bournemouth. During that year also wireless was used between Osborne House and the Royal Yacht Squadron at Cowes, so that Queen Victoria, who was then nearly 80, could receive bulletins on the progress of the Prince of Wales (later Edward VII), who was on the Royal Yacht convalescing after a fall.

In September Marconi moved to Sandbanks, Poole, where he stayed at the *Haven* coaching inn. (Since 1926 the building has been rebuilt and enlarged to become the present *Haven* Hotel). There he erected transmitting and receiving apparatus and a laboratory and workshop, including a 100 ft.-mast which, to the amazement of people in the area, emitted crackling sparks. Those staying in the hotel often had the pleasure of hearing Marconi playing the piano, accompanied by his brother, Alfonso. One of Marconi's accounts for 1901 in the possession of the hotel shows that four days' board cost him 10s. 6d.

An inscription on a plaque in one of the main lounges reads:

In this room which may truly be called the cradle of wireless
GUGLIELMO MARCONI
during the years from 1898 until 1926 conducted some of his most important experiments in wireless, telephony, telegraphy and laid the secure foundation of a science of inestimable value to humanity.

His practical experiments led to the formation of the Marconi Wireless Telegraphy and Signal Co. Ltd. in July 1897, which has today developed in to the huge firm GEC – Marconi Electronics Ltd. For his successful work in wireless communication the name of Marconi became celebrated and famous throughout the world. He was received at Buckingham Palace and awarded K.C.V.O. by George V, he became a member of the Italian Senate in Rome, and was awarded the Albert Medal of the R.S.A.

After a series of heart attacks he died in Rome on 20 July 1937 at the age of 63. Through wireless communication news of his death was heard all over the world. Stations which had been alive with news and music closed down for two minutes as a token of respect, when the ether became silent as in the days prior to Marconi's inventions.

Probably as a result of the work of Marconi in Bournemouth and Poole, great interest has always been shown in wireless in the area. In 1922 a Bournemouth School of

Wireless was opened in Albert Road to train wireless operators. It was later transferred to 20 Lansdowne Road, now the site of Lansdowne post office.

In the following year a Bournemouth broadcasting station was opened at 72 Holdenhurst Road, above a bicycle shop. The new medium with its range of 25 miles was the beginning of radio mania. The *Echo* of September 1922 stressed the influence of the wireless on the countryside, 'reducing distance to a minimum and bringing the voice of the city to isolated places'. An advertisement by Beale's department stores praised the new source of pleasure, which could be enjoyed by the fireside: 'no need to turn out on cold winter evenings, no seats may be booked or cabs need be called'. Bright's department stores advised people to buy quickly to avoid the inevitable rush for 'the exciting moment when for the first time in the history of our town you will hear coming across space the magic words – *Bournemouth calling*'. Wireless sets were advertised at prices ranging from 7s. 6d. to 150 guineas.

On the opening night there was great excitement. Two hundred and fifty guests were invited to Beale's roof-top restaurant to hear a Marconiphone wireless demonstration. Bright's toured the town with a set on the back of a lorry, and those without sets were able to hear broadcasts from loudspeakers attached to lamp-posts in the town. The atmosphere was electric when Mr. A. R. Burrows, Programme Director of the BBC, announced: 'This is Bournemouth. Hello everyone! 6BM, the Bournemouth Station, sends hearty greetings to the world. We hope you can smell the pines . . .'. Amusing incidents occurred in Holdenhurst Road, as microphones and pianos sometimes had to be moved to another part of the room, during which time listeners were requested to wait for a few minutes!

As more advanced regional broadcasting centres developed with better transmission many of the local stations became redundant, and by the 1930s 6BM mainly dealt with local news and sport. In 1939 a new, powerful transmitter came into service at Start Point in Devon, and proved adequate to cover the Bournemouth area.

Regional stations came under review in 1962 with the Pilkington Report, and, much to the disappointment of Bournemouth, Southampton was chosen as the site for a local radio station. Radio Solent opened on the last day of 1969 and, with the help of a satellite transmitter in Grafton Road in Bournemouth, that area was supplied with radio programmes. In 1980 the local transmitter was moved from its old home to the Fern Barrow, Talbot Heath site, with a resulting increase in power; but in the same year local independent radio returned to Bournemouth in the form of Two Counties Radio. It is the only major radio station in Britain to have its own call sign, 2CR. Its studio is in Southcote Road, about four hundred yards from the spot where radio began in Holdenhurst Road in 1923. (The original site is now the forecourt of Abbey Life Assurance Company.)

D. H. Lawrence's short association with Bournemouth was also due to poor health. Mainly as the result of the death of his beloved mother from cancer, coupled with his frustration concerning the publication of his novel *The Trespasser* (originally *The Saga of Siegfried*), and his estrangement from his childhood sweetheart, Jessie Chambers, Lawrence had a serious breakdown followed by tubercular pneumonia which affected both lungs. He was close to death and at that time had little will to live.

On the advice of his doctor he came to Bournemouth on 6 January 1912 for a month's recuperation. He was further instructed to give up his work as a teacher and live an outdoor life. Instead of being depressed by the thought of losing his only reliable source of income, he was greatly relieved that he would not have to face a class again.

Many of his ideas were unconventional and rebellious, and he viewed his proposed convalescence in Bournemouth with mixed feelings.

Lawrence, like other literate Victorians, was a prolific letter-writer. On 3 January 1912 he wrote to Edward Garnett, 'I am actually going to Bournemouth on Saturday, to Compton House, St. Peter's Road, Bournemouth – a Boarding House, God help us'.[4]

Some of his other letters reveal varying and conflicting opinions about the town. On 7 January he wrote to Garnett;

> I don't like it very much. It's a sort of go-as-you-please boarding house where I shall be far more alone than if I had gone into apartments as I wanted to . . . one is always churlish after an illness. When I am better tempered I shall like the old maids and the philistine men and the very proper and proprietous maidens right enough. It is always raining – so stupid of it.[5]

A few days later he wrote; 'We have had three beautiful days – most lovely. I am very sensitive to the exquisite atmospheres of down here. I am sure I make good strides. But at the bottom I am rather miserable . . .'. On 21 January we read; '. . . I am pretty well . . . The weather is soft and inclined to fog . . . Here I get mixed up in people's lives – it is very interesting, sometimes a bit painful, often jolly. But I run to such close intimacy with folks, it's complicating, but I love to have matters in a bit of a tangle.'[6]

In letters to Louie Burrows, to whom he was engaged for 15 months before his elopement and marriage with Frieda Weekley, he described life in the boarding house, commenting on the four large meals served daily, continuing;

> It is really rather jolly. You must come sometime. I get such a lot better – the air suits me. The weather is wet, but it is not cold. The town is very pretty. When you look at it it's quite dark green with trees. There is a great bay and long smashing waves always close to the prom because there are four tides a day. I don't flirt with the girls – there are some very pretty ones – only with the old, old maids and I do about two hours work a day. (8 January 1912.)[7]

To Jessie Chambers he wrote; 'I advise you never to come here for a holiday . . . It's like a huge hospital! At every turn you come across invalids being pushed or pulled along . . . I shall be glad when I get away'.

Owing to criticisms of *The Trespasser* Lawrence had begun to rewrite the book before he left for Bournemouth, and while there he continued to improve it; by 29 January he had rewritten over three hundred pages.

Gerald Durrell, the conservationist and popular writer of amusing animal stories, was born in Jamshedpur, India, in 1925. His love of animals seems to have been inherent, and according to his mother the first word he spoke clearly was 'zoo'. After leaving India the family spent some time in Bournemouth, but the damp, wintery weather caused them to move to the island of Corfu when Gerald was about eight years old. There he lived a carefree life among the animals, insects, birds and wildlife which he loved so much, but when war seemed imminent the family was advised to leave the island and return to England.

To further his ambition of owning his own zoo Durrell became assistant keeper at Whipsnade in 1945, after which he made several animal-collecting expeditions abroad. By 1948 he had acquired various animals, including monkeys, chimpanzees and several species of birds, all of which he kept in his sister's garden in Bournemouth.

Bournemouth seemed an ideal place in which to start a special zoo where conservation, scientific research and the breeding of animals would be the main concerns. As he already possessed the animals there would be no cost to the council, and a zoo could be a welcome amenity for both residents and its many holiday visitors. Bournemouth council, however, flatly refused permission to start a zoo. Durrell's attempts to start his project in Bournemouth (and later in Poole) lasted for a year and were met 'with stubborn refusal and myopic indifference'.[8]

As Christmas was approaching, it was suggested that he offered his animals to some of the large stores as part of the Christmas festivities. The idea was accepted by J. J. Allens (now Dingle's), which put part of its basement at his disposal. Durrell was happy to be able to move his animals from the cold, damp winter weather to the warmth of the store, where there was a constant temperature. An amusing incident occurred when Georgina, a baboon, escaped one Sunday, climbed into a window and created havoc among the bedroom furniture displayed there, gaily jumping up and down on a bed to the amazement of shocked churchgoers. With difficulty and the assistance of the local police she was finally trapped. When the collection was removed from Allens he was allowed to house the animals temporarily at Paignton Zoo while he continued to look for a site.

As is now well known, the zoo was eventually established in Jersey after a fortunate introduction to Major Fraser of Les Augres Manor, Jersey, who, fortunately for Durrell, was finding the upkeep of his large house too expensive and was prepared to rent and later sell it. As Durrell stated, 'in three days I had accomplished what I had been unable to achieve in over a year of fighting with a fumbling bureaucracy in England'.[9]

Several writers came to Bournemouth in the early part of their lives and took away with them recollections of a sunny, pine-clad coastal resort.

John Galsworthy (1867–1933) attended Saugeen Preparatory School for Boys at 30 Derby Road (now a modern house) for five years from the age of 9. The school was close to St. Swithun's Church, and Galsworthy and some of the other boys used to sing in the choir. As the boy's home was in Surrey his father's clerk, Joseph Ramsden, used to bring him to and from school; in 1921 Ramsden re-appeared in literary form as a clerk called Thomas Gradman in Galsworthy's novel *To Let*, one of the books in *The Forsythe Saga*.

The poet and playwright **James Elroy Flecker** (1884–1915) was inspired to write the mournful and descriptive poem 'Brumana' when on holiday in Bournemouth from his school at Uppingham in Leicestershire:

> . . . And – dark militia of the southern shore,
> Old fragrant friends – preserve me the last lines
> Of that long saga which you sang me, pines,
> When, lonely boy, beneath the chosen tree
> I listened, with my eyes upon the sea . . .

After consular service in Constantinople, Beirut and elsewhere he died of consumption in Switzerland in 1915.

A plaque on a house called Grantchester Dene, No. 12 Littledown Road (now used as holiday flats) reads 'Here Rupert Brooke, 1888–1915, Discovered Poetry'.

Rupert Brooke was 9 when he first came to Bournemouth to visit his grandfather and two maiden aunts, Fanny and Lizzie: after that he came several times. During World War I he became a frequent visitor as he was stationed for a time at Blandford. Often he was able to attend Holy Trinity Church, Old Christchurch Road, and he did so for the last time shortly before Christmas in 1914. To a friend he wrote, 'but now, alas! I shall expire vulgarly at Bournemouth and they will bury me on the shore near the bandstand', and 'I have been in this quiet place of invalids and gentlemanly sunsets for about 100 years, ever since yesterday week'. In 1915 he was sent out to the Mediterranean, where he contracted a fatal illness. He was buried at Scyros on 23 April 1915.

Many political figures and statesmen have been associated with Bournemouth, some of whom have already been referred to.

Benjamin Disraeli, the brilliant politician and novelist, stayed at the *Royal Bath* Hotel from November 1874 until January 1875 on the recommendation of Queen Victoria, who considered that Bournemouth's salubrious air would improve the gout which prevented him from presiding at Cabinet meetings. When he left he felt much better.

In February 1898 **William Ewart Gladstone**, that great liberal statesman of outstanding ability who was four times Prime Minister, came to Bournemouth when he was elderly and in poor health and stayed for one month at Forest House, an Elizabethan-style house in Grove Road on the East Cliff. It had been his intention to stay for longer, but his sufferings increased, and when a specialist was called in he diagnosed that his illness was fatal. A few weeks before his death in 1898 he took his last Communion at St. Peter's Church (see chapter V).

He received the news of his impending death with calmness and serenity, but as he wished to die at his home in Hawarden among his own family he decided to leave Bournemouth. A sad crowd assembled outside the station to await his departure. As one person called out 'God bless you, sir' he responded, 'God bless you all, and this place and the land we love'.[10] This benediction was his last public utterance. He died at Hawarden in May 1898.

Earl Cairns, a lawyer and statesman, was for many years Lord Chancellor. During this period he lived at 'Lindisfarne' in Gervis Road, a large Victorian house of terracotta and buff brick, which was built for him in 1873. His former home, which is a listed building, is today a block of flats known as 'Earls Court', No. 9, Gervis Road: a fine original carved staircase, Gothic-style windows and other features still remain. While Cairns was Chancellor, Disraeli came to Bournemouth for health reasons, and because he was a frequent visitor to the house it is sometimes wrongly referred to as 'Disraeli House'.

Cairns died in Bournemouth on 2 April 1885 and was buried in Bournemouth Cemetery, at Rush Corner (now known as Cemetery Junction). The Cairns' Memorial Hall was unfortunately destroyed by bombs during the last World War.

In 1910, as part of Bournemouth's centenary celebrations, the first international aviation meeting was held. Prizes were awarded for weight-lifting, attaining the greatest altitude, alighting and other events. The joyous occasion was marred by the tragic death of the **Hon. Charles S. Rolls**, co-founder of Rolls-Royce, a motor-car and balloon enthusiast and a skilled aviator. When the accident occurred he was flying a Short-Wright biplane and attempting to land on a marked spot. To the horror of the spectators there was a sudden snap, parts of the tail plane broke away, and the machine hurtled down with a thud and turned over on the ground. Although Rolls was thrown clear, he died shortly afterwards of brain concussion.

In 1978 a plaque was unveiled on the spot where he crashed, at the end of the playing field of St. Peter's School, Southbourne, which had been prepared as an aerodrome for the special display. On the circular plaque of Purbeck stone is a carving of the biplane in which he was killed and the words 'This stone commemorates the Hon. Charles Stewart Rolls who was killed in a flying accident near this spot on the

12th July 1910, the first Britain to die in a powered flight'. Nearby Rolls Drive also commemorates his memory.

On 8 September 1979 another plaque was unveiled in the Lower Gardens in memory of **Freddie Mills**, who was born in Bournemouth at 7, Terrace Road, and became the World light-heavy-weight Boxing Champion in 1947. He died in 1965 aged 46. The fine marble memorial was designed by Mr. Rabin, a former boxer, who is also a distinguished local artist and art teacher.

The renown of **John Reuel Tolkien**, Professor of Anglo-Saxon and English Literature at Oxford University, derived from his interest in inventing new words and languages. He achieved fame after the publication of *The Hobbit*, with its well-known opening line, 'In a hole in the ground there lived a Hobbit', and his other best-seller, *The Lord of the Rings*.

His association with Bournemouth commenced through his wife, who enjoyed many happy holidays at the *Miramar* Hotel on the East Cliff during the 1950s and '60s. There her health and spirits improved; she made many friends who treated her with the respect due to the wife of a distinguished author, and with whom she often found it easier to talk than with the wives of Oxford dons.

After Tolkien retired, the couple decided to live in Bournemouth permanently. In 1968, when he was 76 and she was 79, they bought a modern bungalow at 19, Lakeside Road, Branksome Park, close to Branksome Chine and the sea. Although Tolkien missed the stimulating academic atmosphere of Oxford, they found new friends, in particular the local doctor and his wife, and acquaintances also resulted from their attendance at the Catholic church. They still paid frequent visits to the *Miramar* Hotel and used it for entertaining their guests.

It was a shock to Tolkien when his wife died in 1971. After her death he returned to Oxford, where he became resident Honorary Fellow and received many other honours. He died in Bournemouth on September 1973, aged 81, during a visit to his friends Dr. and Mrs. Tolhurst. While in Bournemouth he continued to work on the *Silmarillion*, which he had commenced when he was 25, but which he had found difficult to link with the *Rings* trilogy. It was unfinished when he died and was completed by his son, Christopher.

Leslie Ward, a well known local artist and engraver, was born in Worcester, but he lived and worked in Bournemouth for the greater part of his life. In 1895 he was awarded an art scholarship at the former Drummond Road Art School, followed by a staff appointment as Art Master. In 1913 he moved into the new Art Department of the College of Technology at the Lansdowne, where he stayed until his retirement in the 1950s. He became a member of the Royal Society of Painter-Etchers, and exhibited both at the Royal Academy and in America. Shortly after the conclusion of a most successful art exhibition held at the Russell-Cotes Art Gallery and Museum in 1978, he died at the age of 90.

His work has been reproduced in many books on etching and engraving, while many local artists of today owe their early training to Leslie Ward's skilful and devoted instruction.

So many famous people have been associated with Bournemouth during its short history that it is difficult to name them all.

Past residents also include Sydney Horley, P. C. Wren, John Creasey, Bill Cotton (the band leader), Mantovani and others. Among today's residents are Max Bygraves, Jimmy Saville, Tony Blackburn, Anita Harris, Roy Castle and John Piper. Virginia

Wade lived in Bournemouth as a young girl when her father was vicar of Holy Trinity Church: and Robin Cousins' skating career undoubtedly owes much to a visit he made to the Westover Road Ice-Skating Rink while on holiday when he was seven years old!

Finally, one of Bournemouth's most colourful personalities is Ken Baily, in his grey suit and topper, both of which are decorated with the colours of the Union Jack. He is always to be seen at civic, social and holiday events. Bournemouth is proud of Ken, who has become internationally known for his devotion to English football teams, travelling with them as a cheer-leader to all parts of the world.

Chapter XXI

THE TOLSTOY COLONY

FEW TRACES REMAIN TODAY of Bournemouth's Russian connection at the turn of this century. From 1897 a settlement was formed in the little village of Tuckton consisting of a number of Russian exiles who had fled from Czarist oppression.

The colony was headed by Vladimir Tchertkoff, formerly a great favourite in the Imperial Russian Court, a man of considerable wealth, an intellectual and a close friend of Leo Tolstoy, the novelist and reformer. After participating for some time in the life of excesses and dissipation of the Court, Tchertkoff decided to quit his aristocratic mode of living and devote his time and energy to alleviating the squalor and ignorance of the downtrodden peasants.

For his outspoken views, which had been influenced by those of Tolstoy, he was given the choice of exile or police supervision in a small Baltic town; and, together with about thirty other intellectuals, he decided to come to England. The group of exciles bought an old house with 20 bedrooms in Saxonbury Road at Tuckton and an old water-works in Iford Lane, Tuckton. The latter consisted of a pumping station, an 80 ft.-high chimney, outbuildings and a house, which had been erected in 1875 by the Bournemouth Gas & Water Company to pump water from the River Stour to the Southbourne water-tower. The venture had proved unsuccessful owing to quantities of silt and sand in the water, and by 1898 the pumping station had been sold and the machinery and pumps removed. The building remained empty until it was seen by Tchertkoff, who realized its suitability as a printing works where the banned writings of Tolstoy could be published.

People often wonder why the unknown hamlet of Tuckton, which was then surrounded by woods and cornfields and contained a few cottages, was chosen for the colony. One reason was that Tchertkoff's mother had a holiday residence there called Slavanka, where she passed many happy summers. Tchertkoff also hoped that the soft, warm air of the Southbourne spa and its health-giving pine trees would improve the delicate health of his wife.

At Tuckton House, which had been built by Mr. Moser, the colony lived simply, practising a truly Christian type of communism by sharing all they had. There was an entire lack of personal comfort in the house, and everything was utilitarian and spotlessly clean. There were deal tables and chairs in all the rooms, and army beds in the sleeping quarters. Besides being devout Christians, the exiles were vegetarians and grew and produced their own food. They were kindly and friendly towards everyone and visitors were always welcome to partake of their simple meals.

A Russian type-face was shipped to the printing works so that those works of Tolstoy that were forbidden in Russia could be printed. Tolstoy made Tchertkoff his literary agent outside Russia and was relieved to be able to send his works overseas for publication and safe-keeping. At the printing works the Free Age Press was established, which sold books as cheaply as possible and with no copyright. Refugees were employed as compositors, binders, photographers and printers. The walls were lined with cases of Russian type and everywhere the Slav tongue could be heard. Here many of Tolstoy's books, including philosophical and religious pamphlets, were printed and then shipped through private channels to Russia and to other countries where Russians were living.

The refugees also produced a 16-page prohibited newspaper, which had a good circulation among Russians all over the world. In order to smuggle copies into Russia a special edition was printed on thin rice paper, which was folded into four and slipped into an envelope as an ordinary letter. Although some copies were intercepted by officials, others reached wide areas of Russia, and were even received by exiles in Siberia. Besides Tolstoy's works, other prohibited material was published that gave information about the sufferings of those who were oppressed and badly treated in Russia. Many of the works were translated into different languages.

Originally the manuscripts received from Tolstoy were kept in strong, carefully guarded boxes at Tuckton House. Instructions were issued that in the event of fire or danger the bundles must immediately be thrown in the garden. In 1906, to further safeguard the precious manuscripts, a specially-constructed strong-room was built with reinforced concrete walls 18 in. thick and steel grill doors; it was concealed from a connecting room in the house by a wooden door and a glass corridor, and a pit under the floor was boarded over with detachable pieces. There were no windows, only narrow, iron-barred ventilator slits. The roof was fireproof, damp-proof and even earthquake-proof, and alarm bells were switched on every night.

In 1908 Tchertkoff was overjoyed to be given permission to return to Russia and to be able to live near and assist Tolstoy, who had been banished to the Baltic, and also to continue working for the welfare of the peasants. Thomas Tapsell, a Christchurch photographer, accompanied the returning exiles as their official photographer. He lived with the community at Chulah, 30 miles south of Moscow, where he took many outstanding photographs of Tolstoy and his family. He became homesick, but before he returned to England he contracted pneumonia and died in Russia.

Tolstoy died in 1910 at the age of 82, having made Tchertkoff his sole literary executor. Tchertkoff also died at the age of 82, but 26 years later than his beloved master.

His mother, Countess Tchertkoff, a wealthy and exceedingly religious woman, donated vast sums of money towards the improvement of the slums of St. Petersburg. For her kindly work she fell out of favour with the authorities and just managed to escape, although her husband was executed by the Czarist regime. In 1917, exiled and penniless, she returned to Slavanka, her summer residence in Tuckton, accompanied by Anna Pinikoski, an old family nurse. Slavanka was sold to a syndicate of business men and in 1921 became a Christian conference centre, but the Countess was able to remain there for the rest of her life. She died in 1922 and was buried in Christchurch Cemetery, where her gravestone was inscribed 'Madame Elizabeth Tchertkoff, one of the first of Russian nobility to accept Christ through the ministry of Lord Radstock, who fell asleep in Christ, January 25th 1922, aged 91.'

Among the exiles at Tuckton was an Estonian, Ludwig Perno, who joined the colony

146

in 1903 and who returned to Russia after the Revolution in 1917. Unfortunately he did not find there the peaceful brotherhood that he had envisaged. Because of his pacifist views he was forced to flee with his wife, a schoolteacher, who had already been imprisoned in Sibera for bringing educational ideas to the people.

Together with their three-month-old baby daughter they escaped to England, and in 1922 they again stayed at Tuckton House. In 1929, however, Tuckton House was sold to Mrs. C. Angus as a nursing home. Ludwig Perno was given power of attorney for documents still remaining in this country, and he continued to live in the South-bourne area, where he translated many of Tolstoy's pamphlets into English and other languages.

On the retirement of Mrs. Angus in 1965 Tuckton House was sold to property developers, and it was demolished to be replaced by an estate of bungalows. The demolition of the Russians' strong-room proved exceedingly difficult: after two labour-ers had worked for a complete week, they only managed to cut a hole 15 ins. in diameter because of the thickness of its walls. The destruction of the unique building where the works of Tolstoy had been so securely stored has been bitterly regretted by civic-minded residents. The printing works was bought by Harry W. Kiddle & Sons in 1918 as a commercial vehicle body-building works, and it was there that the first motor-car body and motor-coach body in Bournemouth were built.

When one reads of the persecution and restrictions imposed during the Czarist régime and again after the Revolution of 1917, it is gratifying to know that under our democratic system Russian exiles were able to come to England for safety, and that in Tuckton they were able to publish some of the forbidden works of Tolstoy.

After the Russians' departure some of the Free Age Press leaflets (which cost 3d. per dozen) were discovered in the printing works. Here is an extract from one by Tolstoy entitled 'In the name of God, stop a Moment':

If I were asked for the most important advice I could give that which I considered to be the most useful to the men of our century, I should simply say: In the name of God, stop a moment, cease your work, look around you, consider what you are and what you ought to be – think of the ideal.

Chapter XXII

THE PRESENT AND THE FUTURE

WHAT OF BOURNEMOUTH today and tomorrow? Its development in 170 or so years from wild, uncultivated wasteland to a large, fashionable coastal resort is considered to be unique. Its former image of Bath chairs, consumptives and an élite class of society has given place to a popular, holiday area, and a town with a population of about 154,000. Today Bournemouth, with its seven miles of golden sands and gorse-clad cliffs, caters for a wide range of families from this country and abroad.

The Victorian character of the town diminishes with each succeeding year due to demolition in the interests of so-called progress, and the need for modern roads, high-rise blocks of flats and office buildings. However, as a result of the Town and Country Planning Act of 1947 buildings of historic interest are to be kept as a reminder of the town's early heritage. The Civic Society, the East Cliff Action Group and other bodies strive for the preservation of Victorian villas and buildings, whether listed or not, and for an overall conservation plan in Bournemouth. Regrettably, in the past a number of outstanding buildings have been demolished. Today a more enlightened policy ensures that where it is essential for a listed building to be destroyed in the interests of town development, its Victorian styled façade will be retained. At the time of writing these remarks apply to Granville Buildings, Richmond Hill, which were built in 1885 in memory of Dr. Granville (see chapter VI) in an imitation Franco-Flemish style, with red and buff bricks. Terracotta sculptures of lions with swags and eagle corbels on chimney-breasts are further examples of this style. The frontage of the former *Dalkeith* Hotel (1893) is listed and will also be preserved.

Much of Victorian Bournemouth remains in its many 19th-century churches, which were designed by such eminent architects as G. E. Street, Decimus Burton, Norman Shaw and J. D. Sedding, amongst others. Victorian architecture was mainly based on the styles of earlier centuries. The Gothic form was considered to be the most suitable for religious buildings, while a Roman style was used for secular public buildings; and the designs of many of the Victorian detached villas range from Italianate to Tudor and Jacobean, with a variety of ornamental details and differently-shaped gables. In some houses mullioned windows, tall chimneys and curved arches produced a strange mixture of Gothic and Elizabethan styles.

The present demand for convenient-to-manage, modern houses and flats means that Victorian houses, with their narrow passages, steps and high ceilings lack the amenities and ease of heating required for the late 20th century. The days of servants, when basements and attics provided accommodation for the domestic staff, have long since

Fig. 11. Pediment and Lintels in Victorian Boscombe.

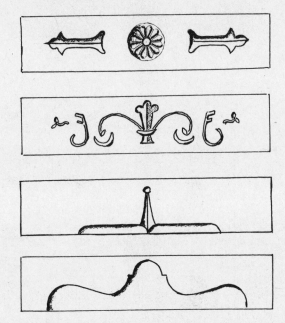

passed. While it is realized that not all Victorian villas can be retained indefinitely, it is hoped that groups of typical ones, often with delicately patterned cast-iron balconies and turrets, will be preserved, whether listed or not, as a reminder of a bygone age when a queen was on the throne for more than sixty years.

During the 1960s plain, utilitarian tower blocks were constructed. Fortunately a more attractive style can be seen in some of the newest structures, such as the Abbey

149

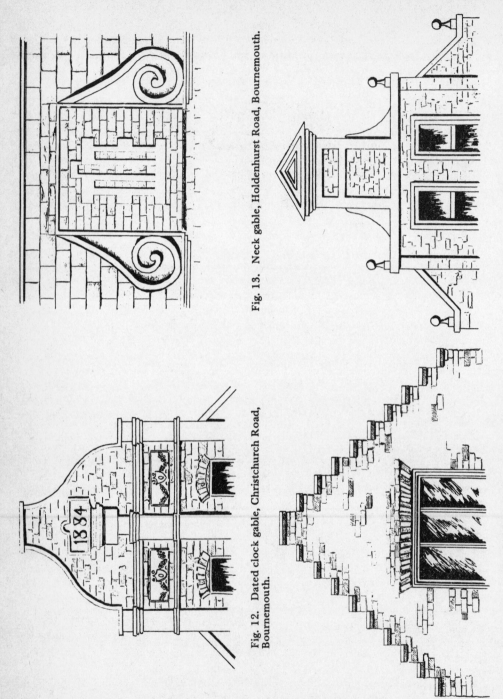

Fig. 13.   Neck gable, Holdenhurst Road, Bournemouth.

Fig. 15.   Neck gable, Christchurch Road, Bournemouth.

Fig. 12.   Dated clock gable, Christchurch Road, Bournemouth.

Fig. 14.   Stepped gable, Holdenhurst Road, Bournemouth.

150

Life Assurance Company buildings in Holdenhurst Road, and there are several well planned, variously-designed bungalows and Queen Anne-style houses. A much-admired example of modern church architecture is the elegant Punshon Memorial Church in Exeter Road, which was designed by Ronald Sims (see chapter XV).

Bournemouth, like many other pleasant coastal resorts, attracts a high percentage of retired residents, but besides the elderly the town also caters for young people. Many educational and cultural facilities attract students from home and overseas. The Dorset Institute of Higher Education at Wallisdown was opened in 1976 and offers a variety of major degrees and diplomas. Among these are videotape and television techniques, computer courses, arts and sciences and one of the most advanced catering schools in Europe. The Bournemouth and Poole College of Further Education specializes mainly in business and commercial subjects. The Bournemouth Centre for Community Arts, Haviland Road, is housed in the first Free Church school in Boscombe, the British School of 1875. Despite its ugly red-brick exterior it is a source of stimulation and enthusiasm for the many Dorset schoolchildren who participate in its colourful, expressionistic and practical classes and creative work in the fields of drama, art and meaningful projects. As a caring community concerns itself with the welfare of its less fortunate members, so the Centre's creative courses involve the maladjusted, the mentally handicapped and young offenders, and many of its students discover talents and interests of which they were completely unaware. While young children play among sand, clay and toys, their parents train to become play-group leaders. A well-developed literacy scheme caters for those with reading and writing problems, and a talking newspaper and magazine for the blind helps them to overcome feelings of isolation, besides keeping them up-to-date with current events. Wherever there is a need for a beneficial community activity the Centre will endeavour to provide it.

As Bournemouth was created as a holiday town, it seems almost unnecessary to mention that it has hundreds of hotels, many of which started as Victorian detached villas. It is the only town outside London that can boast two five-star hotels; of these the *Carlton* is the only five-star hotel in Europe that is still privately owned, and it is still represented by some descendants of its original board of directors. The hotel started as a 'Boarding Establishment for Gentlefolk' after a group of business men purchased a fine Victorian villa called Brumstath on the East Cliff.

Trade and industry have never played a very large part in the life of the town. It is largely due to the original landowners and town planners that industry and residential districts have been kept separate. Former working-class areas such as Winton, Pokesdown, parts of Boscombe, and Springbourne were created outside the main part of the fashionable town in order to provide the services essential to its well-being. Today, industrial complexes have been situated on the outskirts of Bournemouth, mainly in the areas of West and East Howe and Wallisdown, where small-scale industries such as light engineering, furniture removal, printing firms and service firms provide some employment and cater for the requirements of hotels and residents. Changes continue, but a number of residents of long standing fear that some of these do not improve the town. Concern is often felt about the proliferation of discos, casinos, coffee bars, late-night cafés and pin tables, and the resulting loss of tranquillity and calm. It is sometimes felt that the wishes of big business and property speculators are allowed to override the need for inexpensive homes; that it is difficult to appreciate the beauty of art, porcelain, period furniture and antiquities in the cramped conditions of Rothesay Museum, a former administrative office for buses; and that if more youth centres,

Olympic-type stadiums and community halls could be erected, perhaps the youth of the town could be encouraged away from coffee bars and vandalism.

It is sincerely hoped by those who love Bournemouth that it will never become just 'another town' and a replica of so many others. However, its natural beauty remains undisturbed, with its well-planned, tree-lined roads and unique woodland chines. Everywhere one sees the tall, stately pines, with their fragrant aroma, the curative powers of which brought the sick and invalids to Bournemouth in the 19th century. Bournemouth's forests of firs, oaks, beeches and other splendid trees, its well-kept pleasure gardens, open spaces and parks, and its safe sea-bathing and fine beaches are greatly appreciated by young and old.

While Thomas Hardy's description of Sandbourne (Bournemouth) as a city of detached and fanciful residences applies less with each passing year, his remark that it is a Mediterranean lounging-place on the English Channel still seems appropriate.

Pulchritudo et Salubritas – beauty and health: long may this apply to the Bournemouth of today and tomorrow.

NOTES

Notes to Chapter One

1. Calkin, J. Bernard, 'Around Bournemouth in Prehistoric and Roman Times', in *The Book of* *Bournemouth*, written for B. M. A. (1934)

Notes to Chapter Two

1. Hardy, Thomas, *Tess of the D'Urbervilles* (Wessex edition, 1920), p. 487
2. *The Victoria History of the Counties of England*: *Hampshire and the Isle of Wight*, vol. 5 (1912), p. 133
3. *VCH*, vol. 5, pp. 81, 82
4. *VCH*, vol. 5; p. 133
5. Ferrey, Benjamin, *The Antiquities of the Priory of Christchurch, Hampshire* (2nd edition, 1841), p. 8
6. Chilver, Kathleen M., *Holdenhurst, Mother of Bournemouth* (1956), p. 41
7. Dyson, Taylor, *The History of Christchurch* (1954), pp. 135, 137
8. Chilver, Kathleen M., op. cit., p. 63
9. *VCH*, vol. 5, p. 133
10. Chilver, Kathleen M., op. cit., p. 71
11. ibid., pp. 75, 76
12. *VCH*, vol. 5, p. 133
13. Chilver, Kathleen M., op. cit., p. 81
14. *VCH*, vol. 5, p. 135
15. By his son, *Farmer West and Muscliff Farm 1800–1804* (1975, originally an appendix to *Then and Now* by William Mate, 1883), p. 19
16. ibid, p. 22

Notes to Chapter Three

1. *VCH* (vol. 5), p. 133
2. Young, J. A., *Iford Bridge* (1978), pp. 7, 8
3. ibid., p. 4
4. ibid., p. 4
5. ibid., p. 10
6. Chilver, Kathleen M., *Iford on the Stour, Hampshire and its neighbourhood* (1974), p. 10
7. Barnes, Frederick, W., *Iford the Lost Village* (1974), p. 12
8. Dyson, Taylor, op. cit., pp. 235–6
9. Popplewell, Lawrence, *Wick, The Last Village on the Dorset Stour* (from the *Dorset Year Book*, 1975–6)
10. ibid., p. 1
11. Lands, S. J., *Old Kinson* (1972), pp. 8, 9
12. ibid., p. 61

Notes to Chapter Five

1. By his son, *Farmer West and Muscliff Farm 1800–1804*, p. 5
2. Hardy, Thomas, op. cit., pp. 487–8
3. Young, David S., *The Story of Bournemouth* (1957), p. 60
4. Granville, Augustus B., *The Spas of England and Principal Sea-Bathing Places: Southern Spas* (1841), p. 531
5. ibid., p. 531
6. *Bournemouth Observer*, 8 March 1884
7. McQueen, Ian, *Bournemouth St. Peter's* (1971), p. 68

Notes to Chapter Six

1. Young, David S., op. cit., p. 55

153

Notes to Chapter Seven

1. Popham, Mrs. Cecil, *Rambling records of Stourfield, Pokesdown, and St. James's Parish* by 'Jasper' (1930), p. 1
2. ibid., p. 2
3. ibid., p. 11
4. Bright, Frederick, J., *Bright's Illustrated Guide to Bournemouth* (1889), p. 89
5. Young, J. A., *The Village of Pokesdown* (1978), p. 24
6. Ordnance Map 1870, Red House Museum, Christchurch
7. Popham, Mrs. Cecil, op. cit., p. 6
8. Taylor, J. J., *A short article on the History of Southbourne* (written for and in the possession of Galleon World Travel)
9. Compton, Thomas, A., *Southbourne's Infancy* (1914), p. 21

Notes to Chapter Eight

1. Mate, Charles, H., and Riddle, Charles, *Bournemouth 1810–1910. The History of a Modern Health and Pleasure Resort* (1910), p. 9
2. State Papers, Domestic Eliz. I. (S.P.12), vol. 97, no. 32, I
3. In Red House Museum, Christchurch
4. Young, David S., op. cit., p. 191
5. *Funk and Wagnall's Practical Standard Dictionary* (1925)
6. Ordnance Map 1870, Red House Museum, Christchurch
7. By 1923 the thatch structure was destroyed as it had become decrepit and was no longer in keeping with the surrounding buildings
8. Sydenham & Co., publishers, *A Little Book About St. Clement's Bournemouth* (1923), p. 36
9. ibid., p. 19

Notes to Chapter Nine

1. Bell, Mrs. Nancy R. E., *From Harbour to Harbour: the Story of Christchurch, Bournemouth and Poole from the Earliest Times to the Present Day* (1916), p. 179
2. Brannon, Philip, *The Illustrated Historical and Descriptive Guide to Bournemouth and the Surrounding Scenery* (14th edition, 1880), p. 96
3. McQueen, Ian, op. cit., p. 26
4. Lands, S. J., *The Growth of Winton* (1976), p. 6
5. ibid., p. 17
6. ibid., p. 9
7. Bournemouth became a municipal borough in 1890.

Notes to Chapter Ten

1. Mate, Charles H., and Riddle, Charles, op. cit., p. 186
2. Brannon, Philip, *The Illustrated Historical Guide to Poole and Bournemouth* (10th edition, 1869), p. 31
3. Ordnance Map 1870, in Reference Library, Bournemouth
4. *Observer & Chronicle*, 21 February 1885
5. Wood, Charles W., 'On the South Coast' (in *The Argosy*, 1881), pp. 278–91
6. 'A Sketch ffrom Bournemouth', (in *Blackwood's Magazine*, December 1883), pp. 740–53
7. Furniss, Harry, 'An English Wintering Place' (in *Good Words*, 1891), pp. 118–26

Notes to Chapter Twelve

1. Closed 1980. To be demolished as part of a scheme for extending a dual carriageway and linking it with the Wessex Way
2. Robinson, Son & Pike, publishers, *An Illustrated Account of Bournemouth* (1893), pp. 44, 48
3. Ford, R., *History of Bournemouth Police* (1963), p. 8

Notes to Chapter Fourteen

1. The founder of homoeopathy. (*Funk and Wagnall's Practical Standard Dictionary*, 1925)
2. *Royal Victoria Hospitals, 1859–1959*, p. 8
3. ibid., p. 19
(Publication of the above booklet was sponsored by the League of Patients and Friends of the Royal Victoria Hospitals)

Notes to Chapter Seventeen

1. Miller, Geoffrey, *The Bournemouth Symphony Orhcestra* (1970), p. 59
2. ibid., p. 157.
3. ibid., p. 174

Notes to Chapter Eighteen

1. Russell-Cotes, Sir Merton, *Home and Abroad; an Autobiography of an Octogenarian* (1921), vol. 1, p. 35

2. Jones, John Daniel, *Three Score Years and Ten; the Autobiography of J. D. Jones* (1940), p. 77

3. ibid., p. 80

Notes to Chapter Nineteen

1. Award Map 1805, Lansdowne Reference Library, Bournemouth

2. Ordnance Map 1811, Red House Museum, Christchurch

3. Ordnance Map 1870, Red House Museum, Christchurch

Notes to Chapter Twenty

1. Darwin, Francis, *More Letters of Charles Darwin* (1903), vol. 2, p. 285

2. ibid., p. 288

3. Hammerton, J. A., *Stevensoniana: An anecdotal life and appreciation of Robert Louis Stevenson* (1907), p. 77

4. Huxley, Aldous, *Letters of D. H. Lawrence* (1932), p. 18

5. ibid., p. 19

6. ibid., p. 23

7. Boulton, James T., ed., *Lawrence in Love: Letters from D. H. Lawrence to Louie Burrows* (1968), p. 159

8. Durrell, Gerald, *The Stationary Ark* (1976), p. 19

9. ibid., p. 21

10. Mate, Charles H., and Riddle, Charles, op. cit., pp. 258–9

BIBLIOGRAPHY

Bell, Mrs. Nancy R. E., *From Harbour to Harbour: the Story of Christchurch, Bournemouth and Poole from the Earliest Times to the Present Day* (1916).

Bishop, Barbara, *Secondary Education in Bournemouth from 1902 to Present Day* (1966).

Boulton, James, T., ed., *Lawrence in Love: Letters from D. H. Lawrence to Louie Burrows* (1968).

Bournemouth Fire Authority, *Bournemouth's Fire Brigade* (1954).

Brannon, Philip, *The Illustrated Historical Guide to Poole and Bournemouth, and the Surrounding Country* (1855 and 1867).

Bright, Frederick J., *Bright's Guide to Bournemouth and Christchurch* (1896).

British Medical Association (Watson Smith, S., ed.), *The Book of Bournemouth* (1934). Written for the 102nd Annual Meeting of the B.M.A., held at Bournemouth in July 1934.

Brough, James, *The Prince and the Lily* (1975).

Bussby, Federick, *The Story of Holy Trinity, Bournemouth, 1867–1953* (1953).

Calkin, J. Bernard, 'Around Bournemouth in Prehistoric and Roman Times', in *The Book of Bournemouth* (1934), by the British Medical Association.

Chacksfield, K. Merle, *Smuggling Days* (1966).

Chilver, Kathleen M., *Holdenhurst, Mother of Bournemouth* (1956).

Clegg, A. Lindsay, *Bournemouth, Saga of a Famous Resort* (booklet, 1969).

Compton, Thomas A., *Southbourne's Infancy* (1914).

Croft, Henry Page, 1st Baron Croft, *My Life of Strife* (1948).

Dale, Richard, Reminiscences of Stourfield, by Mr. Dale of Tuckton (*Notes and Queries*, 30 September and 7 October 1876).

Darwin, Francis, *The Life and Letters of Darwin* (3 vols., 1887).

Darwin, Francis, *More Letters of Charles Darwin* (2 vols., 1903).

Davies, John Trevor, *Richmond Hill Story* (1956).

Dobel, Horace, *On the Mont Dore Cure and the Way to Use it* (1881).

Dobel, Horace, *The Medical Aspects of Bournemouth and its Surroundings* (1885).

Durrell, Gerald, *My Family and Other Animals* (1956).

Durrell, Gerald, *A Zoo in my Luggage* (1960).

Dyson, Taylor, *The History of Christchurch* (1954).

Ford, R., *The History of Bournemouth Police* (1963).

Forse, Rev. Edward J. G., *Fifty Years of Southbourne Parish 1876–1926* (1926).

Godfrey, Sir Dan, *Memories and Music; Thirty-five Years of Conducting* (1924).

Granville, Augustus B., *The Spas of England and Principal Sea-Bathing Places: Southern Spas* (1841).

Hadley, Watkins, *Twenty-one Years of Municipal Music, 1893–1914* (1914).

Hammerton, J. A., *Stevensoniana: An anecdotal life and appreciation of Robert Louis Stevenson* (1907).

Hardy, Thomas, *Tess of the D'Urbervilles* (Wessex edition, 1920).

Hern, Anthony, *Seaside Holidays* (1967).

Hutchins, John, *The History and Antiquities of the County of Dorset*

Jervaise, Edwyn, *The Ancient Bridges of the South of England* (1930)

Jolly, W. P., *Marconi* (1972).

Jones, John Daniel, *Three Score Years and Ten; the Autobiography of J. D. Jones* (1940).

Lands, S. J., *Old Kinson* (1972).

McQueen, Ian, *Bournemouth St. Peter's* (1971).

Malmesbury, James Edward, 2nd Earl of (ed. by F. G. Aflalo), *Half a Century of Sport in Hampshire being Extracts from the Shooting Journals of an Autobiography* (1905).

Malmesbury, James Howard, 3rd Earl of, *Memoirs of an Ex-Minister; an Autobiography* (1884).

Mate, Charles, H., and Riddle, Charles, *Bournemouth: 1810–1910. The History of a Modern Health and Pleasure Resort* (1910).

Mate, W., & Sons, *Boscombe Illustrated* (1886).

Michael, T. N., *Pokesdown Congregational Church – The Story of 150 Years, 1820–1970* (1970).

Miller, Geoffrey, *The Bournemouth Symphony Orchestra* (1970).

Lord Montagu of Beaulieu, *Rolls of Rolls-Royce – A Biography of the Hon. C. S. Rolls* (1966).

Nicolson, Nigel, *People and Parliament* (1958).

Oakley, E. Russell, *The Smugglers of Christchurch, Bourne Heath and the New Forest* (1942).

Peters, John, Couling, David, and Ridley, Michael, *Bournemouth, Then & Now* (1978).

Pevsner, Nikolaus, and Lloyd, David, *The Buildings of England: Hampshire and The Isle of Wight* (1967).

Popham, Mrs. Cecil, *Rambling Records of Stourfield, Pokesdown, and St. James's Parish*, by 'Jasper' (1930).

Popplewell, Lawrence, *Bournemouth Railway History: An Exposure of Victorian Engineering Fraud* (1973).

Porritt, Arthur, *J. D. Jones of Bournemouth* (1942).

Robinson, Son & Pike, publishers, *An Illustrated Account of Bournemouth* (1893).

Russell-Cotes, Sir Merton, *Home and Abroad: An Autobiography of an Octogenarian* (2 vols., 1921).

Short, Bernard C., *Smuggling in Poole, Bournemouth and Neighbourhood* (1927).

Sydenham & Co., publishers, *A Little Book about St. Clement's, Bournemouth* (1923).

Sydenham, J., *The Visitors' Guide to Bournemouth* (1840, 1887 and 1890).

Taconis, Mrs. F. M., *The Russian Colony at Tuckton, 1897–1908* (1918).

Talbot, Mary Anne, *The History of Talbot Village* (1873).

Talbot Village, The Growth of a Village. To the Memory of Georgina Charlotte and Marianne Talbot (1943).

The Victoria History of the Counties of England: Hampshire and the Isle of Wight, vol. 5 (1912).

Wade, Virginia, *Courting Triumph* (1978).

Webb, Alfred, *The Churches of Bournemouth. The History of the 56 Churches in the Borough of Bournemouth* (1910).

Young, David S., *The Story of Bournemouth* (1957).

I wish to express my thanks to the authors of the Bournemouth Local Studies Group booklets for giving me the opportunity to study some of their many publications and for granting me permission to quote from the same. The booklets, which are researched and prepared by members of the Group, have helped to foster a growing interest in local studies in schools and elsewhere, and have been most helpful in the preparation of my book.

Local Studies Publications

Barnes, Frederick W., *The Lost Village* (1974).

Chilver, Kathleen M., *Iford on the Stour, Hampshire and its neighbourhood* (1974).

Cooksey, Alfred J. A., *Local Radio* (1976).

Gillett, Mildred, *Wandering in Talbot Village* (1976).

Lands, S. J., *The Growth of Winton* (1976).

Lavender, Ruth, *From Pocket Borough to Parliamentary Democracy* (1976).

Mabey, William, *Bournemouth in 1868* (1930).

Popplewell, Lawrence, *Wick; The Last Village on the Dorset Stour* (from the *Dorset Year Book*, 1975–6).

Sherry, Desmond, *Bournemouth, A Study of a Holiday Town* (1978).

By his son, *Farmer West and Muscliff Farm 1800–1804* (1975, originally an appendix to *Then and Now* by William Mate, 1883).

Wills, E. G., *Pokesdown and Neighbourhood, 1895 to 1910* (1975).

Young, J. A., *Iford Bridge* (1978).

Young, J. A., *The Winton Urban District Council 1898–1901* (1976).

Young, J. A., *Southbourne-on-Sea 1870–1901* (1976).

Young, J. A., *The Village of Pokesdown* (1978).

Young, J. A., *The Development of Railways in Bournemouth and District* (1972).

Other booklets

Ridley, Michael, *The Iron Age Settlement, East Cliffs* (reprinted from the *Proceedings* of the Bournemouth Natural Science Society, 1969).

Young, J. A., *Corpus Christi, Boscombe* (1976).

INDEX

160